A Milwaukee Woman's Life on the Left

The Autobiography of Meta Berger

Edited by Kimberly Swanson

Foreword by
Genevieve G. McBride

STATE HISTORICAL SOCIETY OF WISCONSIN
Madison
2001

Published by the
State Historical Society of Wisconsin Press

© 2001 by the State Historical Society of Wisconsin

All rights reserved. No part of this book may be reproduced in any manner or in any medium without written permission from the publisher, except by reviewers, who may quote brief passages in critical articles and reviews. To request permission to reprint passages or quote from this copyrighted work, write to Permissions, State Historical Society of Wisconsin Press, 816 State Street, Madison, WI 53706-1482

Publications of the State Historical Society of Wisconsin are available at quantity discounts for promotions, fund raising, and educational use. Write to the above address for more information.

Printed in the United States of America
05 04 03 02 01 00 5 4 3 2 1

Library of Congress Cataloging-in-Publication Data
Berger, Meta Schlichting, 1873–1944.
A Milwaukee woman's life on the left: the autobiography of Meta Berger
/ edited by Kimberly Swanson; foreword by Genevieve G. McBride.
cm.
Includes bibliographical references and index.
ISBN 0-87020-322-3
1. Berger, Meta Schlicting, 1873–1944. 2. Women socialists—United States—Biography.
3. Women social reformers—United States—Biography. I. Swanson, Kimberly. II. State Historical Society of Wisconsin. III. Title.
HX84.B42 A3 2000
335'.0092—dc21
[B]

00-057394

0942442

Contents

0942443

Foreword

Meta Schlichting Berger (1873–1944) lived a life of service, and in her autobiography she left a significant legacy to serve anyone with an interest in women's history or socialism and other reform movements whose imprints remain strong in Milwaukee and Wisconsin. The State Historical Society of Wisconsin's publication of Meta Berger's manuscript ensures a wider audience for the lessons bequeathed by this school commissioner's daughter who became a school board president and educational reformer who educated her city and state—and to some extent, her country—to reforms that continue to revolutionize classrooms today.

By Meta Berger's time, Milwaukee was among the most ethnically heterogeneous cities in America. Foreign-born immigrants—among them her parents—and first-generation Milwaukeeans comprised more than half the city's population. More than half its newspapers—including her husband's first effort—were published in languages other than English, and many children were educated in bilingual schools. The task then was to build bridges between more than centuries. Meta Berger was among the Socialists who showed their fellow citizens how to span both ethnic traditions and assimilationism without sacrificing a rich, multicultural heritage. In the twenty-first century, Milwaukee could do worse than to emulate her example and become once more a model of urban progress.

Meta Berger's reminiscences are noteworthy because she scored so many important firsts for women, not only in Milwaukee and Wisconsin but also nationwide. Such achievements by women pioneering in public office, well before they won the ballot, became persuasive arguments wielded by the woman suffrage movement to win the ballot for all women—a movement in which she was a leader in Wisconsin. Her story serves as a reminder that major political reforms are achieved at the national level only after many obstacles are overcome and many milestones passed at the state and local levels. It was, and is, difficult for women to win elective office in Wisconsin, but Meta Berger was one of the first women in Wisconsin to do so, even at the local level, just seven years after Wisconsin women finally secured the limited right to vote in school elections. To put her achievement in perspective, it bears pointing out that almost another ninety years would pass before Wisconsin elected a woman to Congress. And Meta Berger won reelection for more than thirty years—a record rarely matched in the state.

That Meta Berger and others of her era won heroic as well as historic victories does not, of course, mean that they lived heroic lives—nor that, with publication of her autobiography, she ought to be enshrined. Many of our heroes were not born to greatness, or even to great goodness, but instead were self-made. Understanding this, we too can realize change as reformers did decades ago. Luckily, Meta Berger left us many useful lessons on how to win against the odds and obstacles and how to transform a city, a state, even a Constitution.

Meta Berger met obstacles in both her public and private lives. She overcame many of them—but not all. In her autobiography, she writes primarily of her private life, yet reveals little of a truly personal nature. Her account of a childhood of genteel comfort suddenly ended by the death of her father, followed by her mother's endless work and worry to avoid poverty and provide for her daughters, suggests clearly that this was a formative experience. In Meta Berger's brief career as a teacher, she saw her students confront similar obstacles and learned lessons she later would bring to her study of socialism. But she wrote most about her many years of marriage and motherhood, especially of her husband's instruction on the role of socialism—and of her years as a housewife and mother. She did not shrink from the role of *hausfrau*, if she chafed under it. She loyally served a husband who knew little and cared less about housework, shopping, or doing the dishes—and who was mildly disappointed when their firstborn was a girl. In time she became "something more than Mr. Berger's house-keeper," in her own words, and achieved a "true partnership" in her marriage.

Eventually she evolved a new role as a leader among women in Socialist Party politics and—although belatedly and briefly—among Wisconsin women in suffragist politics. But she had waited to be asked to join the Wisconsin Woman Suffrage Association only a few years before the end of the "century of struggle" for social justice to which other women had given their lives. And she had only just joined when she departed the organization for the newer National Woman's Party, which had little power in local politics in Wisconsin, where women could not yet vote even in state elections. She discusses the circumstances of her switch in suffragist allegiances, but her recollection of events—by then, decades earlier—does not gibe with the record of her resignation from the WWSA. Nor does her account of a debacle she caused at a state teachers' convention in 1917 coincide with those of other women embroiled in the internal feud that embarrassed all sides and embroiled suffragists in unwelcome publicity.

The historical record is also ambiguous about Meta Berger's work for and with women in the Socialist Party. She was swift to criticize suffragists as "middle-class" and "conservative," but in truth she retained many such bourgeois attributes herself. Paradoxically, because she valued the bonds of marriage and family, the trappings of home and children, she surreptitiously practiced birth control so that she and Victor could afford the lifestyle to which they both aspired. They attempted to be paragons of respectability, too, and were patronizing about working-class comrades who did not dress or behave properly. She wrote that "the women socialists are surely no good," that it was "far easier to work with men than with women." But the latter may well have been a shrewd move on her part, owing to the subservient role of women's auxiliaries in any party. Progress is always easier to achieve when working with those who hold it, yet it could not have been easy for her. Her own husband was among the most conservative of men, both personally and politically. As late as 1910— a year after her first victory at the polls, ahead of his—he qualified his half-hearted support of the Socialist Party's platform plank for woman suffrage by publicly worrying that "the great majority of women" were more "illiberal, unprogressive and reactionary" than their male counterparts.

Meta Berger's reaction to this and many other telling moments in their marriage and life together can only be imagined, because she actually tells little and leaves much to be deduced between these lines about the struggle of a "political wife" attempting to have a life of her own. As she ruefully wrote, "anyone trying to serve the public is subject to the fierce light of publicity." In many respects, this is the familiar story of a wife and mother with responsibilities both at work and at home, a strong-minded woman wary of subordinating herself to her husband—as well as the hardly unfamiliar story of a husband who apparently was the weaker of the two in terms of marital fidelity. Faithful to Victor's memory, as she was to him in their marriage, Meta refers to his failings only obliquely. But her assessment of him otherwise offers insight into an enduring partnership with its full share of endearments and affection— a partnership that sustained them through an episode of virulent wartime hysteria and one of our history's most turbulent Congressional careers.

But there is more than their unconventional personal, political, and professional partnership that sets Meta Berger's story apart from the histories of many prominent women, then and now. It departs from the usual elitist genre of wealth and privilege, and Meta Berger managed to shape her own life in an era when few women were able to escape their husbands' shadows. Her story differs from those of many women whose stories now are better known, not only owing to Meta Berger's marriage to a German immigrant, a Jew, a journalist, a cofounder of the Socialist Party, an outcast in Congress—and a businessman always in debt—but also because of her own background. Her immigrant parentage, impoverished upbringing, and self-supporting years as a schoolteacher were uncommon among prominent women of the time.

She is significant among her peers in Wisconsin because she was one of the first women to serve on the Milwaukee school board, and because she lasted thirty years, making an impact on her city for generations to come. Most important, Meta Berger brought a different perspective to the board from her first meeting, when she defended women's rights and defeated a proposal to prohibit women as department heads in high schools. From the outset, and throughout her years on the board, she asserted a female—if not always a feminist—agenda. This was not surprising, since her agenda of playgrounds, vocational schools, free libraries, and public health was borrowed from campaigns waged by her cohort of Wisconsin clubwomen, who comprised one of the most powerful lobbying forces in the state at the time.

Meta Berger was also a woman of her time as an autobiographer. She devotes but few pages to her own political career and fewer yet to her work for woman suffrage; thus, she brings upon herself this ambiguity about her place in history, because ambition was not then part of women's place. Like many women of the day, she faced the necessity of at least appearing to be self-effacing, of subsuming ambition even as she assumed power. But she did not always subordinate herself to her husband's work and wishes, as is evident in these pages. She could and did confront him on differences ranging from housewifery to how to conduct political campaigns. As evidence of his wisdom, she apparently often won—or at least won him over in time. Unfortunately, her modesty sometimes obscures her role in the arena of public policy.

This ambiguity is perhaps most prevalent in the last chapter of Meta Berger's life and autobiography, during her paradoxical progression from socialism to communism. Her visit to the Soviet Union in 1935 did not follow but preceded her apparent political conversion, as she resigned from the Socialist Party only after it publicly rebuked her in 1940 by asking her to withdraw from "communist-front" organizations. Here again, Meta Berger omits much that historians would wish to know about her life and beliefs. She provides a travelogue of places and events, a series of profiles of the Soviet people, but she offers few insightful political thoughts, especially into her own. It may be, as Meta Berger herself wrote, that she "did not have to agree with the political philosophies" of the people she met, from factory workers to the president of the USSR. Perhaps she simply was, as she writes, naive not to see the political significance of the time of larger events unfolding around her, when she had to be edified by the American ambassador. Still, she seems at the least disingenuous in downplaying the Stalinist purges, which must have reminded her of the persecution of her husband and newspaper by the U.S. government barely two decades before. It is left to Kimberly Swanson, the expert editor of this autobiography, to explore, in the afterword, the possible reasons for Meta Berger's leftward shift in her final years. As Swanson notes, Meta Berger always had relied on the political judgment of others, especially her husband and lifelong mentor who, by then, had been gone from her life, and from the Socialist Party, for more than six years. A careful reading of the last chapter suggests that by 1935, Meta Berger lacked an anchor in her life and probably was more susceptible than ever to being influenced or even led by others.

Yet in her final years, she was not was the docile *hausfrau* and helpmeet that her husband and other Socialist men had wanted her to be. Meta Berger had both suffered and committed hurtful personal and professional betrayals. When the invitation had come to visit Russia, she had accepted it almost impulsively, as a way of escaping painful "home conditions" in the wake of her elder daughter's divorce. She also sought surcease after a series of rebuffs by the Socialist Party leadership—first to sustain the *Milwaukee Leader* now that she had inherited the newspaper, and then to support her candidacy for Victor's old seat in Congress. (By contrast, when Robert M. La Follette had died in 1925, the Republican Party beseeched his widow to accept appointment to the U.S. Senate to replace him—but Belle Case La Follette opted instead to write her late husband's biography, not her own. One can only wonder, had Meta Berger had her party's backing, how different Wisconsin politics in decades since might have been for men as well as for women.) Thus the closing chapter in Meta Berger's life is shrouded in ambiguity and subject to various interpretations.

However, there is nothing ambiguous about the merit of publishing this lasting testament to her mettle that is Meta Schlichting Berger's autobiography. Above all, she mattered—and that is what she wanted to be said of her life. Because she achieved that aim, her life story matters still today. She tells the reader much about life in her era and about the life of significance she led. She tells enough for the reader interested in the history of women, of Milwaukee and Wisconsin, of political and social reform. She tells enough even for the reader interested only in a good story, couched in a straightforward and most readable style, by a woman worth meeting more than a century since she began her "new life" with Victor Berger at the dawn of a new century. Meta Schlichting Berger served her community and her country, as well as her husband and family, by helping to shape her century for the better. There is no better testament to a life lived well, nor to the lessons she left for the next century.

Genevieve G. McBride
Milwaukee, Wisconsin

Acknowledgments

This book grew out of a course project in historical editing. It followed me through several jobs, another degree, three states, and illness. Meta Berger has been part of my life for years, and I am pleased to share the story she did not live to publish.

I would like to thank Meta Berger's granddaughters, Deborah Hardy, Polly Keusink, and Bridget Dobson, for granting permission to publish the autobiography. John Kaminski of the University of Wisconsin–Madison instructed me in historical editing and encouraged me to edit the full manuscript. Michael Stevens of the State Historical Society of Wisconsin brought the manuscript to my attention, advised me generously throughout the project, and allowed me to examine his research files. This book is stronger because of his guidance and his knowledge of Berger family history. Frederick Olson of the University of Wisconsin–Milwaukee provided copies of his notes on the autobiography and answered questions. Many others helped me in small but important ways during the course of research. I began work on the footnotes in a practicum experience directed by Louise Robbins; Lester W. J. Seifert and Mary Devitt assisted with several footnotes; Sharon Hamrick helped me locate and borrow materials; and Lian Partlow commented on the introduction, to name only a few. I am especially grateful to my husband, Jesse Hay, for his encouragement and support.

Kimberly Swanson
Ann Arbor, Michigan
September 2000

Introduction

In 1909 the Socialist Party of Milwaukee nominated Meta Berger as a candidate in the city's first public election of school-board directors. "Surprised, shocked and frightened" by the nomination, she wired her husband, Socialist Party leader Victor Berger, asking him what to do. He advised, "Do nothing, except to accept the honor. You won't be elected anyway." She accepted the nomination and, despite Victor's prediction, won the election.

Meta Berger's election to the school board launched her career in educational administration and social reform. A shy housewife and mother who joined the Socialist Party, held political office, and became influential in suffrage and peace groups, Meta participated in many of the most significant political and social movements of her time. In partnership with her well-known husband, she chose an exciting and demanding life of public service over conventionality and respectability. Through her political involvement she witnessed the rise and fall of the Socialist Party, the early-twentieth-century women's-rights movement, and the patriotic hysteria and repression of World War I. Her autobiography, though incomplete and unpolished, provides an engaging firsthand view of this era.

Meta Berger was a determined and spirited woman. Although she portrayed herself as insecure and "stupid" in her youth, she had the strength to educate herself, to speak openly of her convictions, and to stand up to a domineering husband. Her autobiography chronicles her transformation from dutiful wife to confident activist, revealing both her fears and her enduring hope for the future.

Meta Schlichting was born February 23, 1873, in Milwaukee, the second of five children. Her German-born parents, Bernhard and Matilda Schlichting, had immigrated to the United States as young children. Meta's father was a Civil War veteran, a bookkeeper, and a local politician. An agnostic, he helped his daughter to "unlearn" religious lessons. He served as a Republican member of the Wisconsin Assembly in 1875–1876 and held an appointed position on the Milwaukee board of education from 1878 until his death in early 1884. Meta was ten years old when her father's death plunged her middle-class family into poverty, forcing her mother to take in boarders and her older sister to go to work as a clerk.[1]

A year before his death, Bernhard Schlichting had interviewed a recent immigrant from Austria-Hungary, Victor Berger, for a teaching position in the public schools. Victor accepted the position as German instructor and developed a friendship with the Schlichting family that continued after Bernhard's death. Meta, who was thirteen years younger than Victor, attended the school in which he taught; she studied German language and literature in his classroom. The German language was hardly foreign in turn-of-the-century Milwaukee: the city had a thriving and well-established German-speaking community, and residents considered their city the "most German in the United States." Newer immigrant communities, especially Polish, Slavic, and southern European groups, were growing more quickly, but a wide range of German institutions still flourished, including churches, theaters, newspapers, and clubs. When Victor began courting Meta, he frequently took her to German-language plays, and when he founded his first newspaper, the *Wisconsin Vorwärts,* he published it in German.[2]

Meta trained as a teacher at the Wisconsin State Normal School in Milwaukee, thus qualifying for one of the few professions open to educated women. She graduated in 1894 and taught primary school for three years. In December 1897, at age twenty-four, she resigned her appointment to marry Victor Berger, who was thirty-seven. Her first daughter, Doris, was born one year after the wedding, and her second daughter, Elsa, was born in 1900. Meta's three-year-old nephew, Jack Anderson, also joined the family after the death of Meta's older sister, Paula, in 1902.

In the early years of their marriage, the Bergers experienced a period of "adjustment and readjustment," as Meta phrased it, when their initial expectations of marriage conflicted. She valued financial security and hoped for a cooperative relationship, but Victor's income was irregular, and his political work often kept him away from home. In her view, his devotion to socialism caused unnecessary hardship for the family. Victor, more traditional in outlook, expected Meta to accept his decisions and share his goals and interests. He had little patience for her political naivete and no intention of relinquishing his leadership role in the burgeoning socialist movement. Raised in a poor but culturally middle-class family, Meta felt uncomfortable at socialist rallies and ignorant among Victor's well-read, intellectual friends.

---

[1] Miriam Frink Notes, 1943, Victor L. Berger Papers, State Historical Society of Wisconsin (hereinafter cited as VLB Papers).

[2] Bayrd Still, *Milwaukee: The History of a City* (Madison: State Historical Society of Wisconsin, 1948), 257–278.

Even more distressing to her was the flattering attention paid him by other women as a result of his stature in the socialist movement—attention that he probably failed to discourage. Meta referred only indirectly in her autobiography to Victor's flirtations or affairs with other women, but her daughter, Doris, wrote quite bluntly in her unfinished biography of her father that he had been unfaithful. One of his affairs, according to Doris, was with a maid, Anna, who confessed her involvement with Victor at the lunch table in Doris's presence.[3]

Meta was determined to improve her marriage and to become "something more than Mr. Berger's house-keeper." In an early attempt to participate more fully in his life and all-consuming work, she followed Victor to a Socialist Party convention in 1904. "Perhaps you think this didn't take a certain amount of perseverance!" she wrote in her autobiography. "To a person of my temperament it took all I had." Somewhat to her surprise, the convention inspired her, unlike the books she had tried to read and the discussions she had overheard, and she was thrilled to meet national Socialist Party leaders such as Morris Hillquit and Algernon Lee. At her insistence, she accompanied Victor to additional conventions, including an American Federation of Labor meeting where she first encountered the nation's most powerful labor leader, Samuel Gompers. Slowly, Meta came to appreciate Victor's work for social and economic change. Although in 1907 she still doubted whether his sacrifices for the "rabble" were worthwhile, by 1910 she was writing to him that "the time was when I thought that if you gave up your work and devoted yourself to money making I would be happy. . . is past."[4]

Meta's marriage evolved along with her commitment to socialism. In the early years of their relationship she deferred to Victor in many ways because of his greater age and experience. When Meta questioned Victor about political issues, "sometimes he just laughed at me and said," 'Du bist eine dumme Gans' " [You are a silly goose]. At other times he was reassuring, telling her that she could not possibly know as much as he did, considering her youth. She always accepted Victor's theories, but she began to offer her own ideas on many practical matters as she gained administrative and political experience. In May 1911, she observed that it would be a "dreadful mistake" for the city's new Socialist administration to insist on Socialist appointees if none were qual-

[3] Doris Berger Hursley, biography of Victor Berger, ca. 1926–1980, rolls 12–13, Victor L. Berger Papers (microfilm edition, 1994), State Historical Society of Wisconsin, hereinafter cited as VLB Papers (microfilm).

[4] Doris Hursley, interview with Meta Berger, 1936, roll 33, VLB Papers (microfilm); Michael E. Stevens, ed., *The Family Letters of Victor and Meta Berger, 1894–1929* (Madison: State Historical Society of Wisconsin, 1995), 86, 105.

ified. She also challenged Victor at home, where they argued about child-rearing methods and his flirtations or infidelities. In August 1911, he declared in a letter that no other woman could replace her: "I have had a very severe lesson, as you know." Three years later, on trips to New York, he noted carefully that he had not visited with suffragist Inez Milholland, according to several accounts a close friend and great admirer of Victor's, because he knew that Meta would have disapproved.[5]

As she approached middle age, Meta forged a real partnership with Victor. Working together in the socialist cause, they became "more than husband and wife," she wrote. "We became comrades in the real sense of that word, and as a result we certainly were happy." Their relationship was warm. Elsa remembered that her parents were "very much in love with each other," even through "all kinds of weather and financial difficulties." Late in her life Meta regaled friends at a dinner party with stories of the gifts, letters, and other attentions admirers had lavished on Victor over the years. She had clearly forgiven him.[6]

Meta did not enjoy domestic work—indeed, she employed a maid to help with housework and cooking—but she did enjoy her daughters, especially as they matured. According to Doris, Meta often told Victor that she married him "to share his life, not to take charge of children," but in Meta's letters and in her autobiography she frequently expressed happiness with family life. "The children are all seated around me doing homework," she wrote to Victor in 1913. "I do take such comfort & pleasure in our home." Both daughters found their father's expectations difficult to meet, but Meta was a more understanding parent. Elsa recalled that her father was never satisfied with her grades, no matter how impressive, but her mother "didn't demand anything special. She accepted me as I was." Meta was accepting but also enormously proud of her daughters, who did well in school and later pursued careers in law and medicine.[7]

Meta's 1909 election to the school board, which first thrust her into a public role, was a sign of the Socialist Party's growing political momentum in Milwaukee. Under Victor's leadership, the city's branch of the party had become an efficient organization that advanced a practical, pragmatic form of socialism. The Socialists won the support of the city's trade unions—especially the work-

[5] Stevens, ed., *Family Letters,* 116, 138, 172, 174; Hursley, biography. For references to Milholland, see also Irma Hochstein, account of a dinner party, June 4, 1929, Irma Hochstein Papers, State Historical Society of Wisconsin.

[6] Elsa Berger Edelman, "The Second One," ca. 1973, roll 13, VLB Papers (microfilm), 4; Hochstein, account of dinner party, June 4, 1929.

[7] Hursley, biography; Stevens, ed., *Family Letters,* 151; Edelman, "Second One," 4.

ing-class German community—by emphasizing local problems and offering specific reform proposals, including public ownership of utilities, woman suffrage, tax reform, free medical services, and more. In 1910 the Socialists won their greatest success and fame, capturing both the mayor's office and a majority on the Common Council. Shortly after the Socialists swept the city government, Victor was elected to Congress, the first Socialist in the nation to serve in that role. These successes inspired party members around the country and gave them tremendous hope for the future. The Milwaukee Socialists were never able to replicate these successes, but they remained prominent in local politics and elected a Socialist mayor from 1916 to 1940 and again from 1948 to 1960.[8]

The party's 1910 electoral success in Milwaukee attracted national and even international popular attention. Prominent journalists and reformers, among them Ida Tarbell, Oswald Garrison Villard, and Lincoln Steffens, came to the city to report on its politics. Victor's subsequent election to Congress also drew reporters. Meta joined Victor for part of his term in Washington, where she made a feeble attempt to fulfill the social obligations of a proper congressman's wife, explored the city with her children, and took delight in invitations to a White House reception and dinner at the British embassy.

Meta eventually took advantage of the opportunities for public service that her marriage provided. At her first school-board meeting she felt so ill prepared that she asked a fellow Socialist to signal to her—discreetly—how to vote, but she learned quickly and soon enjoyed the work. In her autobiography she portrayed Victor as supportive of her school-board service, but in a 1913 letter he expressed some doubts: "When I am alone and thinking the matter over— then it always comes to me again that I *don't want* either you or the children to take a prominent part in public life. . . . *You* are not adapted to it at all,— although (I am sorry to say) that you have acquired a little taste for it through your work on the school board. When your term is over I don't want you to run again." Meta ran for office again anyway in 1915 and was reelected. She ran and won three more times in succeeding years and served a total of thirty years on the school board before her retirement in 1939. In 1915–1916 she served as president of the board. By this time Victor had accustomed himself to her public role, and he noted with pride her accomplishment in a letter to his daughter, Doris: "Sometimes I wonder whether you girls sufficiently prize the fact that your mother is the first woman in *America* who has ever achieved

---

[8] Marvin Wachman, *History of the Social-Democratic Party of Milwaukee, 1897–1910* (Urbana: University of Illinois Press, 1945).

the honor of being elected president of a school board. And the first Socialist president at that,—man or woman."[9]

As a school director, Meta supported progressive measures such as playground construction, "penny lunches," free textbooks, and medical inspection of schoolchildren. She was also a teachers' advocate and worked for their tenure, a firm salary schedule, and a pension system. Though she was not always successful in her efforts—she failed, for example, in her attempt to provide free textbooks—her fellow school directors nonetheless respected her "clear thinking, fresh interest and enthusiasm, [and] consideration for Board employes." Her work for the school board eventually led to appointments to the Wisconsin State Board of Education (1917–1919), the Wisconsin Board of Regents of Normal Schools (1927–1928), and the University of Wisconsin Board of Regents (1928–1934).[10]

Meta participated in Victor's work as well. She advised him informally and assisted in the office of the *Milwaukee Leader,* the socialist daily newspaper he founded in 1911. During election campaigns she supervised literature distribution and helped to formulate strategies, eventually gaining enough confidence to "scold" party members for running a poor campaign or to lament decisions made while she was ill in bed. After Victor's death, she was elected to his seat on the Socialist Party's National Executive Committee, an honor accorded very few women.[11]

————

Meta's efforts and skill also brought her influence outside educational and party circles. She joined numerous reform organizations and frequently accepted leadership positions in them. Prior to passage of the Nineteenth Amendment in 1920, she participated most notably in suffrage organizations. She joined the Wisconsin Woman Suffrage Association (WWSA) in 1914, serving as second vice-president for one year and as first vice-president for two years. The middle-class suffrage leaders found Meta's political and administrative experience valuable, but as a Socialist she felt an "undercurrent of suspicion and distrust." She resigned from the organization in 1917, noting candidly that the WWSA was "not sufficiently radical to suit me." She disagreed with the group's tactics and, more importantly, with its strong support for World War I. A week after her resignation she established a chapter of the National Woman's Party,

[9] Stevens, ed., *Family Letters,* 157, 192.

[10] "Twenty-two Years Ago . . . ," ca. 1931; "Mrs. Meta Schlichting Berger Served the Children of Milwaukee . . . ," July 5, 1944; both roll 33, VLB Papers (microfilm).

[11] Stevens, ed., *Family Letters,* 361.

a competing suffrage organization, and soon afterward shared a podium with the first woman elected to the U.S. House of Representatives, Jeannette Rankin of Montana. In the following decades Meta turned to peace work, serving on the national committee of the Women's International League for Peace and Freedom (WILPF), an organization established and led by social reformer Jane Addams. Meta valued efforts to secure peace but found the WILPF unimpressive. "Generally speaking," she remarked, "it is a conservative groupe, well meaning but not courageous."[12]

In her suffrage and peace work, Meta joined millions of educated middle-class female reformers who built a large network of organizations in the late nineteenth and early twentieth centuries—organizations ranging from temperance campaigns to settlement houses to suffrage associations. These women created a place for themselves in public life and shaped their society, but they kept their organizations distinct from those of men. In fact, many of them justified their involvement in social and political affairs by pointing to their feminine values and by using metaphors about motherhood. These reformers sought to improve the condition of women and of the working class, but they did so without directly challenging the gender or economic systems.[13]

However, Socialist women—even those of middle-class origin, like Meta—identified with the working class and questioned economic arrangements; Socialist women were also more likely to question social traditions. Socialist women did build organizations separate from men, but a few women of Meta's generation succeeded in achieving influence within the regular party organization and urged other women to follow suit. Meta may have found rhetoric about so-called feminine values resonant or useful at times, but she nevertheless took at face value the party's pledge of sexual equality. She demonstrated her commitment to expanding women's roles through her educational and suffrage work, for example, by defending the right of married women to teach. She once criticized a fellow Socialist for making a "purely moral" argument in favor of woman suffrage, meaning that she disapproved of arguments for change based solely on supposed moral differences between men and women. A firm proponent of equal rights, Meta may have sensed that emphasizing differences hindered rather than furthered women's integration into public life.[14]

[12] "Mrs. Berger Dies, Aged 71," *Milwaukee Journal,* June 17, 1944; Stevens, ed., *Family Letters,* 339.

[13] Mary P. Ryan, *Womanhood in America: From Colonial Times to the Present* (New York: Franklin Watts, 1983).

[14] Mari Jo Buhle, *Women and American Socialism, 1870–1920* (Urbana: University of Illinois Press, 1981); Stevens, ed., *Family Letters,* 151.

Meta found that her methods and goals sometimes conflicted with those of middle-class reformers, but she shared many of their values, including a concern for community standing. Victor believed in a gradual, evolutionary socialism, and he sought to affect events and institutions by gaining a position of influence. This stance placed Victor and Meta in the Socialist Party's right wing, at odds with the party's revolutionaries. As a political figure, taking part in the life of the community and gaining recognition and respect—even grudging respect—was important to Meta. She enjoyed her own prominence and, by association, Victor's. Encouraging Doris and her husband, Colin Welles, to raise their public profiles, Meta urged them to go out and "be seen" in Milwaukee.[15]

Meta was decisive and politically adept in her middle and old age. A woman of action, she knew how to get things done. She managed a household, often in her husband's absence, raised three children, and served as an adviser to her temperamental husband—all while pursuing her own career on the school board and in reform. Although she had never expected anything more than a conventional life, after her initial election to the school board she pursued her career in public service with great zest. "In spite of her gentle and helpful personality," Doris wrote, "Mama was really not essentially domestic. She fooled people. In a way she fooled Papa. She was wholly without domestic interests. And not as meek as she seemed." This comment suggests that Meta, like many of her fellow reformers, used an image of domesticity to help achieve her ends. But as Doris noted, though Meta was generally pleasant and respectful of others in her work, she was also quite capable of defending unpopular positions. Exemplifying her forthrightness is the speech she made on her first day as a regent for the Wisconsin normal schools: "I finally told the board that I personally [believed] that by figuring so closely that we positively allowed the schools to deteriorate was poor public policy and that instead of trying to shield the poor legislators by not being too hard on them in our requests for money that I for one would go before them and put the responsibility squarely upon their shoulder. If we maintain a fire-trap then the refusal for the money to repair such conditions must be theirs. . . . Well,—I guess I threw a bomb alright enough. The whole board was up in arms at once and didn't know just what to do with such an unruly member."[16]

Meta could be assertive, even blunt on occasion, in defense of her convictions, but she was also sociable and compassionate. By midlife she chatted

[15] Stevens, ed., *Family Letters,* 377.
[16] Hursley, biography; "Mrs. Berger Dies, Aged 71," *Milwaukee Journal,* June 17, 1944; Stevens, ed., *Family Letters,* 376–377.

easily and well with both laborers and dignitaries, meeting brewery workers, schoolteachers, international socialist leaders, and U.S. presidents in the course of her and Victor's public careers. She took pride in her ability to raise money for the many causes she championed. Her idealism was not an abstraction but an extension of her compassion for others: she believed in socialism because she expected it to improve people's lives. Her goal was simply "the greatest good for the greatest number." Never a theorist—indeed, she never read the works of Karl Marx—she left the interpretation of events to Victor.[17]

Meta attributed much of her own success to Victor and devoted a great deal of her autobiography to his career, sometimes leaving the impression that her own work was a peripheral concern. This seems unlikely, given the extent and the nature of her accomplishments. Her focus on Victor can be explained, at least in part, by Meta's desire to write with an eye to the audience curious about her well-known husband. It may also result from a modesty she shared with other women of the Progressive era, who often implied in their auto-biographies—though not in their letters—that their successes simply occurred rather than elaborating on their part in creating them. In writing about their unconventional lives, these women still tried in some ways to make them fit conventional expectations. Meta emphasized that she played a supporting role in her husband's career, and she minimized her own ambition. She portrayed her election to the school-board presidency as unsought and uncertain, though her letters reveal otherwise, and she decided against writing a chapter about her successful fund-raising efforts because she thought it "immodest" to high-light her skill. It is even possible that she exaggerated her surprise and con-sternation at her initial nomination to the school board.[18]

The United States' entrance into World War I dramatically changed the Bergers' lives. Meta and Victor opposed American involvement in the war and were shocked by the repressive measures used to squelch dissent. The day after Congress declared war on Germany in 1917, the national Socialist Party made a formal statement of opposition to the war. This action provoked a wave of anti-Socialist sentiment throughout the country, but in Milwaukee—long iden-tified with both German culture and with socialism—feelings ran particularly high. The anti-German sentiment fostered by the war speeded the assimilation of the city's German population and ended the prestige of its culture. During the course of the war, hysterical superpatriots attacked every aspect of German

[17] Frink Notes; "Mrs. Berger Dies, Aged 71," *Milwaukee Journal,* June 17, 1944.

[18] Jill K. Conway, "Convention vs. Self-Revelation: Women's Autobiography in the Progressive Era," June 13, 1983, Project on Women and Social Change, Smith College, Northampton, Mass.; see also Jill Ker Conway, *When Memory Speaks: Reflections on Autobiography* (New York: Knopf, 1998); Stevens, ed., *Family Letters,* 189–192n; Frink Notes.

culture in Milwaukee—language, music, art, and politics—and by 1920 few outward signs of this culture survived.[19]

The Socialist Party's antiwar position attracted federal scrutiny, resulting in a rash of indictments against its leaders and the loss of mailing privileges for their newspapers and party organs. Victor was one of several party leaders, including the popular Eugene Debs and Kate Richards O'Hare, who were convicted and sentenced to long prison terms under the Espionage Act, a wartime measure employed by the federal government to silence antiwar agitators. The party had grown rapidly before the war, but the indictment and imprisonment of party leaders took a heavy toll, and the party's membership fell dramatically during and after the war. Some Socialists left because they objected to the party's antiwar position, while a postwar struggle for party dominance prompted the radical wing to leave and form the Communist and Communist Labor Parties.[20]

These war years were traumatic for Meta Berger. Her antiwar activism and German heritage provoked hostility in suffrage meetings and in the school superintendent's office. Angry war supporters anonymously threatened her and vandalized her home. Despite such treatment, the withdrawal of mailing rights from Victor's *Milwaukee Leader* caught her by surprise, and his arrest and indictment turned her shock to fear. Indicted by the federal government for publishing antiwar editorials, Victor and four other Socialists were tried in Chicago during the winter of 1918–1919. All five defendants were convicted. (The Supreme Court overturned their convictions on a technicality in 1921.) At the close of the trial, Meta played a central role in collecting bond money to secure the defendants' release during the appeal process. She returned home exhausted and disillusioned, and in later years she frequently remarked that her hair had turned white during the course of the trial. Her only pleasant memory of the Chicago trial was a quiet Christmas Eve at Hull House with pacifist and social reformer Jane Addams, who had closely followed the trial.[21]

Victor's troubles continued. Elected to Congress by the Fifth District of Wisconsin in the fall of 1918, Congress refused to seat him in the spring—following his conviction—and instead formed a committee to study the question of his eligibility for office. The committee found him ineligible the following October, and in November the full Congress voted to exclude him. Milwaukee's Socialist Party nominated Victor to run again in the ensuing special election, and the voters stubbornly elected him once more. Congress barred

---

[19] Still, *Milwaukee,* 455–464.

[20] Sally M. Miller, *Victor Berger and the Promise of Constructive Socialism, 1910–1920* (Westport, Conn.: Greenwood, 1973).

[21] "Mrs. Berger Dies, Aged 71," *Milwaukee Journal,* June 17, 1944.

him a second time, leaving the Fifth District without representation for the remainder of the term.

Elected to Congress again in 1922, after wartime emotions had cooled, Victor took his seat without debate and served three full terms before losing office in 1928. Meta resided in Washington during part of his congressional service but continued to serve on educational boards in Wisconsin. In Washington she was restless: "This life is easy—lazy—has some charm," she wrote, "but I sort of miss my active home life with all its interests & ups & downs." She joined new organizations to keep busy and to serve. In 1924 she accepted a position on the WILPF's national board and helped to organize the Progressive movement that nominated Robert M. La Follette for the presidency.[22]

Meta traveled widely after the war. In 1921–1922 she toured Asia on her way to the Philippines, where she visited her daughter and son-in-law, Doris and Colin Welles. Still bitter about her wartime experiences at the start of the trip, she returned six months later in good spirits. The following year Meta accompanied Victor to an international socialist convention in Germany, where they witnessed the ravages of currency inflation. In 1932 she attended a disarmament conference in Geneva as a delegate for the WILPF, and in 1935 she visited the Soviet Union.

In the postwar years Meta also followed with great interest the education and careers of her grown daughters. Both succeeded in entering demanding professions with few female practitioners. Doris studied at the University of Wisconsin in Madison, where she earned undergraduate and master's degrees, and at Marquette University in Milwaukee, where she earned a law degree in 1926. She subsequently practiced law in Milwaukee, and from 1936 to 1941 she served as the state unemployment compensation examiner. During World War II she wrote for radio, and after Meta's death she and her second husband, Frank Hursley, moved to California to pursue careers in scriptwriting. Elsa joined her sister at the University of Wisconsin for her undergraduate education and in 1923 received an M.D. from the University of Pennsylvania. She trained at the Central Dispensary and Emergency Hospital and the Episcopal Eye, Ear, and Throat Hospital, both in Washington, D.C.; studied for a year at the University of Vienna; and in 1927 became licensed to practice medicine in Massachusetts, where she worked until 1930. From 1930 to 1964 she practiced medicine in Milwaukee.

Victor died in Milwaukee on August 7, 1929, twenty-two days after a streetcar accident. In the years that followed, Meta's relationship with the Socialist Party became strained. On her return from the Soviet Union, she openly

---

[22] Stevens, ed., *Family Letters,* 352.

sympathized with the Communist Party, favoring united action among leftist organizations in response to the rise of fascism. Her affiliation with Communists and support for socialist-communist cooperation provoked the disapproval of Socialist Party leaders, whose objections eventually led to her resignation from the party in 1940. Although she retained ties to individual Communists, she never formally joined the Communist Party.

In Meta's final years a heart ailment forced her to curtail her political activity. She retired from the school board in 1939 and lived quietly on a farm near Thiensville, just north of Milwaukee, together with Doris; Doris's husband, Frank Hursley; and Doris's three daughters. In 1943 Meta undertook the writing of her autobiography. She included much biographical material about Victor and undoubtedly intended to provide an intimate, inside view of him and his work. Probably, she wished to explain or defend her own actions as well. The writing project gave her a sense of purpose in her final months, but it was incomplete at her death on June 16, 1944, at age seventy-one. Friends held a memorial meeting in her honor on April 26, 1945.[23]

Throughout her life, Meta Berger juggled many responsibilities—marriage, child raising, school-board service, political and reform work—more or less simultaneously. Naive and uncertain in her youth, she grew to become a confident and capable woman who thrived on activity and made a strong effort to improve the lives of Milwaukee's schoolchildren and working people. Once anxious about attending her first school-board meeting, she later interacted easily with national and international leaders. At age seventy, she looked back with pride on her development from politically uninvolved housewife to public figure, and she portrayed her sometimes very difficult life as full and interesting despite its hardships. Her views on the political questions of her day come from a participant's perspective, and her choices and accomplishments stand as an example of what a determined and spirited woman of her era could do.

[23] "Field Cites Need for Open Minds," *Chicago Sun*, April 27, 1945.

A Note on the Text

Meta Berger wrote her autobiography during the final year of her life, working mostly alone in bed. Her close friend, Miriam Frink, former associate director of the Layton School of Art, believed that the writing gave Meta comfort, but Meta was denied the satisfaction of completing the manuscript or of seeing it in print. The loose, handwritten pages that she left at her death constituted a first draft: the story contained gaps in her experience, awkward and unfinished sentences, repeated material, and factual errors. She had organized some sections into chapters, but most she had not. A planned final chapter or two on her support for the Republicans in the Spanish Civil War, her resignation from the Socialist Party, and her subsequent activities remained unwritten.[24]

Frink assisted Meta throughout the writing of her autobiography. "We would talk," Frink remembered, "and then by herself she would write material for me to take or go over." Frink occasionally changed or added to the manuscript during her review. She believed that Meta's "mind was clear and her memories vivid," and she noted that Meta frequently referred to the manuscript as an autobiography. In 1971 Frink deposited two versions of the manuscript with the State Historical Society of Wisconsin: Meta's handwritten original and a version prepared by a typist. Frink never examined the typed copy.[25]

The autobiography of Meta Berger is thus a document intended for publication but existing only in rough form. The editor has attempted to discern Meta's plans for the manuscript as much as possible, not to complete the manuscript but to make it more accessible to readers according to her intent. The typed version of the autobiography is easier to read, but it is missing a substantial portion of the text and contains numerous transcription errors. For these reasons, the transcription in this volume is based upon the handwritten original. The unfinished narrative, which ends abruptly in 1935, is followed by an afterword, written by the editor, summarizing Meta's final years. The editor has formed, numbered, and titled the chapters. Meta's own headings, when they exist, serve as titles; otherwise, titles are from phrases within chapters. The documents Meta intended to append—speeches, a party proclamation, trial transcripts—have not been reprinted here because they refer to Victor Berger's work and are available in other published sources. (Citations for the sources are provided.) Factual mistakes in the narrative, when detected,

---

[24] Frink Notes.

[25] Miriam Frink, "How I Happened to Work with Mrs. Victor Berger on Her Unfinished Autobiography," June 6, 1969, VLB Papers.

have been corrected in the footnotes. Miriam Frink's additions to the manuscript appear in footnotes as well, along with a few ambiguous corrections made by either Frink or Meta. Meta's grammar has been preserved, with a few minor exceptions, but some punctuation has been added, and her capitalization has been corrected to aid the reader in following the story and to clarify meaning. For the same reasons, most spelling errors, including errors in names, have been silently corrected; abbreviations and numbers have been spelled out; and a few paragraphs have been condensed. Words in brackets have been added by the editor.

CHAPTER 1

"A Happy Family"

We were a happy family of the so-called middle class living on the south side of Milwaukee. My father, Bernhard Schlichting,[1] was a genial big man with twinkling blue eyes who passionately loved his family and often played and danced with his children. A large room, boasting of the only hard-wood floor and containing an old-fashioned square piano, provided the dancing space and music.

My mother, Matilda,[2] was a tiny frail dark-haired woman, and my early recollection always placed her in the hopeful condition of soon having another baby. There were five living children, an older sister very beautiful, myself the ugly duckling, a younger sister good looking too, and two younger brothers.[3]

Father had a federal job with a fair salary, was interested in politics in a way, and was a member of the Wisconsin legislature at that time. He was also quite a figure in the life of the Masonic groups and in the Turner's Society—which was an organization mainly for gymnastics, but also it had splendid lecture courses and many very delightful social affairs.[4] Mother of course was

[1] Bernhard Schlichting (1838–1884) was born in Germany and immigrated to the United States in 1847. A Civil War veteran and a bookkeeper, he married in 1868 and served in the Wisconsin Assembly (1875–1876) as a Republican and on the Milwaukee school board (1878–1883).

[2] Matilda Krak Schlichting (1847–1905) was born in Germany and immigrated to the United States in 1852.

[3] The Schlichting children were Paula (1871–1902), Meta (1873–1944), Hedwig "Hattie" (1874–1959), Ernst (1876–1920), and Walter (1883–1898). Paula married Archibald Anderson and had one son; Hattie married Frank Schweers, a widower with five children, and had one daughter; Ernst married Arline Warnke.

[4] Turner societies, or *Turnvereine*, were social and athletic clubs established in this country by German immigrants.

busy at home. Living with us was a very crotchety old grandmother,[5] my mother's mother, who was so much a martinet that we feared her more or less and I wish I could honestly say that we loved her. Well, we loved her but not too much!

Due to father's outside activity, he was elected a school commissioner. As a result we were more or less favorites in our public school. I remember once when he came to visit my school, I had opened my geography book, stood it up, and behind it had my head on my folded arms and was sound asleep. You see I was a thumb sucker and could always fall asleep. The teacher was very embarrassed. Not father! He laughed, picked me up and took me home.

When I say we belonged to the middle class I meant we were comfortable, well fed, owned our home and even owned a horse and a two seated rig. This meant countryside drives and visits to the farmer friends in the suburbs. These Sunday jaunts were the high spots of enjoyment for the whole family. It was great fun to pick apples and hickory nuts in the fall and to visit the barns and pig-pens.

As school commissioner, father had the responsibility of seeing that the school was properly run. He was empowered to recommend for appointment teachers whose qualifications had been okayed by the superintendent of schools. So one summer day while we were playing and romping through the house and yard, I suddenly bounced into the music room when I was very surprised and a little shocked to see, sitting on the edge of a chair, a young man. He was tall, brown eyed, wore glasses, had a high pompadour hair comb, shoes shined, well tailored suit with a silk handkerchief carefully showing out of a breast pocket. He seemed as surprised as I was. He was visibly shy, for he wasn't relaxed enough to sit comfortably on the whole chair. Naturally I got out as fast as I could. Little then did I know that that young man, Victor L. Berger, was the man who would years later become my husband. After a rather long interview with my father, he was appointed teacher of German in the eighth ward public school of Milwaukee. That was in 1882.

The years following were uneventful as school life is for any child. Victor Berger was a fairly good teacher. He had a difficult time, as I later discovered, to get his mind and thoughts down to the level of child-life and the ABC of learning. This is easily understood when we realize that his entire training and education was European.

Victor L. Berger was born in 1860 in a tiny village called Nieder-Rehbach in Austria Hungary.[6] His parents in his early youth were well-to-do, owning

---

[5] Matilda J. Krak (1813–1890) was born in Germany and immigrated to the United States in 1852.

[6] Victor Luitpold Berger was born on February 28, 1860, to Ignatz and Julia Berger. The family moved to Leutschau in north-central Hungary when he was seven.

and operating the only respectable inn in the village. Apparently they had a good trade, for Victor's mother was an excellent cook and manager and every afternoon the towns-people gathered at this inn for a string-concert.

Unfortunately the public schools at that time were few and far apart and according to Victor's parents not good—at least not good enough for him. So at a very early age Victor was sent to a private tutor, to live in his house and to receive his early education there. Mrs. Berger, his mother, provided him with all the necessary things such as plenty of clothing, shoes etc. However when she went to visit her son and gave him a coin to spend, he immediately bought himself bread or a roll. This was a surprise to Mother Berger. Upon investigation she found that Victor and two other students were not given enough to eat. Immediately another school was found. So the early years were always spent finding schools and better schools.

During this period, the country was being developed. Railroads were built where none had been before. But the new railroad by-passed the little village where the Bergers lived, and as a result the business of the inn grew less and less until finally they were forced to give it up.

However—Victor was now ready for the university. He attended the University of Budapest and later the University of Vienna. Before he graduated from the latter institution he had reached the military age which required him to join Emperor Franz Jozef's army. This he was unwilling to do since he did not then believe in militarism. Therefore he left the country for America.[7]

Here he had a hard time, like all immigrants. He did not know the language and he had little money. His first job was selling leather goods. This did not pay. Then he became a metal polisher which at least brought in enough so he could eat. But soon he found other and for him more congenial work, such as tutoring. While tutoring he learned the English language, but he never quite got over a German accent. He finally came to Milwaukee as a tutor to the son of A. W. Rich, a shoe manufacturer, and was later employed as a teacher of German in the public schools.

However he was a good mixer in those days and it was not very long before he became quite a figure in the community. He joined the Turner's Society, organized the then famous "reading circle" of contemporaries, joined the Masonic lodge and made friends with the so-called real people of the south side of Milwaukee. He also became a good friend of my father and his family.

A warm heart, a generous spirit and a sense of keen justice endeared him to the whole population of the south side of the city. He need only to have heard of distress in some family and quite without anyone knowing—help

---

[7] Victor Berger studied history and political economy but never graduated. He immigrated to the United States in 1878. His family followed later and settled in Bridgeport, Connecticut.

arrived. At Christmas time, he would hire a horse and wagon and drive to the home of every child who attended our school and present each one with a story book (German of course), an orange, an apple and a bag of candy.

Discipline in the classes where German was taught was always more difficult and Victor Berger's classes were no exception. I still recall the time when he thought I had exceeded the rules and asked me to stay after the class was dismissed so that he could mete out punishment. Needless to say I was interested and waited with bated breath. When my turn came, I was asked to put on my mittens. Surprised, I did so. Then the ruler came out and I was asked to open the palm of my hand for the blow. It came! But so gently that both teacher and pupil burst into a broad grin and we became the best of friends.

During my last year in that school, Victor Berger invited five of the students to come to his home every Saturday morning for private lessons in the German classics. Here, I had my first introduction to reading of Schiller, Goethe, Heine and scores of other German writers and playwrights. After these classes he always walked home with me.[8]

To augment his income he wrote for the newspapers, and became the foremost dramatic critic of the town.

During the summer vacations, he attended the summer sessions of the University of Wisconsin, but soon gave up attending classes, because he said he knew as much as and more than the professors, and preferred to lie on the grass and enjoy the sunshine and scenery from Observatory Hill in Madison.[9]

And now, the first real tragedy came into our lives. One January 3—1883[10]—we children were summoned home from school because father suddenly died from a heart attack. Not realizing fully what this meant, we eagerly sought our little mother. One look at her tragic face told us that something terrible had happened. Mother collapsed and was unable to attend the funeral. I was commissioned to stay with her during those sad hours.

Soon afterward we all felt her worries, the lack of things we needed, saw mother always planning for the future of her brood. It was at this time that Victor Berger again came forward with friendship and help.

To help pay the grocery bill, mother took in boarders. The teachers from the school came in a body to get their noon day meals and thus helped. Victor L. Berger was among them. And each day—he left his pie or *Kuchen* [cake] or dessert, first to one and then to another of the children. Many years later I

---

[8] The preceding sentence probably was added by Miriam Frink.
[9] Victor Berger attended summer school at the University of Wisconsin in Madison in 1890.
[10] Bernhard Schlichting died on January 3, 1884.

discovered that he too had a yearning for sweets. Then I realized what he had given up as a kindness so we could have his share.

He called regularly to see if we needed anything, always bringing good things to eat. I remember I had my first taste of fresh pineapple because he presented us with one. Then he, who had never been taught to use his muscles, helped mother stretch and tack down an ingrain carpet. How he sweat and swore too.

By this time I had left the grammar school. Times were very very hard for the family. My oldest sister chose to get a job as a clerk in a dry-good store; my younger sister gave music lessons at twenty-five cents an hour. My two younger brothers were too young to do anything. As for myself; I begged to go to high school some four miles across town, agreeing to do the housework, washing and ironing on Saturdays and Sundays so that I could earn the fifty cents a day a cleaning woman would have cost. After much debate and pleading I was allowed to try it for a semester. As a result I hurried through my chores, packed a roll and perhaps an apple and walked the four miles to school. I still vividly remember how I froze with the cold during the four mile walk, especially if I got caught at the railroad tracks when long long freight trains held me up. But I was not discouraged; cold yes! Hungry yes! But the high school beckoned to me always. So one year stretched to two, then three and then four!

During these years, I never had a new dress but always wore those my oldest sister, who was earning a little money, didn't choose to wear anymore. Once mother made me a dress out of some old cloth but unfortunately she wasn't much of a seamstress. The result was she cut the left side of a basque [bodice] narrower than the right. Consequently the revers [lapels] which should have pointed exactly to the center at the lower end of the basque always pointed some inch or more to the left. I was embarrassed and kept pulling the point towards the center. Finally a well-to-do pupil at the school asked, "What is the matter with your dress anyway?" It was then my oldest sister bought me a beautiful lace collar and cuffs, hoping thereby to distract attention from the crooked basque.

It was during these high school years that Victor Berger, who was then the best known dramatic critic, came to the house again. He wanted to give us the opportunity to get acquainted with drama and music. So in all fairness he took each of us in turn to the theater. First my oldest sister, then myself and then my youngest sister. Thus we girls had the great opportunity of seeing and hearing the best the stage had to offer. Olga Nethersole, Richard Mansfield, Sarah Bernhardt, Mrs. Leslie Carter, Eleanor Duce, Julia Marlowe, Emma Calvé and all the stars of those years. Not only did we see them in one play but in their entire repertoire of plays. Not only drama but opera were treated to us. We heard all the famous operas, learned the music and story of Wagnerian saga, the Italian, French and other operas, in fact everything produced at that time was shown us. We certainly had a marvelous background.

Besides all these opportunities, there was conducted in Milwaukee a German theater to which we went every Wednesday night. Here we not only saw the best German plays but also heard the German language spoken. This helped immeasurably to keep us familiar with that language. Then there was the open air opera given each summer at the famous Schlitz Park. These too were enjoyed by all of us.

So while it is true, we were deprived of every luxury at home, while we constantly were worried over the payments of the most necessary bills, there was this bright side to our lives, giving us privileges the benefits of which were to last throughout life.

The years were slipping by. My oldest sister suddenly found she had an ardent admirer, and so that Victor might not interfere with this budding romance, she was crossed off the theater list. Therefore my younger sister and I had our pleasures increased by going that much oftener.

There was still another institution peculiar to Milwaukee which for *Gemütlichkeit* [a cozy, congenial atmosphere] couldn't be surpassed. This was a Sunday afternoon concert, given in the West Side Turner Hall by Bach's Orchestra. Here the good German burghers met weekly around the coffee table with their entire family to listen to exquisite music. Victor Berger frequented this hall and always took either my sister or me with him.

So much for the background. The years were passing and I was now a student at the normal school.[11] In the meantime, there were changes taking place in Victor Berger's life. He had left the teaching profession to become the editor of a German weekly paper called *Die Wahrheit*.[12] Just why he took this step was laid to the fact that once while debating with Johann Most, the famous anarchist,[13] the Turner Society had voted Victor the honors. This was easily

---

[11] Normal schools trained teachers. Meta Schlichting graduated from the Wisconsin State Normal School in Milwaukee in 1894.

[12] Victor Berger resigned from his teaching position in December 1892. In January 1893 he began publication of the daily Wisconsin Vorwärts (formerly the *Milwaukee'r Volkszeitung*), titling the Sunday edition of the paper *Vorwärts* (Onward); in the same month he took command of the weekly *Die Wahrheit* (The Truth). In 1898 he ceased publication of Wisconsin Vorwärts but continued to publish the weekly *Vorwärts* and *Die Wahrheit* as organs of Milwaukee's Social Democratic Party. Berger discontinued *Die Wahrheit* in 1910 and relinquished editorship of *Vorwärts* in 1911.

[13] Johann Most (1846–1906) was a German-born anarchist who immigrated to the United States in 1882. A powerful speaker and writer, Most became influential among American anarchists and served multiple prison terms for inciting violence.

understood since all members of the Turner's Society were middle class and very conservative and hardly followed Mr. Most. Victor however told me later that he did not deserve the honor since Johann Most had all the reasons and the best arguments which decried the social and economic system. He then and there began to study and read with the final result that he emerged a Socialist. Confirmed in the belief that socialism was the way out, he dropped his teaching of little children and decided to go in for teaching the grown-ups. There was only one way to do this, and that was through the printed page. Therefore the weekly German paper. This required money and he had none. He took on new responsibilities and burdens and these worried him.

He now became serious, impatient, critical.

I recalled the little place on State Street, a little store, which became the home of *Die Wahrheit*. The presses were in the basement; the editorial office, mailing room and business office were on the street floor. Money was scarce but sometimes credit was good—good for the extreme emergencies such as buying print paper. Salaries were on the books, seldom paid in full. In the winter months coal was scarce. The editor worked with his mittens on to keep his hands warm. When a business acquaintance came into the place unexpectedly, a twenty-five cent bushel of coal was hurriedly gotten and a slow fire was maintained. Throughout those early years in newspaper life Victor carried a heavy load. But not once did he lose faith in the work he had set out to do.

He was now much more serious and weighed down with care. But still he came to see us and take us to the theater. It was on the way home from the theater that I became engaged to Victor Berger. To say I was scared was putting it mildly. He was thirteen years older than I was. He was so much wiser than I was. I was just a stupid, uninformed girl ready to graduate as a teacher in Milwaukee. How often during the intervening years I have condemned the training of teachers. How very little the great mass of teachers know of the world and all its complications. Few indeed have any idea of the Industrial Revolution and the building of a great capitalist world. Imperialism! Power politics! Raw materials elsewhere! Trade! The struggle of the masses for living standards! All and more of these important questions were wholly foreign to the teachers of my early days. And even now our new teachers and many of the older ones are unfit to teach.

Victor Berger, like a true continental European, undertook to remake me according to the pattern he thought a wife should be. Mostly it was difficult for me, and sometimes I spent unhappy moments trying to understand and catch up.

If it were not for the relaxation we got from the theater, I wonder if we could have made a go of it. And now I must tell you of a queer conduct by

Victor. Although I was to be his wife, he continued to take my sister Hattie to the theater as often as he did me. I was hurt and a little shocked the first time it happened. Then I sort of adjusted myself to the situation but was always a little hurt. I loved my sister very much but felt doubtful of my own status. One Sunday afternoon I had attended Bach's concert with him, and walking home from the concert he told me that in the evening he was taking my sister Hattie to the German theater. Again I was stunned and for a while said nothing. Finally I told him that I would go with him that evening, or he need never take me again. He just smiled and we walked on. He had supper with us and finally at theater time he came to me and said, "If you insist, then come!" Well! I went! That evening he acted sort of gay and joked quite a bit and finally told me that through the many months he was taking Hattie, he had waited for me to assert myself and now he was happy I had finally found the courage to do it. After that whenever Hattie went with us, three of us went. I guess I needed that experience for I began to feel that I too must assert myself and have confidence in myself.

It was about this time that Victor Berger and a few—very few—comrades started to organize the Socialist Party of Milwaukee.[14] The group met in a tavern run by John Doerfler,[15] who also became an ardent Socialist. That meant they were going into local politics. Now, Victor Berger lost for the time being his respectable standing with the so-called well-to-do middle class. He became known as a radical, he was charged with having imported his radical ideas from Germany, where the workers were well organized in labor and political movements and where much good social legislation had been enacted.

And now my education as the future wife of a radical began in earnest. Victor insisted that I accompany him to many many meetings at which the workers gathered. So when the meetings were on street corners (a new innovation at that time) I stood in the shadow of a building or a tree. I went into attic rooms and basement quarters and in tavern halls. Most of the talk was in German, way above my head and hard to follow. I didn't tell mother or my friends where I had been. Some kind of shameful reticence kept me quiet.

So the years went by, and the great American Railway Union strike was threatened. This was my introduction to labor's weapon, the strike! For a week

[14] Victor Berger and fifteen others established the Milwaukee branch of the Social Democracy of America in 1897. In 1898 Berger and Eugene Debs led a faction out of the Social Democracy of America and created the Social Democratic Party. In 1901 this party joined with another group of socialists (former members of the Socialist Labor Party) and named the new organization the Socialist Party. The Milwaukee members retained the name Social Democratic Party for their local organization until 1916.

[15] John Doerfler (1854?–1933) helped found Milwaukee's Social Democratic Party. The bar in the boardinghouse he ran for brewery workers became a common meeting place for party members.

I didn't see Victor. Later I found that he attended the Chicago trial of Eugene V. Debs,[16] tried for contempt of court. Victor traveled to Chicago daily, came back at night to write the story, and [went] back to Chicago the next day to watch the trial. It was due to a contempt of court charge that Eugene V. Debs—the idol of the ARU and of the workers in general—received a three year prison sentence in the prison at Woodstock, Illinois. Debs was made of the stuff that heroes and martyrs are made of. He went to Woodstock and became an avid student of the economic theories which he hoped someday might save civilization. It is needless to say that Victor Berger was a faithful visitor to Debs at Woodstock. Berger went armed with books, pamphlets and reading material. He was well repaid for his interest and trouble. When Debs emerged from prison he had become an avowed Socialist. The two men had become bosom friends, which lasted throughout the life of both.[17]

"It was at this time, when the first glimmerings of Socialism were beginning to penetrate, that Victor L. Berger—and I have loved him ever since—came to Woodstock, as if a providential instrument, and delivered the first impassioned message of Socialism I had ever heard—the very first to set 'the wires humming in my system.' As a souvenir of that visit there is in my library a volume of 'Capital,' by Karl Marx, inscribed with the compliments of Victor L. Berger, which I cherish as a token of priceless value."—Eugene V. Debs by David Karsner.[18]

A new world was unfolding for me. To be initiated into political life and labor struggles and the radical movement all at once, seemed to me more than I could absorb. When I asked my future husband to explain, sometimes he just laughed at me and said, "Du bist eine dumme Gans" [You are a silly goose] or he would with some irritation say, "Das verstehst du nicht" [You don't get it]. That hurt. And we would quarrel and I'd slam the door with an angry "Good night," not knowing whether or not I'd ever see him again. But strange as it may seem, he had forgotten all about the quarrel long before the next evening, and while I hadn't, I was quite careful not to ask questions which might provoke answers I didn't like. So now I was also learning to be tactful. Victor Berger was kind and generous enough but he was also arrogant and an egotist. But he was wise and far-sighted too.

---

[16] Eugene V. Debs (1855–1926) was a labor organizer and popular leader in the Socialist Party who received his party's presidential nomination five times. In 1893, before becoming a socialist, Debs organized the American Railway Union, the first industrial union in the United States. The following year he led the union in a strike ended by federal injunction that resulted in a jail term for him and others.

[17] Berger and Debs represented opposing factions of the Socialist Party and for much of the period after 1905 were hostile to each other, though they reconciled in the final years of Debs's life.

[18] David Karsner, *Debs: His Authorized Life and Letters* (New York: Boni and Liveright, 1919), 178.

And so three years went by. I had been teaching in the Island Avenue School under Mr. Kriesel.[19] I guess I was a fairly successful teacher, judging by a nice letter I received from my principal upon my resignation[20] and by the very touching farewell the school (both children and teachers) gave me. I remember when I left for home, flowers from every window of the street car which carried my children home from a school picnic were showered upon me and I was laden with touching and beautiful gifts. Mother and I both wept when I arrived home that last day of teaching. Besides, I had given up a forty-five dollar a month job to marry. No one today can imagine the innumerable little luxuries forty-five dollars could provide for my youngest brother, Walter, who was a bed-ridden invalid with tuberculosis of the hip. And no one can imagine the love and boundless care my devoted mother gave to him. There was nothing that I wouldn't have done to ease the sad situation at home and to give momentary pleasure to my mother and brother. Consequently the thought of leaving a troubled home was saddening to a considerable degree.

However on December 4, 1897, at eight o'clock in the evening, I was married to Victor Berger. Judge Emil Wallber[21] officiated. After some very slight refreshments I left for my new home and a new life.

[19] Meta Schlichting began teaching in the Sixth District Primary School in the fall of 1894; she resigned in November 1897. Christopher A. Kriesel (1853?–1937) served as principal of Island Avenue School from 1893 to 1899.

[20] The letter from Kriesel, dated June 23, 1898, read, in part: "Without exception, teachers who taught the grade above hers, solicited, to be given that class, and since she left the school, her worth has become still more apparent. She will be gladly received back into this school, should she ever apply for a vacant position" (Roll 33, VLB Papers [microfilm]).

[21] Emil Wallber (1841–1923) served in the Wisconsin Assembly (1872), as Milwaukee city attorney (1873–1878), and as mayor of Milwaukee (1884–1888) prior to serving as a judge (1890–1902). From 1906 to 1917 he was a German consular agent in Milwaukee.

CHAPTER 2

No Pie Baker

We moved to a large sunny upper duplex for which we paid the large sum of fifteen dollars a month rent when we had it to pay. But oh! It was a beautiful duplex—measured by the standards of those days. It was furnished completely with carpets, furniture, curtains and all. Later I found out how Victor Berger paid for all this comfort. I knew he had little or no money. He was earning fifteen dollars a week and was paid only when the paper could afford to pay. And yet, here I was in a completely furnished duplex. Well—he had a weekly paper. The paper took advertisements from furniture stores etc., and instead of receiving cash he was paid in kind. Thus it was I was able to start my new life in what I considered luxury. But how long can one live on the satisfaction of looking at a stove or a carpet or a chair etc.? A good meal was also necessary. So we went on a budget. Victor was to take care of rent, coal, light and gas and I was to have five dollars a week for food. Well—we tried it. But party affairs and dues and outside expenses more often than not cut into his budget, and while he tried hard to give me the five dollar a week food budget, that too came in a dollar now, fifty cents then and so on. I do not believe I saw many five dollar bills that first year. Fortunately, his appetite was always good and he never complained about food those early days.

The period of adjustment and readjustment was difficult. Three weeks after I was married I discovered I was pregnant, and [I was] feeling ill most of the time. Added to this, my husband tried to make me the kind of wife he had always imagined a wife should be. Truly continental. I was married now and

11

all of my own interests and friends were to be dropped and I was to be absorbed only in the affairs that he was interested in. A fearful struggle ensued. Again and again I had to assert myself and insist on my own rights and on my own friends. Also he thought I ought now to become his secretary, adopt his political philosophy and even to become a writer of renown. The struggle was hard indeed. You can imagine how often I felt humiliated and frustrated.

His work in the Socialist Party and in the labor movement took him out night after night, leaving me at home wondering what would be the next hurdle I'd have to take. And I did try hard to understand the problems which so absorbed my husband. Finally, when I again asked him to explain things to me, he went to the bookshelves and brought me two books to read: *Merrie England* by Blatchford and *The Cooperative Commonwealth* by Gronlund.[1] "When you have read and understood these books, you will better understand what my work is."

So dutifully I set to work to read. But I hated those books. In my state of health, I wasn't one bit interested in new economic theories. Dry stuff! So no matter how I tried, the books didn't appeal to me. I noticed too how nervous and irritated he was over small things. And how full of care he seemed to be. It was not long after this, that his weekly paper *Die Wahrheit* folded up and Victor Berger, instead of declaring a bankruptcy, assumed full financial responsibility for all the debts.[2] It took him many many years to pay them. The interest on money he borrowed was more than twice the size of the original debts. But pay them he did!

Nothing daunted, he plunged into the newspaper business again, reorganized the old paper, and started another German weekly called *Vorwärts*. This was not only a German newspaper but was mainly a propaganda sheet for the newly organized Socialist Party.[3] Again the financial struggle was fierce. Poor Victor Berger! Little help did he receive from me, who was so absorbed in my coming baby and motherhood. Looking backward now, I often wonder whether I did my full share during those exciting months. Perhaps not! I do not know. At any rate, the prospect of a new baby did not make things easier.

My budget did not allow meat every day. But in those days the butcher

---

[1] Robert Blatchford, *Merrie England: A Plain Exposition of Socialism, What It Is, and What It Is Not* (New York: Commonwealth, 1895); Laurence Gronlund, *The Coöperative Commonwealth in Its Outlines: An Exposition of Modern Socialism* (Boston: Lee and Shepard, 1884).

[2] Victor Berger discontinued the daily *Wisconsin Vorwärts*, rather than *Die Wahrheit*, in 1898.

[3] *Vorwärts* was originally the Sunday edition of the *Wisconsin Vorwärts*. Victor Berger continued to publish the *Vorwärts* on a weekly basis after he discontinued the *Wisconsin Vorwärts*.

saved the sweetbreads, brain and heart of the cows he himself slaughtered and every now and then he made us a present of either the one or the other thing he saved. So I learned to cook brain, heart etc. and make it quite tasty. The only thing we couldn't take with grace was heart. Did you ever cook heart? It is the toughest organ in the body and when cooked it responded to chewing like any tough rubber eraser. Fortunately these days, slaughter houses and packing houses have found better use for that particular organ. And civilization ought to be grateful for it.

Slowly the months of pregnancy came to an end on September 29, 1898. The first signs of the coming of my baby were here. My landlady called the doctor and my husband. Both arrived at about the same time. But the doctor came with his horse and buggy and took me to the hospital. Dr. Kellogg[4] came to get me to take me to [the] hospital. Asked me what it was I wanted most— girl or boy. Then told me fathers were most proud of sons, but girls pulled on the heart strings of fathers more than boys. Hospitals in those days were not overjoyed to take delivery cases. It meant two patients instead of one. Hospitals were really not organized for receiving mother and child. However the Milwaukee Hospital took me in. When my husband arrived, the hospital demanded the two weeks payment in advance. He was stunned! But bravely he issued a check of twenty-four dollars although he feared that night he did not have that much money in the bank. However the next morning before his check came through the usual channels, he had a sufficient amount to cover the twenty-four dollars. Naturally I knew nothing of his financial embarrassment, so as soon as my daughter Doris was born, I felt happy and relieved. [Victor was] disappointed at having a daughter—but adjusted himself within an hour—saying, "This will be a woman's world. She will do her part." [He was] very critical of her, for she must be perfect in every way.

After the regulation time at the hospital I returned home with my baby. Her first bed was the clothes basket, where she slept for many months. And it was really not a bad bed. Of course, now that the baby was here, I naturally believed my husband would take a new interest in home and family and less of an interest in his Socialist Party and the constant meetings held all over the city. I was most disappointed and knew that the entire care of our baby was mine. Well, I loved her so much that this didn't seem a hardship. A two dollar a week maid[5] was added to the household, so that I could devote all spare time to the baby. This new maid was devoted, saving, a good cook, and faithful

---

[4] E. Wells Kellogg (1859–1923) was a prominent Milwaukee physician and Masonic leader and served as a member of the state and city boards of directors of the YMCA.

[5] Josephine "Josie" Rudkowsky (b. 1873).

to us, for she stayed with us twenty-two years.

The Socialist Party was growing. It soon became quite a *national* Socialist Party. This meant that frequently my husband went to Chicago to attend National Executive Committee meetings or he left for a week or ten days to attend conventions. During these months, it seemed to me I was entirely out of his life. It was most difficult for me and often I was saddened because of this. Again and again came the answer to my questions—"Das verstehst du nicht" [You don't get it]. And again I would take down the books which were to be an Open Sesame and read them. Often, after reading page after page—I knew I hadn't gotten anything out of them, merely because I kept wondering whether or not the baby's bottle was too hot or too cold.

Frequently Victor's comrades and friends came to the house. The talk was always about the development of the party, the economic condition of the country, the bourgeoisie, the profiteers, the international situation etc. etc. All I sensed was that I was ignored and not of them. Thus it was when Eugene Debs, Jesse Cox, Corinne Brown and others came to visit frequently.[6]

Secretly I was mortified and then and there made up my mind that things couldn't go on much longer this way. Therefore I listened, learned what I could and began to read. When I was just beginning to follow a little bit, I discovered that I was again pregnant. Now I was not averse to having children. Not at all. But I really couldn't see myself having a large family to support on the meager funds we had to live on. But what to do? I was pregnant! And I had to see it through. But I was determined not to have more children than I could support. Contraceptives were known but were illegal to buy. Anyway I kept brooding on how not to have more children.[7]

In due time another little daughter was born.[8] This time at home. She was a homely little baby with long black hair that stood straight up like a pompadour. I just had to love her, for if I didn't—who would? Often since, I think of that first glimpse of her and I now realize what a fine splendid woman she is and what comfort I got through her. Now my time was well taken up with two babies, and again my efforts to catch up with my husband were interrupted. But not for too long! Money was scarce, times were difficult, but life

---

[6] Jesse Cox (1844?–1902), a Chicago attorney, helped found the Social Democratic Party of America, the precursor to the Socialist Party. Corinne Stubbs Brown (1849–1914), a Chicago public-school teacher and principal, was active in socialist and suffrage movements and served as president of the Illinois Women's Alliance.

[7] Elsa Berger Edelman, Meta and Victor's second daughter, wrote in her memoirs, ca. 1973, "My mother was clever enough to find out that the size of families could be limited, and she obtained a diaphragm. My father never knew the reason for no more pregnancies" ("Second One").

[8] Elsa Berger was born on March 26, 1900.

was interesting even then. My babies were adorable. They began to talk (German) and now Victor Berger was really interested. As a result of this new interest, man-like, he laid down certain rules for the children. Most of them good. Some I disagreed with. The results were constant arguments. Sometimes he won, then again I would win. And it never occurred to me to cheat on the interpretation of rules—no candy—no meat until the children were seven or eight years old but learn to ride and hunt and shoot and swim. How these rules were lived up to will be followed up later. It must not be concluded from what has been written thus far meant that we were unhappy. Far from it! Victor L. Berger was a good provider, far better than his finances permitted. He was kind, generous, loved us in his own way. What reservations I myself had were due largely to my incapacity to follow in the rapid progress made by my husband and by the Socialist Party in the political life in the city and the nation.

Soon a change in my life took place. My husband came home saying he was to attend a Socialist national convention in Chicago within a few days.[9] Again I felt I was left behind. Some quick thinking took place. So without saying a word I determined to attend that convention too. I didn't know quite yet how it was to be managed, but go I would.

So on the day Victor left, he said, "Here, I don't want you to be without money while I am gone" and handed me ten dollars. That was the luckiest ten dollars I ever had. My husband left. I went down town, bought a hat for three dollars and a suit for seven dollars in preparation of my trip to Chicago. But when I got back home my youngest baby was crying with an ear-ache. Now what to do? I called in Dr. Henry Hitz, an old friend and an ear-specialist. When he heard my story about going to Chicago, he took care of the ear and said, "You go to Chicago! I'll take it upon myself to take care of the baby. I'll see her every day and if need be I'll call you at Chicago and you'll be here in two hours. So go to Chicago and be happy!" Now there was a friend indeed.

So the next day I went to Chicago. I couldn't stay at the same hotel with my husband because the cost of a double room cost more than our treasury could stand. That ten dollars was part of my husband's expense account. So I stayed with Mrs. Seymour Stedman,[10] who lived way out on the south side of Chicago. That meant a long ride on the elevated which curved through the streets and alley ways of Chicago and always made me deathly car-sick. But I was in Chicago and as soon as I was able Irene Stedman and I went to Brandt's Hall, where the convention was held. When I entered the hall, and saw the

[9] The convention took place on May 1–6, 1904.

[10] Irene Stedman (b. 1881?) was married to attorney Seymour Stedman (1870–1948), who helped found the Social Democratic Party of America, the precursor to the Socialist Party. Seymour handled many of the party's legal affairs, and in 1920 he was the Socialist Party's vice presidential candidate.

convention in session, I was thrilled. Soon my husband saw me and came over to greet me. "How did you get here?" he asked. I told him how I had managed with his ten dollars and Dr. Hitz. He was so pleased that then and there in the presence of the entire convention he kissed me. Not until later did he worry about where I was to stay. When he discovered I was to be a guest at the Stedmans' he was so relieved because he didn't have money enough for both of us.

This convention was a turning point in my life. I was so interested, so excited, so fired with enthusiasm when I heard those scholarly speeches and arguments, some of which I understood and some I didn't. But the general drift of the purpose of the convention slowly drifted into my consciousness. Anyway I stayed in Chicago throughout the whole period, going to the Stedmans' to sleep while my husband stayed in a rickety hotel with the other bigwigs of the Socialist Party.

Perhaps you think this didn't take a certain amount of perseverance! To a person of my temperament it took all I had.

When we finally arrived back home in Milwaukee, my husband said to me, "Well, *Schatzl* [Sweetheart], what did you learn in Chicago this week?" My reply was—"First of all, all the folks I've been hearing about and reading about became real and human and alive. I know personally now Morris Hillquit, Algernon Lee, Mahlon Barnes, Margaret Haile, James Oneal, George D. Herron and all the others.[11] Then for the first time I got the feeling that a terrific struggle was going on and that you, my husband, were a leader in that struggle and that it was only the beginning of an effort to reach down and help the working masses. And finally—and get this Dear!—I have reached the determination that never again will I stay at home while you go to inspiring conventions. Hereafter I shall attend all conventions with you!"

To say that Victor Berger was a little shocked and a good deal surprised is putting it mildly. And his first reaction was—"Good God! Where will I get the money to take you with me everywhere?"

---

[11] With Victor Berger, Morris Hillquit (1869–1933), a Latvian-born attorney from New York, led the dominant reformist faction of the Socialist Party. Originally a member of the Socialist Labor Party, Hillquit played an important role in bringing that party's dissenting faction into the Socialist Party in 1901. Algernon Lee (1873–1954) edited several Socialist publications and served as educational director of the Rand School in New York City for more than forty years. John Mahlon Barnes (1866–1934) was a Socialist labor leader known for his opposition to Samuel Gompers's leadership of the American Federation of Labor. Margaret Haile, a journalist and women's-rights advocate, helped found the Social Democratic Party of America. James Oneal (1873–1962) was a Socialist Party writer, editor, and speaker. George D. Herron (1862–1925), a well-known minister and writer, joined the Socialist Party around 1899 but left during World War I because of the party's antiwar stance.

"That is your affair, Darling! I'm giving you fair warning. I go to the next convention."

Notwithstanding a certain concern over finances etc. etc., I still believe Victor Berger was secretly pleased that I had finally reached this determination. This was about forty-two years ago.

Next convention was in San Francisco. It was not a Socialist convention but an AFL convention.[12] So I warned my husband to be prepared to take me with him. I hated really to add to his burdens by my insistence, but some Divine Providence stood by me.

When the time came for the San Francisco convention I got my mother and my sister, Hattie, to come to our house to stay with my babies. Victor was troubled about how to get me to attend that convention since the Typographical Union, which he was to represent, paid only ten dollars per diem. To me ten dollars a day seemed like a great future. So I was adamant in my determination to go to San Francisco. Finally one day he came home and said he had secured the railroad passage by accepting small ads from the railroad companies and instead of paying cash for the advertisements the railroad companies issued transportation for both of us. So far so good. But it was agreed that the ten dollars per diem must cover hotel rates for both of us. This meant we could not stay at the hotels which were downtown and large and served as the headquarters of the convention. We had to go to some smaller hotel far from the center of convention activities. This didn't faze me one bit. In fact I was not then aware of the importance of having my husband close to the convention and to the committee meetings. I must say he was a good sport about it. Of course we lost some of the inspiration of a large convention, but I must say I was terribly disillusioned by the character of the AFL convention. It was not on the high level of a Socialist convention. The delegates were on a "spree," having all the drink and fun they could get away from home and acted like naughty half grown youths.

This was the first time I met Sam Gompers[13] and the leaders of the American Federation of Labor. The leaders were better than their followers. But immediately I sensed the vast difference of a trade union movement and a socialist movement. My husband was quite out of tune with the character of the convention and with the conservative trade union non-political stand of

---

[12] The twenty-fourth convention of the American Federation of Labor was held in San Francisco on November 14–26, 1904.

[13] Samuel Gompers (1850–1924) served as president of the American Federation of Labor nearly every year from its establishment in 1886 until his death in 1924. As a labor leader, he was known for his conservatism and political neutrality.

Gompers. In fact the two men were so opposed to each other that often they just snarled at each other. Gompers was determined to keep the trade union movement out of politics or out of any political party. It was his idea to plead with the two old political parties for things labor wanted and then use the labor strength to either support or defeat the party as the case might be. Republican or Democratic party was acceptable provided it supported an eight-hour day or two cents more an hour for workers.

My husband always believed this was the wrong way to get political strength and stood firmly for a political party which represented the workers and espoused the things workers wanted and needed. But Gompers was firmly entrenched as the president of the AFL and when it was time to re-elect a president, the AFL steamroller worked beautifully. VLB prevented a unanimous vote by insisting that the several hundred votes he carried as representative of the International Typographical Union be cast against Gompers.

It was a rather exciting moment when the vote was taken. For about twenty minutes my husband tried to get the floor amid hisses, cat-calls, stamping of feet and derisive shouts. I was up in the gallery watching the performance when a lady sitting next to me said, "Who is that persistent man?" "That persistent man is my husband," was my reply.

Gompers was of course re-elected—[but] not unanimously. I did meet many very fine people however, most notable was Max Hayes—editor of the *Cleveland Citizen*.[14] Emil Liess and his beautiful wife, residents of San Francisco.[15] Both of these were Socialists too.

The next convention was held in August in Boston and was the convention of the Typographical Union.[16] Again finances threatened to keep me home. But once more my husband made the same transportation arrangements with the railroad companies; only this time we frequently had to change trains, for our tickets only carried us part of the way, i.e., as far as that particular segment of the ticket was accepted by the company. This meant changing trains two or three times before we could get to Boston. Since it [was] August and the weather was exceedingly hot, we needed our trunk badly when we arrived. But to our dismay—there was no trunk. It had been carried to Canada due to

---

[14] Max S. Hayes (1866–1945) edited the *Cleveland Citizen*, a publication of the Cleveland Central Labor Union, from 1892 to 1939. He was active in both the Socialist Party and in the American Federation of Labor, but he left the party in 1919 and in 1920 helped found the Farmer-Labor Party. He and Victor Berger represented the International Typographical Union at the 1904 AFL convention.

[15] Miriam Frink made the following note about Emil (1864–1917) and Frieda (b. 1876?) Liess: "Liess—lawyer, German—told Meta Berger he was trying to make his wife the kind of woman he wanted—Continental idea."

[16] The fifty-fourth convention of the International Typographical Union of North America was held in Boston on August 10–15, 1908.

.these frequent changes of trains we were forced to make. Now what to do? We needed a change of linen—in fact a complete change. So with what little money we had we visited Filene's Department Store and secured the most necessary and the cheapest wearing apparel we could find. As it happened, we were to meet Lincoln Steffens, Justice Brandeis and Mr. Filene for dinner on the roof garden of the Filene's Department Store.[17] Naturally I was excited and interested. At the dinner, the talk of course swirled around economics, prices, profits and what not. At one point in the conversation my husband told about our predicament and how easy it was to get the things we needed, and turning to Mr. Filene he said, "Now how much do you think my wife paid for that shirtwaist?" Mr. Filene looked me over and said, "Well, she paid $1.98 for it." Filene knew his stock and got the measure of our finances. I felt a little humiliated, but what was I to do about it? Anyway the friendships which started that evening with L. Steffens and later Justice Brandeis richly repaid me for any and all inconveniences.

The convention itself was fine and on a much higher plane than the San Francisco one.

Then followed other meetings such as the Socialist Party conventions in St. Louis, Indianapolis, Toronto etc. Each one was stimulating and almost like a college course in economics. These trips added immeasurably to my understanding of Socialist Party work and were worth all the time, trouble and inconveniences I endured.

And so never again was Victor Berger to say to me, "Das verstehst du nicht!" A new school of thought gradually took hold of me. It was not easy, but it was stimulating and fascinating. No longer did I resent his going to meetings evening after evening. In fact I went with him. Often these meetings were held in an annex to a tavern, or in a basement room, yes—even in attic rooms. But it was always intensely interesting. I learned so much, so very much from workers at that time.

At home we got along as best we could with our meager income. Often we couldn't pay the rent, and had to make the landlord wait. This debt was always the most painful to me, because my own mother was a landlord and I knew how she felt when tenants were not prompt.

[17] Lincoln Steffens (1866–1936) was a muckraking journalist and lecturer. Louis D. Brandeis (1856–1941) was an attorney concerned with public causes, a Zionist, an adviser to President Wilson, and a U.S. Supreme Court justice (1916–1939). Edward A. Filene (1860–1937) was the innovative and reform-minded president and co-owner of Boston's successful Filene's Department Store.

Yet in spite of all, my children were beautiful healthy little girls and that, seemed to count most. The rules that they do not have candy or meat were strictly enforced. Until I found one of them cheating on us by eating the cheapest and most unwholesome stuff. Then there was a show-down between us as parents. We finally compromised on allowing only the kind of candy which was good and which Victor Berger provided. After that, also meat was allowed. So our rules were being set aside.

Then one day Victor Berger got the notion that his children ought to learn to swim and ride and hunt and shoot. But how was this to be done, while we lived in an upper fifteen dollar a month duplex? Victor Berger was passionately fond of his children and wanted to equip them for life by giving them good healthy bodies. So after much planning, and some doubts, we bought a one hundred foot lot on Shawano Lake for $210. We paid $70 as our share, my sister Hattie paid $70 and my mother the third $70. Then both Hattie and mother turned their share over to me so that we had a deed to the lot. Then we planned a cottage which was to be paid for by yearly installments of $240; which was about the amount my sister and mother made up for a number of years. I mention these arrangements because this Shawano Lake cottage figured years later in the political campaigns waged against my husband.[18]

Well, poor as we were, we had a summer cottage and consequently we spent at least nine to ten weeks of every summer at that delightful place. Needless to say the children learned to swim, and to handle a boat.

The vacations spent at Shawano Lake for years were the delight of the children and a relaxation from the heavier life at home. While Victor Berger had notions for bringing up a family, he was also one of the most unselfish of men. He never complained that he had to spend eight to ten weeks alone in Milwaukee away from his family. Frequently he sent us the choicest fruit and vegetables, because Shawano itself didn't provide any luxuries at all. The stores up there were created to provide the dry groceries for the surrounding farmers, all of whom had their own gardens. Occasionally he came for a weekend, but his restless spirit away from his cronies, work, and paper always cut his visits short. His chief joy when with us was walking through sandy roads from one lake to another.

He found many things to criticize at the cottage. For instance, I had put two screw hooks into two pine trees so I could string a clothes line on which to hang out the weekly washing. He was furious at such vandalism. And each year, although the pine trees grew big and sturdy, those two hooks were the

---

[18] Shawano Lake is in northeastern Wisconsin. In later years Victor Berger's political opponents tried to paint him as a fraud and a swindler for owning a "yacht" and a "country home."

cause of great irritation for him. Finally, again I had to give him an ultimatum; either he could see how healthy those trees were notwithstanding the hooks or I'd have the trees chopped down, but I would no longer have an argument about them. That settled it. The trees are still there big and tall. But he loved trees and couldn't bear to think I appreciated them so little.

It was always small things that irritated Victor Berger. A big crisis in life he met beautifully and never fussed about it. And that reminds me of an incident which also happened at Shawano. Because we were poor, I used to buy the children's clothes much too large so that the dresses would do for three or four years if need be. One of these dresses had a habit of slipping over the shoulder of my little daughter. For two years he scolded about the sloppy dress. Well, this time we had a group of our lake neighbors in and were all sitting around a fire in the fire place. Again, the dress and I came in for criticism because it again hung crookedly. So without raising my voice, very calmly indeed, I said, "Elsa, please come to me! Turn around!" I unbuttoned the dress and threw it into the fire place; saying—"So—that's the last time we will hear about that!" Can you imagine the silence in the room at daring to throw a perfectly good dress into the fire? After a pause of some twenty minutes, Victor Berger found his second wind and said quite meekly—"Well, Mama, you might have saved the buttons anyway." That brought loud laughter, and all was well again. I cite these two instances merely because I want you to know that a giant intellect, a far-seeing man (almost prophetically so), a generous man, kind, good, smart and courageous, had nerves which made *little* things irritate him.

Notwithstanding this quality, he was generally beloved by his associates and comrades. And life at home was by no means made of these picayunish matters but was stimulating, rich in friends and books and the events which were shaping so that both Victor and I were thrown into public life.

My husband greatly admired women who took part in the social and political life side by side with men. Therefore it was not long before I too realized that I must take my place and learn to do what the courageous venturesome women whom Mr. B. admired did.

But how was I—just a mother and wife, shy above all, going to become a public figure without any ability or training? That problem puzzled me for days on end. Then one day I went to the University Extension Division, which also was in its infancy here, and asked about a class in public speaking. If there was such a class I'd like to register. The person in charge of that Extension Division of the University of Wisconsin informed me that there was no class in public speaking, but that if I really wanted to have instruction in speaking, he would be glad to organize a class provided I would secure ten students, each paying fifteen dollars for the course. The university would then send an instructor from Madison. I was discouraged for a little while but finally went out to find folks who also wished to become speakers. After weeks of effort I succeeded in getting the ten students, each with fifteen dollars, [and] went back to the University Extension Division.

Of course we got our teacher, but interest soon lagged and one by one the pupils stopped coming until I was the only one left.

What the professor told us was of course common sense as far as public speaking was concerned. The one thing he couldn't help us on was the material or subject matter to talk about. That was up to each student. All of the other students dropped out, leaving me the only one left. Anyway I got a little self-confidence and felt I could face an audience, although sometimes it was difficult when I had nothing to say.

But I was spurred on to make effort after effort because I wanted not only to make my own contribution but I wanted above all my husband's approval and admiration. And right here I may as well tell you that all men in the public limelight, and especially those who were leaders, had a large following of adoring women pay glorious tribute to them. VLB was no exception. He received glowing tribute, mushy compliments and adoration from many spirited, intelligent, independent and beautiful women.[19]

I know. I saw. At first I was shocked, then bewildered and confused. It happened to all or nearly all prominent men. Once while in New York City we met Lincoln Steffens. He was a great friend and admirer of my husband and insisted that both of us come out to his home in Stamford, Connecticut, for an evening's visit and to spend the night. After some polite hesitation we accepted and Lincoln telephoned his wife of our coming. Upon arrival, we were very coldly received by the then Mrs. Steffens.[20] She positively was an icicle and froze us to the marrow. Her behavior was so shocking that shortly after dinner I pleaded a headache and retired. My husband followed soon after. The next morning I found the most charming hostess one could imagine. Surely the morning Mrs. Steffens was altogether different from the Mrs. Steffens of the night before. As soon as it was possible, she apologized for her behavior and then told me she was sick and tired of having women, all kinds of women,

---

[19] As his letters demonstrate, Victor Berger was devoted to his wife, but several accounts suggest that he did not discourage attention from other women. See Hursley, biography; Hochstein, account of dinner party; and Penelope Niven, *Carl Sandburg: A Biography* (New York: Scribner, 1991), 150, 161, 729. In his May 8, 1914, and June 6, 1914, letters, Victor pointedly told Meta that he did not intend to call on New York suffragist Inez Milholland, with whom both Hursley and Hochstein linked him (Stevens, ed., *Family Letters,* 171–172, 174).

[20] Probably Lincoln Steffens's first wife, Josephine Bontecou Steffens (1856?–1911).

admire Lincoln etc. etc. Good Lord! One look at me who weighed about 190 pounds and who was the picture of the typical *Hausfrau* type should have convinced her of any doubts.

However—I understood. Many of these women were like moths flying around brilliant lights. They were good women in a way, frustrated possibly, but just anxious to be in contact with a movement which was new, run by intelligent men and which promised hope for the future. In fact I believe I acted as a balance wheel to an ego which might easily have become exaggerated.

So I had to work hard to make a place for myself and to continue my own education and development.

In the meantime my two adorable daughters were growing up. Doris, the older, was to be the perfect woman according to her father's ideals. Therefore he undertook to chart her education and her conduct. However she was so much like her own father that very often friction arose between the two. She was going to lead her own life according to the ideals she then possessed. Arguments were of no avail, and many is the time I acted as a buffer between two temperaments. Argument was of no avail, and Doris argued.

Elsa was a jolly little girl whose life was not so neatly patterned by her father. I must say Elsa could astonish her father's anger away by the pert or clever or saucy things she said. Therefore Elsa didn't have as hard a time at home.

Time was going on. My contacts with the working class and the Socialist Party became more frequent and slowly—too slowly—I was beginning to identify myself with the labor and political activities of the world outside of my home.

We still had very little to live on, as the *Vorwärts*, a German weekly, was not able to pay more than fifteen dollars a week. About this time a newcomer to the Socialist Party arrived in Milwaukee—Elizabeth Thomas.[21]

Elizabeth Thomas was of Quaker stock, came from a well-to-do New York family, got interested in the socialist movement and came to Milwaukee to contribute her services without salary to the cause. She admired VLB and became his confidant and secretary. Because the Socialist Party was poor—she also acted as the secretary to the party in Wisconsin. She is one of the most

---

[21] Elizabeth H. "Betty" Thomas (1856–1949) moved to Milwaukee in 1900 to work with Victor Berger and the Social Democrats. Among other contributions, she played an important role in editing and securing funding for the *Social-Democratic Herald* and the *Milwaukee Leader*. She served as president of the Milwaukee Social-Democratic Publishing Company (publisher of the *Herald* and the *Leader*) (1902–1929), as state secretary for the Social Democratic Party (1901–1919), and as a member of the Milwaukee school board (1915–1921).

intelligent courageous women it was my good fortune to know. Not only her services but her money went into the cause. Naturally we became good friends and comrades and have been so these past forty years and more.

The national Socialist Party was growing but like all minority parties met a hostile opposition in every state. The national party tried to keep the spark of enthusiasm alive by issuing a weekly paper called the *Social-Democratic Herald*. But finances were scarce and the National Executive Committee finally [had] to let the *Herald* die. Not so Victor Berger. So one very hot summer day Elizabeth Thomas, Victor B. and I took a boat to Chicago, went to the home of Theodore Debs (brother of Eugene) and received from him the mailing list of the national readers of the *Social-Democratic Herald*.[22]

Now we were going to have two weekly papers, one in German and one in English. These two papers could not possibly answer the vicious attacks of four/five daily newspapers. There were the *Milwaukee Sentinel* and the *Milwaukee Free Press,* morning papers, and the *Wisconsin Evening News* and the *Milwaukee Journal*, evening papers. All these papers had money and were supported by the big advertisers. Nevertheless the *Social-Democratic Herald* and the *Vorwärts* struck back at the daily attacks and pointed the way towards a new and better life. In fact any weekly papers that could draw the fire of four vicious dailies, day after day, attracted the attention not only of the citizens of Milwaukee, but even nationally we were going places. With hard work, industry and the enthusiastic support for the cause of the under-dog—we were attracting quite a national subscription list and were becoming a little famous. No one who has never started a newspaper—and especially a paper espousing the minority cause and a cause which threatened an entrenched economic order and the doing away with the exploitation of men by men and abolishing a profit system—well—they just cannot imagine the herculean task. Finances, finances and more finances troubled us. How to pay for print-paper; how to pay the rent; how to keep the old broken down press in repair; how to get enough money for the pay-roll; how to get credit from an unfriendly bank— and put up a convincing story so as to receive the needed loan of money; [how to] borrow money from friendly comrades or from sympathetic unions—these and many more problems made life very difficult. At the same time we had to put on a respectable front, so that some folks might think all was well with us. I remember my husband pleading with me to get some new clothes because he said my appearance hurt his credit. Looking back now to those years I can understand that. When I was married I weighed 112 pounds and at the time

[22] Victor Berger brought the *Social-Democratic Herald* to Milwaukee in 1901 and published it there until 1913.

I was urged to get a new dress I weighed 190 pounds. No wonder nothing fit or that I didn't look well! Anyway I got the dress with some misgivings on a charge account. I hated to charge things but soon learned the art but always was a little worried about charged accounts for fear that these debts could not be promptly paid; and they never were. Victor said, "Schulden sind keine Hasen." (Debts are not rabbits.) And to please let him worry about the finances of the family. So I did! And finances have never ceased troubling me.[23]

———

My new home, to which I came directly after I was married, consisted of a very large eight room upper duplex for which we had to pay fifteen dollars a month when we had it. It was a beautiful duplex because the sun shone in from the east, south and west. Oh, I was happy in my new home! The first two rooms were devoted entirely to house Mr. Berger's big library. He possessed somewhere between ten and twelve [thousand] volumes which represented a private library perhaps larger than any in the state of Wisconsin. The library consisted of books devoted to history, economics, politics, racial problems, international problems and some of the classics. I remember, so well, that when the difficulties of life seemed almost too great to bear, my husband would take refuge reading the Greek classics, which he enjoyed hugely. Besides the two front rooms housing the main library the books overflowed into every other room in the house.

Some folks facetiously in answer to the question—"What is Milwaukee famous for?"—replied beer, books and Berger.

In addition to books, periodicals of every sort came to the house. For years we kept German and French periodicals and even a Magyar newspaper. Early in married life I was trained never to throw any printed or written document away. Consequently the collection of material was tremendous. And since I prided myself on an orderly house it fell to my lot to take care of this material and to keep the books dusted and in order. Nothing irritated my husband so much as to have a careless helper put the books back on the shelves up-side-down. Great indignation and temper was aroused by such illiteracy.

———

[23] The remainder of this chapter consists of two sections that Meta Berger had not yet worked into the manuscript.

In the very early days of my marriage, when both of us were not yet used to our new relationship, it was my hope and shall I say one of my ambitions that our new situation should resolve itself into a true partnership, I to share the problems of my new husband, who by the way was thirteen years older than I was, and he to share the joys and burdens of a common household.

So I tried hard to interest my husband in domestic activities and invited him to help me with the chores of the household. I really laugh today to think of the futile waste of energy. However, then I didn't know!

Many and many are the times I was more than chagrined at the German mothers of those days. Sons seemed to be made of better and more brittle clay. Anyway—when I invited my "better half" to wipe dishes, he was a little ashamed to refuse and yet I know now, humiliated at the task. However, I wouldn't notice. So after a few moments, he hung up the dish towel, saying his chore was done. But upon investigating I discovered that only the upper surface of plates had been wiped, and since he couldn't very well stack plates that were still wet on the underside, he carefully placed all plates separately all around the kitchen until there was literally no more room to place the balance of our dishes. He was most astonished when he was told that both sides must be wiped and then the plates stacked. Consequently there was plenty of room. And so he learned to help with dish wiping.

But not all of the jokes were on my husband. I recall the day I was ambitious and desired to surprise him with a pie which I had baked. The pie looked luscious and juicy; so I set it out on the window sill in the back hall to cool.

As soon as my husband came home, he went to the rear hall to brush his coat, since he just couldn't bear to have dust on his clothes. As soon as he saw the pie, he stood there puzzled, since it wouldn't do to brush the dust off his coat and have it settle on the pie. After a second's thought, he just turned the pie up-side-down and continued brushing his coat. To my astonishment and humiliation the pie behaved itself by sticking to the tin. It was really a very tough pie. And I have never to this day mastered the art.

CHAPTER 3

"The Board of School Directors"

Once more my husband was away, trying to take care of the welfare of the Socialist Party. At home here, the local party functioned as usual. The time had come for the selection of candidates for the first school board people's election. Heretofore school directors had been selected and appointed by local judges. Now the people of Milwaukee were to choose. During the absence of my husband the Socialist Party committee, whose duty it was to OK the party's choice, nominated me as candidate for school director. To say I was surprised, shocked and frightened—puts it mildly. Up to this point I had not taken a very active part in the activities of the Socialist Party. True, I went to party meetings, picnics and balls (for the purpose of raising money for the party) but for the most part just to sit quietly, listen and learn. And learn I did from these workers, who were awakened to their class interests and who were willing to discuss the problems so vitally affecting their welfare and the welfare of their fellow workers.

But to represent this new, young party as its representative on a board of education—well that was a responsibility I felt altogether beyond me. So, I wired my husband telling him the news and said, "What shall I do?" Back came the reply, "Do nothing, except to accept the honor. You won't be elected anyway."

What a comfort that telegram was. Soon however the campaign began. I was a new-comer in the race, but I was also a member of the Socialist Party and that fact gave the campaign its slogan—"Do not let the Socialists control the schools!"[1] And that cry has lived throughout the last thirty-five years. Every campaign was bitterly fought and always around the slogan "Don't let the Socialists control the schools!" What vicious propaganda that was. Or didn't our opponents know the schools were the only socialistic institution we had. What I did to help the campaign—I do not have the faintest notion. The young Socialist Party did the campaigning for me. After the votes were counted—I was elected to the Board of School Directors.[2] Now what to do!

Looking up the law, I found I had to appear before the city clerk of Milwaukee to take the oath of office and then wait for the first meeting of the board of which I now was a member.

I remember going down to that first meeting in the street-car, quarreling all the way with VLB, telling him if he ever *once* criticized me for activities on the board I would forth-with resign. All I can remember now is that my husband chuckled and was kind and re-assuring.

In the board meeting that first night, I was so nervous I couldn't sign my name. Frederic Heath,[3] also a Socialist, was a member and since he sat in front of me, I asked him to scratch his right ear if I was to vote "Yes" on the question and his left ear if I was to vote "No!"

However my fear left me even before the close of the meeting over a question which had aroused my interest and indignation. The board was going to discriminate against women by ruling that no woman, no matter how qualified, could become the head of a department in any high school course and was going to replace a woman who had served in such capacity for a number of years.[4] My shock came when I heard the discussions and recommendations of the old guard principals and board members.

I forgot everything except that I must defend women and their rights; so made my first speech in the school board. It must have been pretty good for I won the fight and women there-after could hold positions equal in rank with men.

My dear old friend, Dr. Charles Kissling,[5] left his seat and walked up and down smoking cigarette after cigarette and saying, "I knew it was a mistake to

---

[1] Six of the school board candidates were Social Democrats.

[2] Of the five new school board directors elected on April 6, 1909, two, Meta Berger and Frederic Heath, were Social Democrats. A third, Annie Gordon Whitnall, had applied to join the party before the election and was accepted afterward.

[3] Frederic F. Heath (1864–1954) resigned from the school board in 1910 to serve as county supervisor, a post he held from 1910 to 1948. He also served as a reporter and editorial writer for the *Milwaukee Leader* from 1913 to 1933.

[4] The discussion concerned the classification and salary of Gertrude Hull, a history teacher at West Division High School still classed and paid at level B. A few other women were already serving as class A department heads at other high schools.

[5] Charles L. Kissling Jr. (1859–1917), a physician, was an appointed member of the Milwaukee school board from 1900 to 1905 and an elected member from 1907 to 1917.

elect women to the board." Dear old Dr. Kissling—he changed his mind some years later when I was up for re-election and called me on the telephone to tell me I was to be the next president of the school board. Of course I was flattered but didn't believe it for a moment. But more of that later.

Now—I began a new phase of education; that of administering to a school system, of which I was a product. It was an inspiration to me. First to get acquainted with a city system, then to watch the administration of it from the top down. Then to know the teachers and to hear of their successes and complaints about the weak spots in the system. And then to discover too, that the great majority of teachers knew little and cared less about the children whom they were teaching. Oh! Yes, there was a Teachers' Association. It was a small group and it was organized originally for social purposes only. I know because I was one of them while teaching school and long before I was a member of the board. But this little social group became the nucleus from which sprang the Milwaukee Teachers' Association—a professional group which through force of circumstances now worked militantly for their *economic* welfare first, and later became interested in pedagogical matters which certainly gave the schools a boost forward.[6]

However the great mass of teachers were content to let the MTA do the fighting. Most girls who taught were content to teach [and] draw their paychecks and cared little about the progress of the rest of the world. Even the MTA considered itself only a professional group and therefore could not, or would not, support legislation which affected the welfare of the fathers of the children they taught or those affecting the general public welfare. Only on matters affecting teachers and their welfare were they active.

I must confess I was disappointed. To me the teachers of a community ought to be in the vanguard for all social legislation which meant progress. However I made it my business to win the confidence of the teachers, which helped me immensely as a director, for I kept in close touch with their problems which in turn helped me understand the weak spots in the system.

The MTA made some progress (for itself and its members) under the leadership of Miss Ethel Gardner. She was sure of herself and able, perfectly fearless. But she was rendered useless [to] the rank and file of teachers when she was promoted to the principalship of a school.[7] Her successor, Miss Frances Jelinek, was able, competent, knew her power but was too timid to do anything except that which the MTA stood for. Never did the MTA under her leadership leave what it called its professional stand.

---

[6] The first Milwaukee Teachers' Association was established in 1874. Its successor by the same name, established in 1901, promoted the interests of elementary school teachers.

[7] Ethel M. Gardner became a Milwaukee public school principal in 1931.

It was during World War I, that the MTA went to Madison and defeated the Milwaukee school board by getting a minimum salary passed over the objection of the board.[8] I was pleased about this because it promised much for the social point of view of teachers and because the then board members were so indignant that "pressure groups" had begun to work.

Soon thereafter another small group was formed, the Teachers' Union, affiliated with the AF of L. Again board members were indignant that still another pressure group appeared on the scene. Not I! I soon became a member of the Teachers' Union and therefore could speak with authority for them. Into this group went most of the men and the more courageous women. Through their clear and dignified approach, they finally won the respect, if not the cooperation, of the board.

Sometimes when I think of the results of my thirty year efforts on the board, I feel that I ought to record a series of defeats. As for example, my first resolution was to provide free text-books for all children. Of course I was defeated. Pencils began to count up the costs of free text-books and the money it would take—would boost the tax-rate. Smaller classes for teachers—well that would require more classrooms, more school houses, more land, more money—and again the tax-rate would go up.

Health inspection, heartily supported by me, met the opposition of parents, wealthy parents who had [a] family doctor and [were] tax-payers; and even school authorities. [A] Jewish mother brought two babies in protest because [the] children had lice. *Zwei aber drei, was ist das* [Two or three, what does it matter]? Children sewed into their underwear full of scabies.

Pensions for teachers, heartily supported by myself and others—soon became a reality and not a dream. But again we had to over-come much conservative and political opposition.

The free use of school houses for the parents to discuss their problems—always promoted and supported by Socialist members, to this day is denied the citizens of Milwaukee.

Nursery schools—still a dream and now so necessary for working mothers—called a thing to break up the home. Penny luncheons instituted by the Woman's School Alliance met snag after legal snag.[9] Monies appropriated for education could not be used for milk. There was great need for milk and luncheons for children during the depression years, and many were the sad incidents related to us by teachers.

---

[8] The legislature established a statewide minimum salary for teachers in 1919.

[9] The Woman's School Alliance, established in 1891, was a group of middle-class women who agitated for school reform on behalf of the urban poor. In 1904 the alliance began a "penny lunch" program, funded initially by private donations, that provided free or nearly free lunches to schoolchildren.

Today, thank God, we do have a distribution of milk and some luncheons in schools. But many times both teachers and principals objected to the work and bother of having milk provided for children.

Again the discrimination against married women teaching was an obstacle over which the board fought long and hard.[10] In this the superintendent[11] loyally supported the conservative members of the board. It was necessary for me to pack the school board halls with all the advocates of freedom, of no sex-discrimination etc. The fact that the board did not employ single blessedness or the marital status but was only interested in qualification and service rendered apparently made no difference. Married women belonged in the home. As one school director said, "A woman's duty is first to her husband, then to her home and last but not least to her children." What a laugh! This school director has served eighteen years and is now asking the support of parents for another term.

Well the meeting was packed. The League of Women Voters, the Milwaukee Woman's Club, the Business and Professional Women's League, the AFL, the CIO, the Socialist Party, the Communist Party and scores of other organizations sent representatives. The meeting lasted until after 1:00 A.M., when finally the above mentioned school director asked for another meeting to continue the arguments. Naturally—I knew he too would pack the next meeting. So once more I sat at the telephone and again gathered more and new advocates for the next hearing on the subject.

Finally—those opposed made a poor hearing—when a motion to adjourn was made by same school director. But a protest went up from those present and not yet heard—i.e., those for the married women's right to teach, that the committee voted to continue until all were heard. The final result was that we carried by one vote—even winning the support of Mrs. Elizabeth Mehan,[12] who although a good Catholic voted to support the measure since she herself—married was working.

---

[10] Waldemar C. Wehe proposed on October 4, 1932 (during the depression), that the superintendent be given the power to dismiss married women teachers at will. The board's legislative committee instructed the city attorney to prepare a bill to provide for such dismissals. The legislative committee and a special committee composed of the three female board members first met to settle the issue on December 1. The full school board defeated the proposal by accepting the committees' recommendation to "file" it on December 6. In 1935 Meta Berger attempted to change the policy of dismissing probationary teachers who married, but this effort failed.

[11] Milton C. Potter (1873–1972) served as superintendent of the Milwaukee public schools from 1914 to 1943.

[12] Elizabeth Moran Mehan (1883–1938), housewife, editor, and leader in Catholic affairs, served on the Milwaukee school board from 1921 to 1938. She served as president of the board in 1930–1931, the third woman to hold that position.

Then came the struggle for progressing in the educational field. The superintendent said, "Let them have their project at 3:30 P.M. every Friday." However with the support of the teachers and the progress made generally in education, the rigid formal school teaching reading, writing and arithmetic evolved into a method of teaching along progressive lines, and no longer is the superintendent able to "sit in his central office and know that each child in the city is busy with penmanship at 10:00 A.M."

The struggle to keep the schools from being platoonized is worthy of mention. It was recommended that we follow the Gary plan[13] of putting twice as many children into a school, in the interest of a false economy, than the building could decently hold. This was to be done by having one group of children come at 8:30 A.M. and a second group come at 9:00 A.M. The children of Group 1 were to have their first instructions early and then move on to the next classroom while Group 2 came in to take the lessons Group 1 had just finished. The children were then expected to go to different classrooms with different teachers for each period of the day. The method didn't appeal to me and therefore I opposed the scheme. However in the struggle to get approval, the school board sent a committee of school directors to visit platoon schools in Gary, Detroit and other places and bring back a report. From the complexion of the committee chosen, I knew that a favorable report would be forthcoming. Therefore in order to fortify myself against the plan I visited the only platoon (rotary) school in Milwaukee, which had been established as an experiment. Mrs. Marie Whitnall,[14] also a Socialist, and I agreed to go together and follow a third grade child through the school for a day. This is what we discovered. At 8:30 A.M. the third grade was in the assembly hall enjoying a movie picture show about Italy. The bell rang at 9:00 A.M., the class jumped up to go to their next class which was in arithmetic. At 9:30 the bell rang and the children rushed into a drawing class where the teacher was showing them free-hand paper cutting. They were to make a canoe. At 10:00 A.M. the bell rang and the children rushed into a geography class where they were to study the geography of Norway. At 10:30 A.M. the bell rang. The children rushed to their penmanship class where the teacher was showing the children how to write the letter j. At 11:00 A.M. the bell rang and the children rushed to their English class where some beautiful poetry was read. And so it went all day long. At the close of the day both Marie Whitnall and I were bewildered and confused with the

[13] The platoon or Gary plan involved splitting the student body into two groups that alternated between regular classroom activities and vocational or recreational activities. Board President Loyal Durand proposed on January 3, 1924, that the board consider this model as a means of reducing overcrowding in specific schools.

[14] Marie Kottnauer Whitnall (1874–1957) served on the Milwaukee school board from 1923 to 1929.

knowledge those teachers tried to put into the heads of seven or eight year old children. Mind you—none of the subject matter taught was correlated and integrated, Italy, Indian canoes, Norway, the letter *j* etc. etc.

But we decided we must be entirely fair, and while this school seemed all wrong we would next visit a progressive school which was conducted in [the] training school of the State Teacher's College. Here we found the entire morning taken up by fifth grade children, getting the history, English, arithmetic, art and all kindred subjects while studying Daniel Boone. The boys were measuring and making log cabins, the girls were measuring and making dresses for the early Americans. Discipline did not enter the classroom, for each child was so absorbed and so interested that there was the most perfect of all discipline— i.e., perfect freedom and interest. It was a most delightful morning and both Marie and I were convinced that the platoon school was wrong—and we were ready to do our best to defeat the measure.

The committee of school directors came back with an enthusiastic report for the platoon schools. It was so much more economical. But we opposed the project and were going down to defeat once more when I tacked on an amendment to the original resolution providing that the next platoon school should not be established until eight years had passed and we could compare the children of the platoon school with children from other schools. That was passed. It is with satisfaction that I can now write that no other school in Milwaukee has been platoonized and that the present director of that school is trying to change that platoon school back to a normal public school.

But the visit to the progressive school made me wish to establish a similar school in the city and accordingly I introduced a resolution to the effect that the Milwaukee board establish as an experiment a progressive school in our system. Well, I lost that too after the superintendent sent out a questionnaire so worded that no educator anywhere in the world would recommend the experiment under the conditions as set forth in the questionnaire.

After my first term of six years was finished in 1915—I ran again as a candidate. World War I was in full swing in Europe and we here in America were preparing to enter the war. The Socialist Party of America was violently opposed to our entrance into the European struggle and said so through their party declarations, editorials, leaflets and speeches. With a war hysteria in the making, I nevertheless was a candidate taking what abuse would naturally come to me because of my affiliation with the Socialist Party. Nevertheless I was again elected. It was the morning after election day that Dr. Charles Kissling called me on the telephone and said, "My congratulations to the next president of the school board." Laughingly I thanked him but did not believe for a moment that he meant what he said. However he went to work and before July 1 he again telephoned me to say that he had only seven votes while it required eight votes to elect and would I vote for myself! No! No! I couldn't do that but thought he still had ten minutes to get the eighth vote. When I entered the board rooms, I didn't know what would happen, as one of the most influential directors opposed me very much and worked against me until the vote was taken. To my surprise eight votes were cast and I was the first woman president of the Milwaukee school board.[15]

The following year was strenuous and I had to be on my toes every minute. The parliamentary procedure wasn't so hard, as I had learned Robert's Rules of Order in the workers' meetings. But the war was on and feeling ran high. Everyone wanted to be a 100 percent American.[16] And the 100 percent citizens usually resorted to abusive unsigned letters. Teachers were also victims of this hysteria and as a result the children often were made to feel most uncomfortable. There was—for instance, a teacher who asked a little child to write the names of three prominent citizens on the board. So the little girl wrote Woodrow Wilson which name the teacher applauded. Then Victor Berger whereupon the teacher quickly erased the name, saying that "she had asked for the names of *prominent* men, not *jail* birds." (Victor Berger was not a jail bird.)

Or again—an unsigned letter to me on school stationery as follows— "Mrs. Berger, why don't you hide your dirty head in shame and take your stinking sausage and go back to Germany." Also the pressure on children to contribute to the Red Cross to make each school a 100 percent Red Cross school, made many a child's life miserable at that time. War hysteria is an awful thing.

But one of the interesting phases of my year as president of the board was the fact that my program included a visit to every school in the city, to ascertain what the physical condition of the school was, as to fire escapes, cleanliness, sanitation etc. During these visits I regularly encountered a lady-reporter from the *Milwaukee Journal*.[17] At first I thought it queer that we just happened to meet accidentally. But finally I asked her how it happened that she always chose to go to the school that I was visiting that day. With a smile she let it be known that it was part of her work to trail me and watch me. What did the *Journal* think? That I was trying to incite unpatriotic or subversive activities.

---

[15] Meta Berger served as president of the board in 1915–1916. A letter to her husband suggests that she was sure of election by June 15, 1915 (Stevens, ed., *Family Letters,* 192n). The formal ballot on July 6, 1915, resulted in eight votes for Berger, five for Charles J. Coffey, one for J. H. Derse, and one blank vote.

[16] Writers and speakers during the war who insisted on conformity, national loyalty, and service to one's country often called themselves "100 percenters."

[17] Mabel Search (1891–1955) joined the *Milwaukee Leader* staff in 1918, the same year she left the *Journal.* In 1924 she moved to New York and became a magazine editor.

So absurd! So I invited the lady reporter to come *with* me and gave her the schedule. As a result the representative of the *Milwaukee Journal* and I became warm friends. A few months later this same reporter left the *Journal* to work for the *Milwaukee Leader*—socialist paper.

At the close of my year as president the school director who had been so antagonistic introduced the following resolution:[18] "Mrs. Victor Berger is about to retire from the presidency of the School Board. She has served as its presiding officer with fairness and fearlessness. Her social sympathies, her knowledge of school affairs, her executive ability, her uniform courtesy and the careful and efficient manner in which she has discharged every duty as presiding officer of this Board has won for her our esteem, therefore, be it RESOLVED, That this expression of our appreciation of Mrs. Berger's faithful discharge of her duties as president be spread upon the minutes of the Board, and that she be presented with a copy thereof."

And so the years rolled by. There were many many difficult pulls. My husband was indicted five or six different times, both in Wisconsin and Illinois.[19] During these hectic war hysterical years I kept on running for the school board. Every campaign was bitterly fought, but hats off to the voters of Milwaukee. They never failed me. When I had finished my twenty-fifth year, an informal coffee party was held in one of the rooms of the administration building. Dorothy Enderis[20] managed the party as only Dorothy can. At this festive occasion the members of the board presented me with a silver water pitcher with all the names of the then school board. Also they released me from work on the building committee, which had called for climbing scaffolds, tearing silk stockings, picking out bricks and opera chairs, but [instead] allowed me for the next five years to attend to the welfare of teachers, librarians, children and pedagogical problems. I used to think that progress marched forward on the feet of little children. And since World War II has thrown the world into blood-shed and chaos and utter ruin, I am more convinced than ever that future generations of children and their education will have to save what little will be left of civilization and democracy.

Before closing this chapter on my activities of school work, which after all took thirty years of effort of democratizing the public school system and making life a little brighter and happier for teachers and children alike, I wish to

[18] The resolution was introduced by William L. Pieplow (1875–1959), a businessman who served on the Milwaukee school board from 1902 to 1919 and held the post of board president in 1908–1909 and 1917–1919.

[19] Victor Berger was indicted three times.

[20] Dorothy Enderis (1880–1952) served as assistant to the director of Milwaukee's recreation and adult-education program from 1912 to 1920 and as director from 1920 to 1948.

say that my personal relationship with the other members of the board, who fought bitterly on all problems on which we were diametrically opposed, was always most pleasant, and we severed our association with mutual affection and respect.

When I finally gave up the post or office a civic dinner was tendered me with five or six hundred friends present. Again the board members presented me with a handsome brooch which I shall cherish during the rest of my days.[21]

———

By-elections never draw the same interest on the part of the voters as do the regular municipal election. Just why this is so—is difficult to explain, except perhaps for the fact that there were a great many political "plums" to be handed out after a city campaign.

And yet it always seemed very wise that school elections and the election for judges should be held separately. Both these departments are terrifically important, especially the election of a wise, socially minded Board of School Directors under whose care the most formative years of the lives of the city's children were entrusted. But not so! Voters considered these civic duties as a side issue and consequently only a small percentage voted for either judges or school directors.

It was not until Socialists entered the race that interest was sharpened and campaigns grew hot. As the wife of the Socialist leader and also because of certain qualification I naturally became the target for greatest attacks. Perhaps now in retrospect I only imagine I was the most abused candidate—abused by a hostile press. On the other hand, I was blessed with the loyal support of the Socialist Party and a large part of the working class and a majority of the thinking and discriminating population. There were four women on the board who became life-long friends, Mrs. Charles W. Norris, Mrs. Simon Kander, the first Mrs. Charles Whitnall and myself.[22] More of these friends later.

Most of the things I proposed and promoted at first went down to defeat, but as the years passed I lived to see many of them come into fruition.

I wish now to give credit to the Seidel administration[23] for having proposed and supported and created through the offices of the school board the very

[21] The remainder of this chapter consists of several pages Meta Berger had not yet worked into the manuscript.

[22] Fannie Wells Norris (1852–1937), a philanthropist, served on the school board from 1907 to 1909. Lizzie Black Kander (1858–1940), founder of a Milwaukee settlement house and author of the famous *Settlement Cook Book,* served as a school board member from 1907 to 1919. Annie Gordon Whitnall (b. 1858), who divorced Charles B. Whitnall in 1912, served on the board from 1907 to 1911.

[23] Emil Seidel (1864–1947) helped found Milwaukee's Social Democratic Party and served as a Mil-

marvelous department of recreation. Harold Berg[24] had the terrific task of initiating it and organizing it. Dorothy Enderis, now nationally known, became Berg's successor and through her ability and love of people Milwaukee's recreation department flourishes and has won great renown. But here again to the Socialist administration of the city, together with a national committee of which Margaret Wilson, daughter of Woodrow Wilson, and Mr. Ward, then organizing playgrounds, must go the credit of this humane and educational venture.[25] The then superintendent of schools[26] was for placing this tremendously important work under the park board. Mayor Seidel and the Socialists fought to have it under control of the school board.

During the years of the First World War, when the frenzy of a war hysteria was at its height, I had a hard time.

Not only were the Socialists opposed to the entrance of the U.S. into the European holocaust but I had to run again for re-election. Again I carried the city. But that didn't soften the war-crazy psychology of the mob. Teachers in the schools were sometimes cruel in their patriotic zeal. It was cruel for a teacher to take a little child of seven or eight or nine years of age and stand it up before the class and say, "Children, see—here we have a little Hun." [27]

Only once I appealed to the superintendent [Potter]—when a child was a victim; but I got no satisfaction from him as he too was rabid in his fanaticism and his so-called patriotism.[28]

Those were difficult years and as I met and surmounted each difficulty I knew I had helped myself and my cause. I received as much and more than I gave.

---

waukee alderman (1904–1908, 1909–1910, 1916–1920, and 1932–1936) and as mayor of Milwaukee (1910–1912). In 1912 he was the Socialist Party's vice presidential candidate.

[24] Harold Berg served as the first director of the Extension Department of the Milwaukee public schools from its establishment in 1912 until 1920. The department developed the city's recreation and adult-education program, the first of its kind in the nation to be managed by a public-school system. The program received national and international recognition.

[25] Margaret Woodrow Wilson (1886–1944), the eldest daughter of President Wilson, was a professional singer who debuted in 1915. During her father's presidency she promoted the use of schools as community centers. Edward Joshua Ward (1880–1943) served as the Wisconsin state adviser in civic and social center development for the University of Wisconsin Extension Division (1910–1915).

[26] Carroll G. Pearse (1858–1948) served as superintendent of the Milwaukee public schools from 1904 to 1913.

[27] Four sentences have been deleted here that repeat stories told earlier in the chapter.

[28] Miriam Frink added here: "Potter crushed the paper with Meta Berger's notation and threw it on the floor."

CHAPTER 4

"The Successful Election"

The success of the Socialists in the campaign for school directors in the spring of 1909, at which time Frederic Heath, Annie Gordon Whitnall and I were elected, fired the enthusiasm of our small but healthy Socialist Party. Every member now felt himself the important member who was responsible for the success of the party. Naturally, the attendance at party branch meetings was almost perfect. And the plans and hopes for the future were discussed in the most energetic way. These branch meetings served as an educational field for the workers, and I myself learned all the parliamentary procedure of conducting orderly meetings right here amongst the workers in the party. Looking back to those years I am amazed at the knowledge I acquired and at the respect those workers won from me. Arguments were not always agreeable, and sometimes I feared blows would follow heated discussions, but always at the close of those meetings I was surprised at the good comradeship which prevailed. It was here too, I learned how to differ with folks and still not allow differences of opinion to alienate me from either love of person or party affiliation. This fact was of tremendous importance during all my later work, whether it was for votes for women, tactics in the peace movement, or work on the school board. In fact, I discovered that it was far easier to work with men than with women. Women sometimes carried differences and resentment to personalities which were always distasteful to me.

Life at home became still more hectic and interesting. While my husband carried the fearful burdens of running and financing two weekly papers, helping to shape the political policy of the Socialist Party and its growth, and struggling to keep the finances of all in some sort of shape, at home I was struggling to raise my family of two girls and my nephew Jack Anderson,[1] who was said to have tuberculosis [and] who had come to live with us after his mother died of the disease. I mention this because our family doctor told me it would be dangerous to take Jack into the home and possibly expose my two little children to the dread disease. And yet how could I refuse to take my dead sister's child into my home? But as usual, my husband came to the rescue. I was permitted to care for Jack and give him a home provided I followed Mr. Berger's instructions governing his health, such as sleeping with open windows, plenty of milk and fresh vegetables etc. That settled it. Jack had a home with us. Fortunately we were all strong and healthy and even Jack never suffered from the illness.

With my outside interests, and I became more and more united with my husband in his work; and [with] the care of a family and a good sized apartment, I could not have managed well if it had not been for the loyalty and the industry of my helper, Josie [Rudkowsky], who was more than maid. She was friend and helper to us for twenty-two years until she was married. She not only did the housework and cooking for us but she was trustworthy with the children. As a result of so much responsibility and trust she soon ruled the family—even my husband and I obeying certain injunctions she laid upon us. I was very fortunate indeed!

The fact that Josie was so trustworthy naturally gave me much peace of mind when I left home. Therefore I became more and more absorbed in the socialist movement. As I said before, the success of the spring campaign made for enthusiasm and solidarity among the working class. Plans were being laid for the municipal campaign for the coming year.

Although there were five daily newspapers fighting us—the *Milwaukee Sentinel,* the *Milwaukee Free Press, Daily News,* later the *Milwaukee Journal,* and a German paper called *Germania,*[2] evening paper, [and] the *Herold,* morning paper, we went ahead to conduct a city-wide campaign with the aid of two weekly papers, *Der Vorwärts* (German) and the *Social-Democratic Herald* (English). At that time, the city was governed by David S. Rose,[3] who was an arrogant, brazen man but very handsome and who enjoyed an unsavory reputation. In fact the charges of graft were so numerous that even David S. Rose could no longer ignore them. He brazenly spoke of the charge of graft in his

---

[1] Jack Anderson (1899–1970) was the son of Meta Berger's sister, Paula. He lived with the Bergers from his mother's death in 1902 until about 1918 and later became an agricultural agent, farm administrator, and highway engineer.

[2] The *Germania* was a weekly newspaper.

[3] David S. Rose (1856–1932), an attorney and Democratic politician, served five terms as mayor of Milwaukee (1898–1906 and 1908–1910).

speeches by saying, "Oh! Yes! But they haven't caught me yet!" Milwaukee had much to gain by cleaning out the then administration. So we went ahead, doing our utmost to call attention of the voters that they had nothing to lose but only good to gain. Not so the daily press. It supported Rose right straight through.[4] It called attention to the fact that our socialist program was alien, was imported from Germany; that we didn't believe in family life, but in free love; that we would take away the homes and property of folks and divide it up etc. etc. And on one election day one of the papers printed huge facsimiles of the American flag and the red flag—saying, "Which will you have?" Sometimes, in retrospect, I wonder if we could have won the campaign if the papers had not over-reached themselves in abusing [us] and thus boosted us into office.

The effect of these daily attacks on the integrity of the party and particularly on the party-leader, VLB, was such that life became too serious, too difficult, and sometimes too unhappy for us all. After all our nerves were taut and sensitive. Troubles outside of the home were brought into the home. Small things, inconsequential things, irritated my husband out of all proportion. And, since his was a dynamic personality carrying a heavy load, his volatile temper would burst over the slightest provocation. Coats that were not hung up, hair that the wind no doubt blew into the eyes of the children, loud noise, a child's argument, papers misplaced, and many other minor things were enough to start a temperamental explosion. And these were not mild or pretty or funny—they were violent to say the least.

I would have been glad to come home and enjoy the serenity of a home and the lovely lively children. Not so Victor Berger. Oh! Yes—he would enjoy everything when the temper had quieted down and a calm had set in. Then he was most contrite and apologetic and with a most sympathetic appeal asked us over and over again if we still loved him. How could you do otherwise? You know always that he was more generous than his purse allowed, that he adored his children and consequently wanted perfect children. And what children are perfect? Then he would rush down town to buy each of us a present to make up for any pain he had caused.

Sometimes—often now after thirty-five or forty years, I smile when I think of the intentions of both of us. At the beginning of each campaign we pledged each other to patience and tolerance and promised that nothing that might happen during the fierce campaign would interfere with our mutual love and respect, and then we shook hands to bind the bargain. But long before the end

---

[4] Rose was not a candidate in 1910; the Democrat was Vincenz J. Schoenecker and the Republican was J. M. Beffel.

of those hectic and bitter campaigns, we didn't speak to one another. It was this sort of an atmosphere that three lively happy-go-lucky children had to endure.

Now, seeing them all grown and healthy and happily married, they survived beautifully and are none the worse for wear.

But to get back to the spring campaign of 1910 when the workers and the Socialist Party were conducting a campaign for the defeat of David S. Rose and for the election of Emil Seidel—pattern-maker, worker, dreamer, idealist. What qualifications did Emil Seidel have to become the mayor of a big city? Well, he was honest, knew the socialist program and had the courage to put it through if that were possible. What better qualifications need he have?

So the campaign progressed, bitterly fought and bitterly contested. The talk in the town, the excitement of big mass-meetings, the fact that our meetings were larger than the meetings of the other side, made us feel that we had a chance to win.[5]

The night of election day happened to fall on a night when the school board met. The school board at that time met on the eighth floor of the city hall of Milwaukee. The large conservative hostile newspaper, the *Sentinel,* had its plant across the street from the city hall. The *Sentinel* had notified the citizens of Milwaukee that it would flash a white light if the opponents of the Socialists won and a red light if the Socialists were winning.

From my seat at the board meeting I had an excellent view of the lights that were flashed from the *Milwaukee Sentinel.* The first lights were always white. This was so because the results of the day's election came from the smaller and perhaps the more versatile counters of votes. Anyway suddenly a red light flashed only to be replaced by a white light. This went on for some time, the white lights representing the conservative wards, the red lights the working man's wards. Great crowds had gathered on the streets below. We could hear the jubilant shouts going up after each light blazed forth.

I was as excited as I could be, for I knew how much sweat and worry had gone into that campaign. Naturally I have not the faintest notion of what was going on in the school board meeting. I do not believe anyone else did either, as all members were watching the *Sentinel* lights. After two or more hours of this anxious waiting, the red light came on again and did not go out again. Then we knew! All I remember now is that I grabbed my hat and coat and without waiting to put them on, got down on the street and ran as fast as I could to the West Side Turner Hall, which the Socialists had rented for the

---

[5] Meta Berger added here: "Bundle brigade—." The bundle brigade was a group of volunteers who distributed party literature, printed in many languages, quickly and on short notice.

evening and where they were to receive the election returns.

As I entered the hall wild and joyous music greeted my ears and bedlam reigned. Every one was embracing someone in the joy of the successful election. The crowds were massed in that big hall and all called for "Seidel" "Speech" "Speech." But Seidel refused to appear on the stage until they traced my husband, who had waged the campaign and who [had] taken the brunt of the abuse. Finally the two men appeared and never before have I heard such unbounded applause. The ovation really was tremendous. Seidel made a speech pledging his utmost to make Milwaukee a better place in which [to] live. Then my husband thanked the workers for their work, support and confidence, and like the optimist he was promised great things for the future of the party and for humanity. I really believe that on that evening, all the Socialists believed we had now gotten a glimpse of the promised land and that it was only a matter of time before the human race was free from any kind of bondage. How mistaken we were! The events of two world wars completely disillusioned us, although the experiment in Russia during and after the revolution gave us a flicker of hope again.

During all this time I have forgotten to mention the fact that my husband was elected an alderman to the city common council.[6] (His first political office.) He was one of twelve or thirteen Socialists elected. Besides these we elected Daniel W. Hoan as city attorney, John Mudroch as city treasurer and some minor officials.[7]

Our joy was not unmixed with a great sense of responsibility. Responsibility not only to our new tasks which lay immediately ahead but a responsibility toward the whole socialist movement everywhere. Milwaukee was the first large city ever to have been captured politically by Socialists. It is true that here and there smaller towns had elected Socialist mayors. But never before in the USA had a whole city administration of a city the size of Milwaukee gone Socialist. We immediately became the focal point of interest throughout the nation. Magazines and newspapers sent correspondents to call upon us to get the "dope" or information for their respective publications. I remember so clearly that Ida Tarbell, Lincoln Steffens, Oswald Garrison Villard, Frederic C.

---

[6] Victor Berger served on the Milwaukee Common Council in 1910–1911.

[7] The Social Democrats captured every city administration position and an overwhelming majority of aldermanic positions in 1910. Daniel W. Hoan (1881–1961) served two terms as city attorney (1910–1916) and seven terms as mayor (1916–1940). He left the Socialist Party in 1941 and later ran for office as a Democrat. Charles B. Whitnall (1859–1949), not John W. Mudroch (1877–1938), was elected city treasurer in 1910. Mudroch was elected alderman in 1916, served on the school board from 1923 to 1932, and served as city treasurer from 1932 to 1938. During his first term as treasurer he clashed with the party, which expelled him in 1934.

Howe, Helen Keller and many others of that day came for interviews.[8]

My husband was always very careful of anything he said for publication. So often a verbal interview was not understood or garbled when it appeared in print. As a result of several sad experiences, we (both of us) made it a point to give only written statements which had to be printed as written or not be printed at all. To this day—when I am suddenly called upon by a reporter from any paper I have this thought in my mind—be careful—say as little as you can—but be honest and be careful.

Life at home became more complicated than ever. Now we had to study municipal problems besides those of party, labor, economics, finances etc. etc. But it was interesting to say the least. And what kind of a wife would I have been had I not encouraged my husband to tell me of all the things that happened and all the difficulties he had to meet and over come.

The fact that the Rose administration had an unsavory reputation soon became apparent. Not many days after the inauguration of Mayor Emil Seidel, the Socialists discovered many slip-shod ways in which the Rose administration had conducted the city's business. One incident long remains in my memory. It was the fact that the former administration had not kept books on the city's finances, or if they did, no trace of books or auditing accounts could be found anywhere. All that was found were loose leaf accounts scattered here, there, everywhere; merely notations of expenditures etc. So one of the first things the new Socialist administration did was to get an auditing company to straighten out the city's finances and to set up a very good set of book-keeping books. They also established an amortization fund, so that in some future years Milwaukee would be debt free. And then there was "Berger's million dollar park" proposition.[9] Berger had a vision of the city beautiful.

And daily the opposition press hammered away, ridiculing every effort and every attempt to bring order out of chaos. The attacks were so fearful, that finally Mayor Seidel declared to us privately that he could not do his best work under the barrage of criticism and therefore refused to read any of the opposition press.

---

[8] Ida M. Tarbell (1857–1944), a journalist, is best known as the author of the *History of the Standard Oil Company,* an exposé of industrial corruption. Oswald Garrison Villard (1872–1949), a liberal journalist and pacifist, published the *New York Evening Post* from 1900 to 1918; from 1918 to 1932 he published and edited the *Nation* (formerly a weekly supplement to the *Post*) and turned it into a leading liberal magazine. Frederic C. Howe (1867–1940), a progressive lawyer, reformer, and author, served as commissioner of immigration at the Port of New York from 1914 to 1919. Helen Keller (1880–1968), an author and lecturer, promoted the education of those who, like herself, were blind and deaf.

[9] The Social Democrats planned to purchase land along the Milwaukee River for a public park. The local press attacked the proposal, calling it "Berger's million dollar park."

We on the other hand did our level best to answer attack after attack with the weekly newspaper. Soon it became apparent that a weekly paper could not possibly do justice to our cause and answer the daily attacks of five papers only once a week. There was nothing we could do but start a daily English newspaper. But with what? Just keeping the two weekly papers (one German and one English) going was as heavy a burden as we could carry. However, the cause merited heroic efforts on our part and on the part of the workers. So after the most serious consideration, a deep breath and all the courage we possessed, my husband and his co-workers started to organize a campaign for a daily socialist *news*paper printed in the English language.

A mass meeting was called at the auditorium of Milwaukee to put the whole proposition before the citizens. The workers responded beautifully. Of course our best speakers were there to explain, enthuse and arousify[10] the meeting. I shall never forget the speeches made by Oscar Ameringer and Carl D. Thompson, among others.[11] Enthusiasm ran high, the spirit was more than willing and the workers contributed generously to our cause. No one expected that enough money could be raised to start a newspaper in this way. But the good-will expressed gave my husband the courage to go ahead. He knew and I knew that he and he alone might have to carry the load, not only of financing such a proposition but of editing the paper, hiring the reporters, the editors, get the features for the paper, press men, typesetters, mail men etc. etc. etc. And that wasn't all. Advertisers to support a daily paper, as no paper could live without advertising.

Many a night, in fact all of the nights, were worrisome and sleepless. We burned the midnight oil until the early hours of the next day, only to have a very troubled night for the remaining hours. My husband would pace the floor and snap his fingers and wonder and wonder how he could meet the next day's problems.

These worried times lasted throughout his life time.

Can you imagine what these problems did to a man of his temperament. I was of much calmer disposition, but then, I never realized what all this meant. Realization came to me only as the months rolled by and I witnessed as a wife, not as a responsible part of the whole business. My job was to keep the home

---

[10] Miriam Frink added here: "A word coined that night by Carl D. Thompson."

[11] Oscar Ameringer (1870–1943), a German-born Socialist writer and party organizer, came to Milwaukee from Oklahoma in 1910 and organized, wrote for the *Milwaukee Leader,* and ran unsuccessfully for public office. He returned to Oklahoma City after World War I and published Socialist newspapers there. Carl D. Thompson (1870–1949) served in the Wisconsin Assembly from 1907 to 1909 and directed the Socialist Party's Information Department from 1911 to 1915. He subsequently served more than thirty years as secretary of the Public Ownership League, an organization that promoted public ownership of utilities.

calm, quiet, good meals on the table and keep the children as healthy as possible and to be as sympathetic as possible.

It was at this time that the cottage at Shawano came as a great boon to the family. My husband was always anxious to do everything possible for the health of the children. He was most unselfish too about staying in Milwaukee to wrestle with his big important problems, while I and the three children left for Shawano and a summer free from care and to play. It was at Shawano that the children learned to swim, to row a boat, to manage a launch shared with my sister and her family. Occasionally—perhaps once during the summer, he visited us. But all he enjoyed was the healthy joyous children. Summer resorting was not for him. All he wanted to do while there was to walk and walk and walk along the sandy hot country roads, or find fault with the neglect of the land or the neglect of trees, or the abuse of trees, such as screwing hooks into trees so we could stretch a clothes-line for our washing. Usually he was very glad to take the midnight train back to Milwaukee.

When I arrived back in town, I realized how lonely he must have been. He spent such leisure hours as he had shopping. And as a result I would be surprised with all sorts of gifts such as new porch furniture or a new carpet on the floor. These gifts were usually wholly inappropriate and out of tune with the rest of the house. Years later I became aware that that was his way of having a vacation.

Now—this Shawano lake cottage which was being paid for in installments figured in the bitter campaigns. Our opponents used to say that my husband lined his pockets with the dues collected from working men. How dishonest and contemptible they were! Union dues stayed in the union treasury as everyone knows. But any and every argument was used to discredit Mr. B.—and to throw dirt into the eyes and the minds of the unthinking.

And right here, let me say that anyone trying to serve the public is subject to the fierce light of publicity.

But to go on with the problem of establishing the *Milwaukee Leader,* which was to be the name of our new daily paper. After months of negotiation, the machinery was finally purchased with a down payment and the balance on notes. The machinery arrived and was ready for operation. Naturally every one was curious and interested. The *Social-Democratic Herald* was merged with the *Milwaukee Leader.*[12]

---

[12] Victor Berger launched the daily *Milwaukee Leader* in 1911 and edited it until his death in 1929. The paper, later published under other names, survived until 1942. Berger discontinued the *Social-Democratic Herald* in 1913.

No one can ever imagine the joy at having arrived at this point. And no one will ever know how the notes plagued us, caused us worries, the sleepless nights, and the fear that we couldn't meet the payments on time. The trouble we had to get enough money to pay for the car-loads of print paper waiting for delivery.

Another big task now was to get the merchants and business people to place their advertisements with us. Can you imagine the difficulties we had to overcome the hostility of all business against us, the tricks these advertisers resorted to, in order to show that the *Milwaukee Leader* was [not] a medium for buying power. The *Milwaukee Leader* carried ads quite different from the ads in the other papers, or they would put "key" ads in the *Leader* to measure how many of our readers responded. And usually these key ads were for furniture or other expensive goods which workers couldn't or didn't often buy.

Very soon Mr. Berger came home and asked me to help organize the buying power of our readers by asking them to save their sales-slips, or to have key-people in all sections of the city to whom we telephoned to tell them of certain trick ads and [to] ask our friends to again telephone to a chain of people, telling them to please go down to the stores and purchase something advertised and to save the sale-slips. Then my husband had to take these sales-slips to the department stores in order to convince the managers that it pays to advertise in the *Milwaukee Leader.* This method worked only in a small way. While the opposition papers carried pages and pages of well paid ads, we got perhaps two columns, sometimes three.

So life went on in its hectic way. The children at home were too young to get its repercussions. Then the summers at the cottage always was a great respite from the troubles and responsibilities at home. Looking back to those years I simply marvel at the way my husband could take it. But his marvelous constitution and his zeal for his [work] sustained him and even gave him a certain amount of joy that his dream was meeting with measured success.

CHAPTER 5

"A Socialist in Congress!"

In the fall of 1910, another election was to take place; this time the selection of members to the House of Representatives in Washington, D.C. It was not only natural but absolutely imperative that the Socialist Party select as its choice the best qualified man. That man was Victor Berger.

And now we were headed for more work, more responsibilities and more and greater interests. The campaign as you may imagine was bitter and hotly fought. But when the votes were counted, to our surprise and joy my husband had won his seat in Congress. Again, this success startled the nation. A Socialist in Congress! Unheard of before!

My reaction was queer. While I had gradually been absorbing the socialist philosophy, I know now that I wasn't ready for the rapid political progress we were making.[1] My husband had to resign as alderman in order to represent the Fifth District of Wisconsin in Washington. Now not only local problems but national problems were brought into the home.

I am so grateful that the children grew up such healthy children because I have often wondered just how to meet still more problems.

Naturally everyone in the whole country wanted to know who this lone Socialist congressman elect was and what he was like. Again we were besieged with writers from everywhere to get the facts. I've always been so grateful to

---

[1] Miriam Frink added here (for Meta Berger): "To be thrown into center of national activity was overwhelming to me. Questions affecting nation—tariff, free trade, international problems being discussed—big jump from civic and local problems to these larger ones. Had been on the school board about one year. That had been a tremendous jump then—whole new world opening up—and now Congress. I couldn't catch up by reading, too much to take in a philosophy of life and economic order—had to get it by absorption. (Has not to this day read Karl Marx but has Marxian philosophy.) Hattie and Paula never graduated from eighth grade."

Frederic C. Howe for being so understanding of our situation and I have always counted him as a friend.[2]

But Milwaukeeans too were jarred into a curiosity about their representative, and new friends appeared on the horizon. In order to meet the situation and in order to give these new friends a glimpse of what my husband was like—we inaugurated at our home a series of dinners, say one a month, the guests always to be from the ranks of the opposition. In order to accommodate my guests a banquet top was made to fit over the dining room table. Then I was able to have eighteen guests at one evening.

So, the members of the press came, the judges came, the clergy came, the educators came, the social workers came, etc. etc. In this way they and we became acquainted and much hostility broke down. After a good dinner and good wine, the guests and my husband and I would retire to the library which was on the top floor (formerly the attic) of a house in which we lived, and there in the most friendly manner the economic, political and party topics were discussed until the early hours of the next day. It is needless to say, that all, everyone, left our home with a feeling of friendship even though we made no converts to our political faith.

I recall especially one member of the clergy who each Sunday in his sermons denounced my husband in no uncertain terms. Monday morning papers always played up these denunciations. Well, this minister of the gospel also was a guest at one of these dinners. He was charming as could be, was my partner at the table, and later on took an active part in a lively discussion. When leaving for home that morning, he came to me and said, "Thank you Mrs. B.—for a lovely and stimulating evening. I shall never again preach against your husband." And he kept his word.

Well—I guess the dinners helped a little.

It was during this time also that Henry C. Campbell of the *Milwaukee Journal,* Dr. Horace Manchester Brown and Victor Berger organized the Milwaukee City Club.[3] The purpose of this club was to bring lecturers and speakers to Milwaukee. The dues were only one dollar a year. This was done so that

---

[2] Miriam Frink added here: "Frederic C. Howe represented a magazine, writer of books—later immigration commissioner at Port of New York (Harding? Wilson?). He came to house when Mrs. B. was running carpet sweeper, she leaned it up against wall and he made her feel perfectly at home, very charming. Cf. Howe Who's Who. Has a sister living here in Milwaukee. Macmillan. Still comes to Milwaukee."

[3] Henry C. Campbell (1862–1923) was a *Milwaukee Journal* editor and amateur historian. Horace Manchester Brown (1857–1929) was a surgeon and hospital owner. Fernando Mock, John Butler, Glenway Maxson, and Charles Norris organized the Milwaukee City Club in 1909. Campbell was one of the club's first members and served as its president from 1919 to 1923 (Milwaukee City Club Records, State Historical Society of Wisconsin).

everyone could join and make it a truly civic organization. But as happens so often, the committees managing club affairs soon wanted permanent head-quarters. These cost money. Consequently the dues went up to twenty-five dollars a year. Naturally the character of the club changed and now only those who could afford it were members.

Also my husband was instrumental in establishing the Milwaukee Press Club.[4] I mention these facts because a few years later during World War I both clubs expelled him from membership. More of that later.

The anticipation and joy of looking forward to the work and living in Washington was tempered a good deal by the difficulties connected with get-ting the *Milwaukee Leader* launched. Always and always the great questions were finances, advertisements, subscriptions etc. etc. After all, the future of our whole movement depended on the life and success of our paper. So Victor Berger as leader carried the greatest of burdens. Not only did he caucus with the Socialist members in the city council, but he had to make the contacts of the larger advertising media, both in the city and in the nation, [and] he had to borrow money from banks, unions, people who were sympathetic and from everyone possible. In keeping the *Leader* going he had the most wonderful and loyal help of Elizabeth H. Thomas.

Miss Thomas was president of the *Milwaukee Leader* publishing company and as such she shared the financial burdens. And now let me say something about Elizabeth H. Thomas. She was a Quaker, coming from very strict Quaker stock from New York. She had means of her own, consequently all her services were a donation. She was one of those human beings who had originally become interested in the welfare of the people by working in Hull House working with Jane Addams[5] [and] had gone to Russia to contact the liberal or protest movement against czarism over there. She is undoubtedly the best read woman of my acquaintance and is the salt of the earth. She was a spectator at the unity convention in New York when the national Socialist Party broke with the Socialist Labor Party which was then under the domination of Daniel De Leon.[6] While there, Elizabeth H. Thomas decided to throw in her lot and also a good share of her fortune with the Social Democratic Party of Wisconsin.

---

[4] According to the *Milwaukee Press Club Book* (Milwaukee: Milwaukee Press Club, 1895), Victor Berger was an active member but not a founder of the club, which was established in 1885.

[5] Jane Addams (1860–1935), a noted reformer and pacifist, established the social settlement Hull House in Chicago in 1889 and served as its head resident until 1935. She was international president of the Women's International League for Peace and Freedom (1915–1929) and a co-recipient of the Nobel Peace Prize in 1931.

[6] Daniel De Leon (1852–1914) led the Socialist Labor Party when a dissenting faction left the party in 1899. The unity convention, held in Indianapolis in 1901, formally joined this faction with the Social Democratic Party and established the Socialist Party.

She became secretary of the Socialist Party here, secretary and confidant of my husband, [and] later president of the Social-Democratic Publishing Company, which published the *Milwaukee Leader*. The responsibility of her various offices very frequently thrust upon her perhaps the most difficult task of borrowing money with which to meet current debts. While these tasks were always distasteful, not once did she hesitate. To Elizabeth H. Thomas and to Victor Berger can be credited the fact that the *Milwaukee Leader* survived the continuous financial storms. And borrowing money is always difficult, but more so for a socialist paper.

Sometimes some good comrade would advance his bit, but always with fear that it might not be repaid. But the *Leader* always repaid those who had helped, timidly but courageously.[7]

And so we launched the daily paper about December 1911?,[8] with which to carry on.

In the meantime, my husband and I were making plans to go to Washington. Some cranks or venomous people sent us threatening letters, saying in effect that if we dared claim the seat in Congress bombs would be planted in our home and my husband and his family would be blown to bits. These letters were never signed, so we considered them "crank letters" which were consigned to the waste basket. It would have made an interesting volume had we kept them.

So with high hopes and a great[9] feeling of responsibility we started out for Washington; taking the three children and Josie with us.[10] William J. Ghent[11] was appointed by my husband as his secretary. This was a happy choice we thought. Ghent was a writer, a scholar and a Socialist. Unfortunately, the two men were temperamentally not qualified to work together easily.

The sight of the Capitol from the station gave us all the thrill of our lives. Never had we seen anything anywhere so beautiful, so wonderful. The im-

---

[7] The *Milwaukee Leader* did not repay all loans. Because the paper ran at a nearly constant deficit, many party members' contributions were essentially considered donations, especially after Victor Berger's death in 1929.

[8] The *Milwaukee Leader* was first published on December 7, 1911.

[9] Meta Berger first wrote "fearful," then crossed it out and wrote "great."

[10] Although Meta Berger was present when Victor Berger took the oath of office on April 4, 1911, she stayed in Wisconsin with their children during the first and third sessions of the Sixty-second Congress (April 4–August 22, 1911, and December 2, 1912–March 3, 1913). The family joined Victor in Washington, D.C., for most of the second session (December 4, 1911–August 26, 1912) but returned to Wisconsin by the end of June 1912.

[11] William J. Ghent (1866–1942), author of several books, joined the Socialist Party in 1904 and helped establish the Rand School of Social Science in New York, serving as its secretary (1906–1909) and president (1909–1911). In 1911 he became Victor Berger's secretary but resigned in 1912 as a result of illness. Ghent left the party in 1916 because of its antiwar stance.

posing dome against a blue blue sky, surrounded by a parkway—up a gentle slope—gave us quite a sensation of reverence.

Mr. Ghent had found us a house quite near the House Office Building. We were delighted at first, but after a night or two there we discovered the house was quite rat-infested. That settled it. At once I went house-hunting. For a stranger in Washington, that was quite a task. After a week of tiresome hunting, we finally found a very pretty house way up on Thirteenth [Street] NW on the outskirts of the city not far from Rock Creek Park. In fact in the next block were meadows on which cows were grazing. It was pleasant to hear the bells tinkling on the cattle. For this home we paid the sum of forty-eight dollars a month, but it was worth it since it was new, clean and comfortable. But it was miles and miles away from the HOB. And since automobiles were not so plentiful, the street car was our only means of transportation.

I really tried to be a good companion and wife to my husband; but I found it a little more difficult to get into his work at Washington and keep house and get the children into school etc. etc.

Also, I thought it was my duty to take the youngsters sight-seeing. There were so many beautiful sights and historical spots to visit. We climbed the Capitol Dome, Washington's Monument, saw the White House in all its simplicity and glory—went to art galleries and did the town up properly. But Mount Vernon captured us all.

Often I would go to my husband's office and try to help. His office was in my opinion the busiest office on Capitol Hill. True, he represented the Fifth District of Wisconsin, but he also felt that he represented the entire socialist movement. As a result of the activities his office soon became a bureau of information. Members of Congress frequented his office, constantly getting facts they needed for their own speeches.

The congressional library was a great boon to us. Not only did we have to be sure of our facts, but we had to be careful to lay the foundation of future social policies. For instance, my husband was the first member to introduce [a bill for] an old age pension system. This policy has not yet reached fruition, but it is certainly progressing to fulfillment.[12]

Perhaps the most colorful and at the same time the most tragic incident in the first term was the Lawrence strike.[13] The textile mills at Lawrence were

[12] Miriam Frink added here: "*Milwaukee Journal* [?] last two or three years had an editorial giving him credit."

[13] In January 1912, textile workers in Lawrence, Massachusetts, went on strike to protest a pay cut; the strike ended in March in the workers' favor. Strikers' children were sent out of town for the purpose of saving money and garnering public support. Although most of the gains were lost within a year, the strike was significant in that it organized an unskilled and ethnically diverse workforce, a group that organized labor had largely overlooked.

not organized, and as a result of a drastic wage cut the workers, mostly of foreign extraction, struck against the wage cut but also against the working conditions in general. Conditions at Lawrence must have been pretty bad, because the strikers were farming their children out to neighboring sympathetic towns. Some two hundred children came to Washington to make a protest. Finally my husband succeeded in getting President Taft to permit a hearing in Washington on labor conditions at Lawrence. To do this legally, a federal law had to be found which would allow such a hearing to be held in Washington. This was done. Both President and Mrs. Taft attended the hearing which was exciting enough, with both sides making heated arguments.

This was the first time I saw and met President William H. Taft. Whatever else his policies were, I wish to state that he was certainly friendly and jovial. Mrs. Taft also took a keen interest in the Lawrence strike.

The results of that strike, as I recall, were beneficial to the workers, and soon after they were organized so that their working conditions improved as well as their wages.

Except for my interest in what was going on in the Congress, life in Washington didn't particularly appeal to me. I was not used to society life and calling on strangers. But the wife of a congressman from Seattle, Washington,[14] told me it was a definite duty to call on certain people, such as the wife of the Speaker of the House, the wives of members of the Supreme Court, the wives of the chairmen of my husband's committee, the wives of the floor leaders of both majority and minority leaders, and the wives of the president's cabinet members. Furthermore, said this good lady—that while they (Republicans and Democrats) clubbed together to get taxis to make the round of calls—so many on Monday—and so many Tuesday etc. etc., she advised me to go alone as I represented the third party in Congress and everyone was interested in looking me over, where as if I went with the group I might be over-looked.

Of course I was aware that the good lady's intentions were of the best. And so were mine. Therefore—being poorer and not being able to hire a taxi alone, I started out to do my social duty alone, taking street cars and walking. I cannot tell you how often I was lost, especially along the winding roads around Rock Creek Park. I walked miles daily for three days and then finally gave up being a socialite in Washington.

Then came invitations to the White House! Now—question—could a class-conscious Socialist accept an invitation to the White House reception given by a most conservative president of the country? We pondered on that important [question] long and earnestly and finally decided that the represen-

---

[14] Helen Humphrey (1870–1936) was active in women's clubs. Her husband, William Ewart Humphrey, served as a Republican representative from Washington from 1903 to 1917.

tative from the Fifth District of Wisconsin was invited because he was chosen by the people back home and that invitations to the members of the House of Representatives were not invited because they were Republicans, Democrats or Socialists. So we went. Can you imagine all the impressions we got that night.

We were used to going out at seven or eight o'clock. But here the time was set for 10:00 P.M. And then we had to go to the White House by auto because that was the way it was done. I remember that car cost us five dollars to take us about six blocks and back again.

But I have appreciated Cinderella ever since. The long line of guests—there were usually five hundred to eight hundred guests at one of these receptions—slowly winding its way up the stairs from the cloak rooms; Secret Service men stationed every ten or fifteen feet along the line, then precisely on the appointed hour the door at the head of the stairs opened and the line proceeded through the rotunda, the Red Room, [and] the Blue Room where the president and his wife and members of the cabinet with their wives received the guests. The military attaché asked your name and then introduced us. This formality over, the famous East Room was for the guests of the evening where dancing took place—if you found enough space to dance on. Usually light refreshments were served in the famous dining room. But here you had to stand and try to eat if you could.

Well—the evening made a great impression on me. I loved the White House. My husband was the center of attraction because the gentlemen laughed and joked with him and I guess they tried him out socially that night. The ladies—well—I don't know what to say of them. I can only hazard a guess that they were a little afraid of the word "Socialist." It took me much longer to get on a friendly footing with them, and then with only a few.

Somehow, I thought that when my husband was earning for the first time in our lives a magnificent salary—that I would have plenty of money to spend. Not so! I was so hard up that sometimes I didn't have a nickel in my purse. Nor did my husband. I couldn't understand our financial situation at all. So one day I said I'd like to discuss with him the question of our financial status, and when I said—"Now why—when you are earning so much money—don't we have enough to get on comfortably?"—with a queer smile he said, "Now Mama—do you remember all those conventions you went to—well—I borrowed money to take you and now I am paying back that money and more besides. Also the money I pay to strike funds, charitable causes etc. etc. takes everything I earn."[15]

---

[15] Miriam Frink added here: "Rent paid first of month. Grocery and meat bills paid back month—no cash left over. Congressman's salary was $650 (check?)." U.S. representatives earned $7,500 per year in 1911.

All right I said—"You pay back the money—I understand and I'll walk." And the walk from the HOB to our house on [Thirteenth] Street NW was between five and six miles. Many is the time my husband and I reached our home dog-tired. And when you are so tired, some of the beauty of Washington just faded out of the picture.

One day—upon reaching our Washington home, I found a man on our porch nailing up a red-flag. My consternation knew no bounds. Hadn't we gone through enough at Milwaukee without having the red flag follow us even into our home in Washington? I ordered him to take it down immediately— thinking the meanwhile—what would the opposition press at home do to us now. The man did remove the flag after some protest, telling me that the owner of that house (a widow) had lost it, and that it was now up for auction and that the red-flag was the auctioneer's flag to notify anyone that the house would be sold. I insisted however that the flag could not be nailed to the house while I lived in it and paid the rent. So very resentfully he planted the flag on the curb; but we did have the flag and I couldn't forbid him the right under real-estate rules to place it in front of the house. Fortunately this all happened in the late spring, so by the time the new owner notified us to move, we were ready to come back to Milwaukee at the close of the congressional session.

Our social life was limited to the official White House functions and a dinner at the British embassy. How did we ever get to the British embassy? Well—I'll tell you. While we were working hard in Milwaukee, we suddenly received a visitor—Lord Eustace Percy[16]—who was sent over to America to study the labor movement but more particularly the socialist movement. Naturally, my husband did his best, spared neither pains, time, or [?] to enlighten the young lord. I guess he must have had an interesting evening because the visit lasted all night.

When we first arrived [in] Washington—he was one of the very first to call on us to renew his acquaintance. Again we enjoyed him and he enjoyed my husband, for one day an invitation came from him to have dinner with him at the British embassy. Have you ever been in the embassies of foreign lands? Well—it's a worthwhile experience. Upon entering the front door opened by a footman or butler, and there half way up a most beautiful wide stairway—on the landing was a gorgeous life sized picture of Queen Victoria. Of course I do not know whether it was a good likeness but it certainly was a gorgeous picture and set the stage for everything that followed.

---

[16] Eustace Percy (1887–1958) served as a diplomat in the British embassy in Washington, D.C., from 1910 to 1914. He resigned from the diplomatic service in 1919 and became a politician and educator.

Lord Percy's guest of honor was my husband. And he had invited the two grandsons of Gladstone who were in the States on a visit, Sir and Mrs. Arthur Willert, representative of the London *Times*, [and] the daughter of James G. Blaine.[17] We had a most interesting evening and as you can imagine the discussion was most animated and inspiring. I shall always count that evening as a mile-stone in my education as well as an introduction into high society. Twenty-five years later I had the good fortune to again meet Lord Eustace Percy while I was in London and where he was a member of the British Cabinet— minister without portfolio. More of that later.

A two year term is hardly enough for a congressman to learn the seriousness of being in Congress. And many representatives were so fearful of not being re-elected, that often they could not or did not vote their convictions, but had their ears to the ground in the hopes that they were making a good bid with their constituents for re-election.

What was the lone Socialist member to do? He felt that a socialist message to the nation was so important, that he could do more good to humanity than catering for votes for re-election. Besides weren't all his proposals as good for San Francisco, Cal., Dallas, Texas, or New York, N.Y. as they were for the Fifth District of Wisconsin?

But how to get all his messages out to the nation? That was a problem. But a solution was found. Daily—reporters from the press called at the office to report to their respective papers. We finally succeeded in getting one of these gentlemen on our pay-roll provided he agreed to send out a daily news item from the lone Socialist in Congress. Thus we succeeded in doing a good bit of constructive work during those two years. Our office was the busiest one on the Hill, we thought.

The next fall, during the federal election for Congress, my husband was defeated to succeed himself. It was a little hard to take, but knowing the political line-up in Wisconsin we were not wholly surprised.

The two years in Washington had been rich in experience, so we came home better prepared to go forward in the political life of Wisconsin. My children—too, had had a change in schools and environment which could only help them better on their road of life. When we returned to Milwaukee, we came home with seven dollars in our family treasury.

---

[17] The other guests included William Glynne Charles Gladstone (1885–1915), the grandson of former British prime minister William Ewart Gladstone (1809–1898); Arthur Willert (1882–1973), American correspondent for the *Times*; Florence Simpson Willert (1876?–1955); and Harriet Stanwood Blaine Beale (b. 1872), daughter of former U.S. Secretary of State James G. Blaine (1830–1893). Arthur Willert wrote that Percy's brother also attended the dinner (*Washington and Other Memories* [Boston: Houghton Mifflin, 1972], 47).

Our next task was to build the Socialist Party and to fortify the *Leader* against the financial hazards with which it was always beset. Both of these undertakings were terrific. And of course much of the burden came home and reflected itself in the family relationship.

Also, since both girls had reached the adolescent period, it became necessary for us to look around for larger living quarters. Finally, we found a large red brick house on the corner of First and Clark Street which formerly belonged to Mr. Ed. Schuster of the Schuster Dry Goods Company. Mr. Schuster had gone to California for his health and died, leaving this magnificent house to his son, who was a doctor in Detroit and wasn't interested in owning the house. Therefore we bought it at a most reasonable price, but we bought this particular house because of the marvelous attic, a room thirty by thirty-three by nine [feet] high with plenty of windows. At once we saw the possibility of using the attic for our ever growing library. We could place nearly all the books up there, but still there was an overflow in three other rooms of the house. The purchase of this house only added to our financial burdens, but it did also provide us with ample bed-rooms, living rooms and kitchen. Here we lived during the rest of my husband's life.

So we settled down to private life except for the fact that we were always the target for criticism by the opposition. Anyone who believes in minority causes and whose convictions are such that he must give voice and action to those convictions, must indeed have a thick skin. We had that. But we were not so immune to criticism that our nerves reacted to much of it. Largely because we felt we were right and the critics were either stupid or motivated by small and selfish interest.

Naturally my husband bore the brunt of it and we in turn suffered through his irritability. I often recall the sort of electric shock that ran through the family when we heard his key in the front door in the evening. A quick glance around the room to reassure us that at least here there was nothing to criticize. Whatever happened during the day at the office would soon be made clear. And it never failed. The burdens of the office were fearful. Money to pay for print-paper on flat cars, interest to be paid on machinery-notes, payrolls to be met, rent, taxes, borrowing more and more money to meet the most pressing demands. The drive for circulation, the effort to increase our advertisements, both local and national, the growth of the party and the quarrels within, all these helped to create a nervous explosive temperament.

Meanwhile, family life went on as best it could. The children were now in high school and doing well.

Occasionally very prominent guests came to visit us; perhaps the most famous of all was Keir Hardie[18] of England, a man we so greatly admired. Philip Snowden, [Henry Noel] Brailsford, Norman Angell and many more. Also a Mr. Greulich, the vice-president of the Swiss Republic.[19] Not only prominent folks came, but the simple poor fellow who wanted to visit us.

I remember so well, a Mexican laborer came and spent several hours with my husband. Fortunately the children had been put to bed; after our Mexican friend left, my husband came to announce that he believed the Mexican had a highly developed case of small-pox. Well—that was the man whom Mr. B. took the time out to teach.

In the meantime the Seidel administration was voted out of office. So the Socialist didn't have much of a chance. Although there were still a few Socialist members in the common council and in the legislature. However no reverses such as losing political office could discourage us. The main and important fact was that the Socialist vote increased slowly but surely.

It was during this period that we had those dinner parties; mainly to get those in high positions to really know us and not believe we had horns etc.

Our progress was slow but sure. We had a very good staff of editorial writers on the *Leader.* Ernest Untermann, A. M. Simons, Winfield R. Gaylord and others whose names do not come back to me at this moment.[20]

Our circulation also increased as did some of the advertising accounts.

———

Now we just saw a bit of blue in what had been a dark and gloomy sky when the fateful year of 1914 approached.

[18] Miriam Frink added here: "Idol of British Labour Party—Scotch, bearded—." Keir Hardie (1856–1915), a British labor leader, helped found the Labour Party and served as a member of Parliament (1892–1895 and 1900–1915).

[19] Philip Snowden (1864–1937) served as chancellor of the exchequer in the first two British Labour Party governments (1924 and 1929–1931). Henry Noel Brailsford (1873–1958) was a liberal British author and journalist. Norman Angell (1873?–1967), a British peace activist and author, won the 1933 Nobel Peace Prize. Herman Greulich (1842–1925) was a Swiss labor leader and Social Democratic politician but never served as Switzerland's vice president.

[20] Ernest Untermann (1864–1956), born in Germany, worked for the *Milwaukee Leader* from 1915 to 1916 and again in the 1920s. He resigned from his editorial position in 1916 because Victor Berger objected to the pro-German slant of his writings. Algie M. Simons (1870–1950), a Socialist Party founder, editor, and theorist, worked for the *Leader* from 1913 to 1916. He supported U.S. involvement in World War I and was expelled from the party in 1917, when he joined the staff of the prowar Wisconsin Defense League, later called the Wisconsin Loyalty Legion. Winfield R. Gaylord (b. 1870), a former Congregational and Methodist minister, was a Socialist Party lecturer, a Wisconsin state senator (1909–1913), and the party's five-time candidate for Congress in Wisconsin's Fourth District. He supported U.S. involvement in World War I and was expelled from the party in 1917.

CHAPTER 6

Suffrage

During the years that passed, I became more and more aware of the work that my husband had dedicated his life to. Socialism became a real cause to me as it had become to my husband. I realized more and more the struggle for existence [of] the workers who had so long been victims of a profit system and [victims] of the great industrialists who fought vigorously against the working man organizing to protect his interests, and [I became aware of the struggle] against the competition of worker against worker; to overcome long hours and starvation wages was the paramount issue. More and more I admired my husband's fortitude and foresight. Sometimes I think that a Divine Providence helped me and guided me to understand and to provide me with the will to go along and become a real worker in the great struggle. Also I became fired with a zeal to do my part, small as it might be. My husband and I became more than husband and wife. We became comrades in the real sense of that word, and as a result we certainly were happy.

As Socialists, we believed in equal rights. That meant I ought to take an active part in the struggle the women of the nation were making to possess the right of suffrage. Naturally my place was with them. However the suffrage movement in Wisconsin as well as in some other parts of the nation was in the hands of the upper conservative middle class women. I considered long about joining, not because I was not in accord with their cause, but because I thought of the effect my entrance into the suffrage movement might have. The Red Scare might easily have alienated the good ladies. Also the anti-suffrage league might fight harder against us if they could use the radical bugaboo. So I waited. I knew that sooner or later intolerance must break down. Finally I received the long looked for invitation to be a delegate to a Wisconsin [Woman] Suffrage [Association] convention. Of course I was glad to go. As might have been expected, I did the unpopular thing by demanding the union label on the *Wisconsin Citizen*—the suffrage paper—printed in Waukesha by the husband of the president of the Wisconsin state suffrage group.[1] If I had thrown a bomb into the meeting, I could not have astonished the good ladies more.

A heated debate took place on recognizing organized labor and the union label etc., but after the vote was taken, all suffrage literature passed out in Wisconsin must hereafter carry the union label. (Prohibition literature also was to be banned by the suffrage [group].)

And when the new board for the ensuing year was elected, I found myself a member of the executive board.[2] That was the beginning of my part in the fight for votes for women.

My association with the conservative middle and upper class women was pleasant enough on the surface. But underneath there was an undercurrent of suspicion and distrust, of which I was aware but which I chose to ignore. My work in the labor movement had made me able to see trends and to use tactics which were useful to the suffrage movement, and so before long I became more or less influential in the community. Furthermore, the fact that the Socialist Party and the working class were solidly behind me gave me some prestige even with these good ladies.

We were part of the national movement and as such were expected to obey the orders coming to us from the national headquarters. There too, the ladies didn't, in my humble opinion, make the most of their opportunity. They were timid politically speaking. Committees were sent to the two dominant political parties (Republican and Democratic) begging them to incorporate [a suffrage plank] in their respective national platforms. These were the same tactics employed by the AF of L under Samuel Gompers. But suffrage was a touchy subject and neither party would incorporate a suffrage plank although they endorsed the principle of votes for women. The Socialist Party at that time was the only political party incorporating a plank for woman's suffrage. As a result, the national office urged only partial suffrage for women. They sent out word to each state that we were to ask for votes for president only.

Wisconsin being far more progressive than that rejected the vote for president only idea and went to Madison to a state suffrage convention[3] and insisted [on] full suffrage for every elective office. Naturally, the loyal followers of Carrie

---

[1] Theodora Winton Youmans (1863–1932) edited the *Wisconsin Citizen* for many years and served as president of the Wisconsin Woman Suffrage Association (WWSA) from 1913 to 1920. Her husband, Henry Mott Youmans (1851–1931), edited and published the *Waukesha Freeman*.

[2] Meta Berger was elected second vice president of the WWSA in December 1914.

[3] The convention took place on January 18, 1917.

Chapman Catt and Dr. Anna Howard Shaw were disappointed in the group which carried Wisconsin for full suffrage.[4] There were some brave souls there who stood loyally by, among these were Mrs. Glenn Turner of Madison, Ada James of Richland Center, Irma Hochstein, and myself of Milwaukee and others.[5]

It was at the close of this meeting I was offered the presidency of [the] Wisconsin State Suffrage Association. Of course I declined the honor in the interest of further progress for votes for women. It would have alienated all the good conservative women in Wisconsin to have a Socialist head the organization. But I did accept the first vice-presidency at that time.[6] The next move was to go to Atlantic City to the national convention at which Woodrow Wilson and his new bride were to be guests and where President Wilson was to address the big mass meeting.[7] It was a most propitious time to hold a national suffrage convention, for President Wilson was running for his second term on the slogan "He kept us out of war."

I need not dwell on the attitude of the Wisconsin ladies towards their Socialist fellow suffragists. Suffice it to say, they were most undemocratic and spiteful; even going so far as to be envious about my most beautiful dress—which was a leftover, but a fine one—from my husband's first term in Congress.

I have often thought of Woodrow Wilson's speech that night. Of course I cannot reproduce it here word for word. But the gist of his remarks was to show the ladies that the history of the United States could really be divided into three periods. First, the period when citizens and politicians were devoting their time into making government, such as writing constitutions and laws which fit the times. Secondly the period given over to develop business, trade and industry—high and low tariffs and free-trade etc. And now thirdly—the period which would devote itself to the human needs and happiness. It is in this third period that woman's suffrage belonged; but since we were in the

---

[4] Carrie Chapman Catt (1859–1947) served as president of the National American Woman Suffrage Association (NAWSA) from 1900 to 1904 and from 1915 to 1920. Anna Howard Shaw (1847–1919), a physician and minister, held that position from 1904 to 1915.

[5] Jennie M. Turner (1885?–1967), Ada L. James (1876–1952), and Irma Hochstein (1887–1974). James was president of the Political Equality League (PEL), a suffrage organization formed by dissidents from the WWSA in 1911; the PEL and WWSA merged in 1913. Hochstein worked at the Wisconsin Legislative Reference Library in Madison (1914–1925).

[6] Meta Berger was elected first vice president of the WWSA in November 1915, at the state suffrage convention in Milwaukee.

[7] President Wilson spoke at NAWSA's Emergency Convention, held in Atlantic City on September 4–10, 1916.

midst of a great world war—why, human needs or happiness had to wait a little while longer. So Woodrow Wilson did not commit himself to our cause and we did not receive the vote until President Harding's time.

During this period there sprung up a new organization called the People's Council.[8] This group called upon all organizations which had ever adopted peace resolutions to join with it to bring about an early cessation of the World War No. I. The Wisconsin Suffrage Association had year after year adopted [a] peace resolution. So being the only one who would do it and as a member of the state board I asked them to join or endorse the People's Council.[9] Then and then only did I realize that I was in the wrong suffrage group. Mrs. Youmans, the president, protested indignantly at my request saying—"This is a holy war." I resigned immediately, and the resignation was accepted.[10] However my resignation did not say I would cease to work for votes for women. On the contrary, I notified my former associates that henceforth I would continue to work but in my own way.

Shortly after this happened Mabel Vernon of the Alice Paul's Woman's Party came to Milwaukee.[11] I entertained for her. There were thirty-eight guests present and thirty-eight joined the Woman's Party of Wisconsin. That was the beginning in Wisconsin.[12] The national members of the Woman's Party had guts and courage. They went to prison, went on hunger strikes, picketed the White House and did spectacular things that brought the question of the woman's suffrage on the front page of every newspaper in the country. To be sure, the publicity wasn't always friendly, but it was publicity. The fact that women finally got the right to vote can be credited to both organizations— the more conservative Suffrage Association for its early organizational contribution and to the Woman's Party for its gallant heroic, if sometimes unpopular, efforts.

[8] The People's Council of America for Democracy and Peace, organized in June 1917, opposed the war and sought a swift negotiated peace.

[9] At the August 3, 1917, WWSA board meeting, Meta Berger did not propose that the WWSA join the People's Council but that the group ask the council—as it had asked the Defense Council—to endorse the enfranchisement of women. See Meta Berger to Zona Gale and S. Quakenbush, August 7, 1917, Ada James Papers, State Historical Society of Wisconsin.

[10] Meta Berger resigned on October 8, 1917.

[11] Alice Paul (1885–1977) left NAWSA in 1914 and in 1916 founded the National Woman's Party, a militant suffrage organization that used tactics such as pickets and hunger strikes. Mabel Vernon (1883–1975) served as the party's national secretary (1916–1920). She and Dora Kelly Lewis spoke at Meta Berger's home on October 14, 1917.

[12] A Wisconsin branch of the Congressional Union (the original name of the National Woman's Party) had been established in 1916, though without a Milwaukee chapter.

Years later, while making a talk in Oshkosh [at] the home of Mrs. Ben Hooper,[13] a good Socialist comrade asked me to have a cup of coffee before going back to Milwaukee; as he had something he would like to tell me.

So over the coffee cup, I was informed that the suffrage ladies were spreading the news that I undoubtedly was in the pay of the brewers since no working [class] wife could possibly afford such a gorgeous gown.

[13] Jessie Jack Hooper (1865–1935) of Oshkosh, Wisconsin, was a reformer, suffragist, and peace activist. She was the Democratic candidate for the U.S. Senate in 1922.

CHAPTER 7

"War Hysteria"

As I recall the summer of 1914, I and the three children were up at Shawano, getting health and sunshine and learning all the sports that go with a cottage at the lake. There was a routine of things to do at Shawano. After breakfast the children and I and my sister Hattie always went to pick blue berries or June berries in the woods behind our cottage, or we hunted pine knots full of pitch for the fire place or the cook stove. This was not only fun but quite hard work. But wood was a little scarce and since we cooked with a wood-stove, the pine-knots were especially welcome for the hot fire from the pitch. And when I stop to think that we baked twenty-seven loaves of bread each week besides the cakes, cookies, and pies needed to feed a healthy growing family, our morning efforts helped quite a bit.

After luncheon, a rest and then a good swim in the lake with much shouting laughter and fun before dinner time. The children usually had guests from Milwaukee to spend the summer with us. This was due first because they were happier to have their friends with them, but also permitted because the prejudices lodged against us as Socialists had reached the children of the village of Shawano. And as a result, they had a difficult time getting anywhere on a friendly basis. Consequently my children brought their own company with them.

The men of Shawano, however, were most cordial when my husband came on a week-end to visit us. Victor Berger was something new to the small town mind and always when my husband came, we had many callers and many warm discussions. They challenged my husband on all political and economic questions and of course he had a really good time, until he left again.

Evenings were spent around bon-fires, with songs and music; or the people from the neighboring beach came and sat around the huge fire place.

These were very happy care-free days. The children learned to handle boats, swim, fish and a good deal about the northern woods. Discipline was not thought of as there was but one rule which governed the household. We all had to be prompt at meal time. This was easy to obey and the rule was made as much out of consideration of the maid as anyone else.

So early in August, the shot at Sarajevo which killed Arch-duke Ferdinand and wife reverberated around the world and the news was heard by us up at Shawano Lake. At first we were terribly shocked and watched the papers eagerly for the news. No one then seemed to realize the far reaching consequence of that tragedy. Not many days passed however when the world knew of the ultimatum Austria sent Serbia; an ultimatum that surely pointed to a European war.

Letters from home were fewer in number and shorter and crisp and that could only mean that VLB was busier than usual, and later I discovered that his concern over the European situation was great indeed.

There was an ominous feeling amongst all the thinking people. We read the news from abroad avidly and hauled out our old geographies.

True, our own country from the president down cautioned us to be neutral in this European squabble.

I was glad indeed when the summer season at Shawano was over. It was the first time since we had gone up there for our vacations that we were glad to come home. And incidentally, that summer was the last summer, I think, we spent at the cottage, which was sold shortly afterward.

Upon our arrival home in Milwaukee I found the house full of new things, such as porch furniture or carpets that didn't harmonize with the other things in the house. I guess I was too stupid or too absorbed in my children to realize that my husband too had to have what you call an "out" for his lonesomeness or pent up emotions. So he just spent money for things he liked or thought were cheap and surprised me with them. Much later in life I could explain this passion for surprises.

Anyway these were small things. We were immediately plunged into the international situation in Europe. Naturally we studied the news most carefully. And there was an ominous feeling in the air. No one knew of course. But it was not very long before declarations of war were issued throughout Europe. Austria declared war on Serbia July 28, 1914. Two days later Russia ordered a general mobilization which was a challenge to the German Empire. August 1—Germany declared war on Russia. August 3 Germany declared war on France, and the following day England broke off diplomatic relations with

Germany and cleared for action on the pretense that Germany violated the neutrality of Belgium by marching through that country to France.

We in America were simply overwhelmed with the news from Europe. And while those in the State Department and in the know were not completely taken by surprise, as is now known for President Woodrow Wilson had sent Colonel E. M. House,[1] his confidential man, to Europe with the idea of forestalling disaster and for the purpose of forming some kind of general entente cordiale capable of preventing the war that loomed on the horizon. Besides being admonished about the imminence of war, Wilson was specifically informed by Colonel House on June 26 that, as all the world knew, the "competition of the money-lending and developing nations" was responsible for "much of the international friction."[2]

The great American public however was stunned by the militarism in Europe going stark mad. In the beginning of those perilous months, we in America were told to be neutral in deed as well as in thought.

How did these tragic events affect me and my home life? Everyone who knew Victor Berger knew what a keen student he was of the economic conditions, not only of the United States but of the European countries as well. Therefore he was better informed than many others about the rivalries and imperialistic ambitions of the European countries. And as a member of the National Executive Committee of the Socialist Party and the editor of the *Milwaukee Leader* he analyzed the whole problem for our readers. He was clear in his analysis, forceful in his condemnation of the capitalist system which in order to survive had to resort to militarism and wars.

Naturally life became very serious for all of us. We loved our country. It was our home land but that didn't mean we were blind to the faults of an economic order. It was our aim to better conditions for the toiling masses and in order to do that, we of course aligned ourselves with organized labor and against the profit system which we felt was at the bottom of the threatened war.

Fortunately my children were healthy children so that I never had to worry on that score. They were now high school students and doing very well. Sometimes now, I wonder just what we did do to bring a little fun or comic relief into our lives. Even my husband must have felt a need for relief from the care and burden of all responsibilities. And as usual he came to the rescue. He insisted on getting an automobile, provided I learn to drive it first. I agreed of

[1] Edward M. House (1858–1938) was a chief adviser to Wilson in foreign affairs.
[2] This and all subsequent quotations in this chapter are from Charles A. Beard and Mary R. Beard, *The Rise of American Civilization*, 2 vols. (New York: MacMillan, 1934).

course. So after that we could get into the car away from everyone and drive. Yes! That was a relief! My husband didn't play cards or dance or drink or play around with women, so the car became a life-saver.

As a Socialist and a member of the international Socialist Party he was very much opposed to the imperialist war in Europe. And to our dismay we watched the rapid change from a country pacific in nature to one which became crazy with war hysteria. Propaganda! Subtle propaganda—crude propaganda was employed to whip up a war psychology.

I well remember the preparedness parades organized every where to encourage voluntary enlistment. But voluntary enlistment did not materialize. I quote now from La Follette's[3] speech as reported by Professor Charles Beard:[4] "The espionage bills, the conscription bills, and other forcible military measures which we understand are being ground out of the war machine in this country are complete proof that those responsible for this war fear that it has no popular support and that armies sufficient to satisfy the demands of the entente allies cannot be recruited by voluntary enlistments." Then came the drive for the conscription act. That was easier, since the big moneyed press [was] owned largely by the same interests that had large investments in Europe.

Slogans were adopted. "This is the war to end war." "This is a war for democracy." "This is the war to establish the right of small nations to choose their own form of government" etc. etc.

The press of the country, the gentlemen of the cloth, the orators, the Four Minute Men[5] all were pressed into the war effort.

And while all this was going on, we in our home were doubly concerned. First because we did not believe in the imperialist war, and secondly—what was to become of the socialist international movement which had grown quite sizable and respectable?

My husband as a member of the National Executive Committee of the Socialist Party of America naturally made frequent trips to the Socialist Party headquarters in Chicago. There he could, as one member of the committee, guide the policy of the party. As a result he became the most powerful member of the committee and also could by cable keep in touch with the international

[3] Robert M. La Follette Sr. (1855–1925), a Republican, served as a U.S. representative (1885–1891), governor of Wisconsin (1901–1906), and a U.S. senator (1906–1925). A progressive leader, he was noted for his liberalism and his reform accomplishments. He opposed U.S. entry into World War I.

[4] Charles A. Beard (1874–1948) was an influential American historian who emphasized economic interests in his interpretations. In 1917 he resigned in protest when Columbia University dismissed several faculty members for their opposition to U.S. involvement in World War I.

[5] Four Minute Men were volunteers in a national program who gave short speeches at theaters and before other audiences in 1917–1918 in support of the war and war-related efforts.

secretary, Victor Adler,[6] if I remember correctly. Naturally he was terribly concerned with the movement and with the activities of the Socialists abroad.

These problems as well as editing the *Leader* and getting the finances to keep the paper going seemed herculean, and our home life became more and more involved as events grew more and more serious. In addition, there were the political campaigns to run and money to get for the expenditure of campaigns. Really I do not remember a care-free moment during the entire period while we were getting ready for war—nor for a good many years after the war.

Meantime, the war hysteria was being whipped into a frenzy. Drives of various sorts were promoted. "No person, native born, naturalized, or alien, escaped the universal dragnet. Workmen in factories, farmers in fields, clerks in stores, members of lodges, children in school, bank depositors, government employees, travelers on trains, pedestrians in the streets, were . . . blacklisted by his neighbors . . . and enrolled . . . in the Department of Justice as a potential traitor."

And yet, we were so naive, we believed so ardently in the constitution and its guarantees of freedom of the press and speech, that quite unconsciously of the dangers that lay ahead we continued our opposition to the war.

Inevitably we were called pro-German by the unthinking and the uninformed and it was not long before yellow paint made its appearance. We escaped yellow paint, but not black ink or garbage and broken milk bottles which decorated our home almost daily. Also there was the threat of personal violence against my husband and I was told never to let him go anywhere alone.

I felt sorry for my children, who had to endure the spirit of the times. I was indeed thankful then that we had a car and could get away from everything for a few hours on Sunday to get fresh air and to take a deep breath for whatever the next day might bring.

The year 1917 was indeed ominous! We watched the propaganda at work. The press, the platform, the church, the theater, in fact every medium to spread the war hysteria was active. Slowly—no rapidly the country became war-mad; and the word *patriotism* soon became *pay*triotism to many Americans.

To those of us who did not believe the U.S. should enter the war on the side of the Allies, dark and dangerous days loomed up. Yet as Socialists, belonging to an international socialist movement, knowing the causes which brought on the war, we stood our ground and we believed in our constitutional

---

[6] Victor Adler (1852–1918) was an Austrian Social Democrat; the secretary of the Second International was Belgian Camille Huysmans (1871–1968). Victor Adler's son, Friedrich (1879–1960), became secretary of the Labor and Socialist International in 1923.

rights of free speech, free press and the right of free assembly.

How little did we realize that these precious rights were soon to be suspended!

So my husband as a member of the Socialist Party executive committee continued his opposition to our entrance, both through the party and as editor-in-chief of the *Milwaukee Leader,* the only English socialist daily in the country at the time. Quite naturally therefore attention was focused on him by all the war-mongers of the day. Also he was quite a political figure in Wisconsin and that too was not liked at all by those who were pushing us into the war.

An emergency convention was called by the Socialist Party to be held in St. Louis early in April of 1917. The purpose for this convention was to draw up a war-proclamation which was to state unequivocally the position of the American Socialists. Just why I did not go to this all important convention—I do not recall. No doubt I was needed at home. Anyway the proclamation issued by that fateful St. Louis convention was issued on April 7, 1917 and is as follows.[7]

I must also call the attention of the reader [to the fact] that a special session of Congress had been called for April 20 or thereabouts, but for reasons I do not now recall, that special session of Congress was moved ahead two weeks so that the declaration of war [by] our country was made April 6. That being the case, the Socialist declaration now became a subject of scrutiny on the part of the authorities; since war had been declared the day before.

The war psychology of the nation now became almost hysterical. Again permit me to quote from Professor Beard's history, *The Rise of American Civilization.* "Never before in history had such a campaign of education been organized; never before had American citizens realized how thoroughly, how irresistibly a modern government could impose its ideas upon the whole nation and, under a barrage of publicity, stifle dissent with declarations, assertions, official versions, and reiteration. Organized to sell the war to a divided and confused nation, the committee on public information succeeded beyond all expectations. With adversaries who were not convinced or cowed by its publicity campaign, the government dealt mercilessly under drastic statutes."

I quote Professor Beard, first because he is a learned man whose honesty and knowledge cannot be questioned and secondly—having been a victim—at least second hand—of this merciless treatment, I may be more sensitive and might under the memory of the agony of those days be tempted to over state

---

[7] The proclamation announced the Socialist Party's opposition to the war. See *Revolutionary Radicalism* (Albany, N.Y.: Joint Legislative Committee Investigating Seditious Activities, 1920), 613–618, for a copy of the proclamation and party program adopted in April 1917.

the condition of those unhappy days. Even as late as February 1917, Wilson was not convinced that the U.S. should enter the conflict.

In June 1917, Congress enacted the Espionage Act. This act provided severe punishment for all persons who by speech, writings, action or any other means interfered with the armed forces of the U.S.[8]

I guess we were very naive for we continued to educate the readers of our paper through its editorial on the causes of the war and its imperialistic foundation, never once realizing that an intelligent analysis would interfere with the armed forces of the country. Never once did we expect to become the victims of the Department of Justice which administered the Espionage Act.[9]

The atmosphere in our town was changing. There were hundreds, thousands of folks who supported our position, some no doubt for reasons other than our own. The circulation of the *Leader* increased, although the large advertisers, both local and national, withdrew their accounts from the paper. Thus we lost accounts that totaled upwards of $500,000 a year.

This made the issuing of the paper a fearful financial problem. Our money problems never ceased to plague us. And during these coming days and months, we should have been relieved of that worry. But instead of getting better things got ever so much worse. But in restaurants, in public meetings, on the street, where ever we met friends who knew us, they would glance around furtively, then pat my husband on the back and whisper to him, "More power to you, Victor."

From July 1, 1916, to July 1917—I was the president of the Milwaukee board of education,[10] and therefore I was much in the public-eye. The task was difficult, but the kindness of friends and strangers far outweighed the petty annoyances of the 100 percent patriots who occasionally sought to embarrass me. Naturally the press of the city was hostile too, for two reasons—first I tried to turn the schools into socialistic institutions (as though they were not that by the very nature of their support and management), and secondly I was the wife of the man who was not considered loyal to the government of the U.S. I still remember the remark of the superintendent of schools, [Milton C. Potter,] who was an ardent[11] supporter of the war but who frequently was a guest at our home, saying to me—"I could sit at your husband's feet and learn

---

[8] Violation of the Espionage Act, passed on June 5, 1917, could result in a maximum $10,000 fine, a twenty-year prison term, or both. The act prohibited obstruction of military operations and recruitment.

[9] On February 2, 1918, a federal court in Chicago indicted Victor Berger under the Espionage Act for the publication of five antiwar editorials in the *Milwaukee Leader;* the trial began on December 9, 1918, and ended on January 8, 1919. He was indicted again on October 28, 1918, in Milwaukee and on December 3, 1918, in La Crosse, Wisconsin, but these charges were later dropped.

[10] Meta Berger served as president of the school board in 1915–1916, not 1916–1917.

[11] Meta Berger crossed out "but reactionary" here.

and learn but I consider him a criminal just the same." I was shocked to say the least.

The summer of 1917 passed. Everyone was studying head-lines and maps as we are doing today. We did too. Very often the stories in the press did not square with the facts. My husband, knowing the geography of Europe well as well as the development of the imperialist policy motivating the cause of the war, later got him into deeper difficulties.

Of course then we did not know what later appeared in the letters since published of Walter Hines Page, Franklin K. Lane and Colonel House—that President Wilson looked rather indifferently on the war, regarding it as a conflict of commercial powers over colonies, markets and power.[12]

September 1917—both my girls entered the University of Wisconsin. Doris had completed her first year and was beginning her sophomore year. However Elsa was a freshman. With what misgivings I saw them go, no one could possibly know. Even I didn't know why the misgivings except that the times were hysterical and hectic.

We had managed to finance Doris's first year but didn't quite know how to meet the expenses of two girls when times were getting more difficult by the month. Then—my husband's sisters[13] came to the rescue and sent us fifty dollars a month so that Elsa too might enjoy the benefits of a college education. Needless to say—the girls didn't have much spending money and got along as best they could.

At home I still had my nephew, Jack Anderson, who was about seventeen years of age.

Then one day—October 2, 1917, the telephone rang and upon answering it, I found my husband saying, "This is the time to come to the office to help! The government has just withdrawn the second class mailing rights from the paper,[14] our mailing room and bags are locked by federal agents. We will have to notify our 17,000 or 18,000 national subscribers of our plight. This is work you can do!" Of course I went immediately, but I confess that not even at that moment did I realize the enormity of the calamity that had befallen us.

At the office I found the whole plant in a turmoil. Everyone looked belligerent, defiant or scared. Then and then only did I begin to feel the terror

---

[12] Walter Hines Page (1855–1918) served as U.S. ambassador to Great Britain during World War I. Franklin K. Lane (1864–1921) served as secretary of the interior under President Wilson.

[13] Victor Berger's sisters were Rose Morganstern (1861–1928), Matilda Weingarten (1863–1957), Anna Gorman (1866–1950), and Rebecca Gottlieb (1868–1936). They lived in Connecticut.

[14] The Espionage Act allowed the postmaster general to ban from the mail material that obstructed the war effort. Postmaster General Albert Burleson revoked the *Milwaukee Leader*'s second-class mailing permit on October 3, 1917; the U.S. Supreme Court upheld the decision on March 7, 1921. The *Leader* regained its mailing permit by order of the Harding administration on May 31, 1921.

that permeated the whole force of workers from the editors down to the press-men, mailers etc. etc.

Before this my husband used to say facetiously that I was more mother than wife. I'm sure he had not appreciated the efforts I made to become "wife." But from this day forward, I am sure that I was more wife than mother, if that were possible.

My task now was to write to all the readers of our paper explaining what had happened but telling them at the same time, if they sent the additional money to cover first class mail, the paper would be sent. Well, you can imagine that our national subscription list dwindled very fast indeed. The same pressure by the federal officials disapproving our party stand must have been exercised elsewhere.

From this time on, my life was closely interwoven with the life of the *Leader*, with the fate of the Socialist Party, and its members who became victims of persecution.

After we lost all of our national readers we tried to serve the loyal ones who lived in Wisconsin by using bundles of papers and sending via the American Express. To our amazement the American Express, being loyal to the federal government or under instruction from the federal government, refused us their service. Consequently our sphere of influence extended only to the city of Milwaukee, where we could still deliver the paper by carrier.

Then followed the withdrawal of our advertising accounts and credit in banks. Many a day we didn't know whether on the morrow we could issue a paper, or whether at the end of the week we could meet the payroll. Often we were on the verge of issuing a weekly paper instead of a daily and as often we considered oiling up the machinery and presses and closing down the plant.

Somehow however we struggled through those first months by borrowing small sums from first one and then another good friend who had faith in us or our cause. The year 1918 had begun! Early in the year U.S. Senator Husting[15]—Republican (?) came back to Wisconsin for a fishing or hunting trip and accidentally shot himself. That left a vacancy which had to be filled by special election. Labor and the Socialist Party nominated my husband to run for the U.S. Senate February 24.

By this time my early amazement and shock had turned into fright. I wasn't at all certain that we ought to get into still deeper trouble and I expressed myself accordingly. So one Sunday morning a committee of labor including

---

[15] Paul O. Husting (1866–1917), a Democrat, served in the Wisconsin Senate (1907–1915) and in the U.S. Senate from March 1915, until his death in a hunting accident in October 1917. He supported U.S. involvement in World War I.

Wisconsin's grand old man, Frank Weber,[16] came to see me and to urge me to give not only my consent but my hearty support. Well—I gave it. I couldn't do otherwise.

At that time we were bitterly disappointed in "Old Bob" as we had affectionately called Senator Robert M. La Follette. Our disappointment was based on Senator La Follette's public declaration that Berger's platform was impracticable although the war issue was the all important issue during that special election and La Follette and Berger's war stand were nearly identical. Consequently La Follette endorsed the candidacy of Thompson (progressive) of La Crosse. That meant a three-cornered race. Thompson, Berger and Irvine Lenroot, Republican.[17]

Campaigns are always nerve-racking. In the first place the work called for long hours and irregular hours. It called for nervous tension and the effort to keep calm and do our work well.

So before each campaign opened my husband would come to me and say, "Now Mama, please don't mind anything during the next six weeks. I may be late for dinner, or I may not come at all. And remember, no matter how often I lose my temper or what I say—please overlook it. Remember we both want the same thing. So shake hands on the resolution to bear with me during these times!" And we shook hands—each resolved to carry on with forbearance. But weeks before the campaign closed we were not on speaking terms. Looking back to those days now, I understand so much that I couldn't tolerate then. After each campaign was finished, even before the results were known, we were the best of friends. Each granting our mistakes and each full of apology.

Now for the first time I was called upon to help run a state-wide election. With the limited amount of money allowed us for campaign expenses, we had to be most careful. So we bought the poll-lists of the counties of the state of

---

[16] Frank J. Weber (1849–1943), known as the grand old man of Wisconsin labor, allied the Wisconsin labor movement with the Socialist Party. He helped to found the Milwaukee Federated Trades Council in 1887 and served as the organization's director from 1902 to 1934. He also helped to found the Wisconsin Federation of Labor in 1893 and served as its director from 1893 to 1917. He served as a Socialist member of the Wisconsin Assembly (1907–1911, 1915–1917, and 1923–1927).

[17] Meta Berger added here: "(Look up blue book of that period to see if there was a Democrat—maybe Joseph Davies.)" James Thompson (1875–1921) and Irvine L. Lenroot (1869–1949) competed for the Republican nomination, which Lenroot received. Lenroot had worked closely with Robert M. La Follette in the past, but Lenroot's support for U.S. entry into World War I caused La Follette to endorse Thompson. Thompson served three terms as district attorney in La Crosse; Lenroot was a member of the Wisconsin Assembly (1901–1907), a U.S. representative (1909–1918), and a U.S. senator (1918–1927). Joseph E. Davies (1876–1958), an attorney and diplomat, was the Democratic candidate. He supported U.S. involvement in World War I. He served as the first chairman of the Federal Trade Commission (1915–1916) and as U.S. ambassador to the Soviet Union (1936–1938).

Wisconsin and carefully checked the names of likely sympathizers to whom literature could be sent. We checked all blacksmith shops, garages, drugstores, creameries and milk depots and barber shops. These were the places where men gathered and talked war or shop. When postage stamps were exhausted we sent bundles of literature with a covering letter asking only that the material be placed where farmers etc. could help themselves. This type of work was entirely in my hands while my husband wrote the pamphlets and letters.

In addition a friend secured the telephone books of towns and villages. It was our opinion that the possessor of a telephone was a little above the average citizen in intelligence and would therefore read.

All work of this type was done by volunteers as every cent went for paper and postage. Many a day I worked eighteen hours a day, taking heavy bags of mail to the central post office at 3:00 A.M. or 4:00 A.M.

How glad I was to be so busy. To work in the interest of our cause was sufficient.

I recall too, that two young women who were employed by the *Milwaukee Journal* (the hostile paper in our town) but who were sympathetic with our program came over to ask me what they could do. So I gave them the checked list of one of our counties together with the literature and allotted postage and asked them to take care of said county.

These two women, unbeknownst to me, sent our material to every citizen in the county with the result that we carried the county. I cite this because I believe that had our program reached many more citizens, my husband could have carried the state.

Mr. Thompson—the La Follette candidate—was eliminated at the primary election as was the Democrat. That meant the final race was between Irvine L. Lenroot and Victor B. It was a hotly contested election. Mr. Lenroot received [163,983] votes and my husband 110,487 votes.[18] A difference of [53,496] votes might have changed the political history for that period. However, we too were surprised at the large vote cast against our entry in the European war.

It also showed that the vote cast was intelligent and informed and not at all on party lines, for the Socialist Party was small; no wonder the politicians were alarmed. It was most exciting and thrilling too to be at headquarters when the votes came in. Usually my husband in his eagerness to get the news walked much faster than I could walk and as a result was a block or two ahead of me. I however couldn't lose sight of him, first because the streets at night

---

[18] Victor Berger finished third, not second, behind Lenroot and Davies, who received 148,923 votes.

are not crowded and secondly because I caught a glimpse of the umbrella which he always carried. The great thrill came always with the knowledge of the great vote cast during those hectic days.

On March 9, 1918, my husband and four members of the national office of the Socialist Party in Chicago were indicted in the federal court in Chicago.[19] When that summons reached us I thought my heart would never beat again. We had no idea, now, to what lengths the administration might go. And of course it is quite terrifying to appear before a federal court on a charge of conspiring to obstruct enlistment. Also—the thought that Judge K. M. Landis[20] [was presiding], known for his hostility towards any opposition to the war, made our position most difficult. Judge Landis's position had been given much publicity in the press of the country. William Bross Lloyd—part owner of the *Chicago Tribune* and an erratic man temporarily sympathetic to our cause— went on the bond of Victor Berger, Adolph Germer, William Kruse, [Irwin] St. John Tucker and [J. Louis] Engdahl, the five Socialists who were indicted.[21] The bond was placed at $25,000 a person.

I have always wondered why the federal government didn't indict the whole National Executive Committee of the Socialist Party which after all was responsible for the party policy. Instead however my husband who was one member of the executive committee and the four paid office workers were grouped under this indictment.

So we began to think of the preparation for our defense. I wish I could separate my life story from that of the difficulties of those days; but that is impossible, because I was as much involved now in the difficulties as anyone. My days were spent in the *Leader* office, the conversation at home was always and always based on our perilous situation, on the financial condition of the paper and speculating on what might happen next.

The atmosphere in our home was so serious that even the laughter of the children made our nerves jump. We couldn't enjoy even a moment of pleasure.

---

[19] The five Socialists were indicted on February 2, 1918, but the federal government announced the indictment on March 9.

[20] Kenesaw Mountain Landis (1866–1944) was a federal judge for the Northern District of Illinois from 1905 to 1922. From 1920 to 1944 he served as the first commissioner of Major League Baseball.

[21] Millionaire William Bross Lloyd (1875–1946) left the party later in the year to help found the Communist Labor Party; he left that party after serving a short prison term in 1922. Adolph Germer (1881–1966), a labor activist and former coal miner, served as national secretary of the Socialist Party (1916–1919). William F. Kruse (b. 1891) directed the Young People's Socialist League and the Young People's Department of the Socialist Party. Irwin St. John Tucker (1886–1982), an Episcopal minister, served as assistant editor for the *Christian Socialist* (1914–1916), as an organizer for the Intercollegiate Socialist Society, and as the Socialist Party's literature director for six weeks in 1917. J. Louis Engdahl (1884–1932) edited the *Chicago Daily Socialist* (1910–1912) and the *American Socialist* (1914–1917) until it was suppressed in 1917. Kruse and Engdahl joined the Workers' Party in 1921.

In the meantime I was a member of the Milwaukee Board of School Directors and had to behave so that I was a credit to myself, my family, and the party and citizens which elected me. To be in the public service while an indictment hung over a member of the family was most difficult. Fortunately friends and teachers (most of them) were kind and elected me for five successive terms.

Events now happened in rapid succession. My husband was nominated to run for Congress for the Fifth District of Wisconsin August 3, 1918. We made the best campaign we could under the difficult circumstances, never for one moment expecting to be successful. Again we resorted to a literature campaign as no one would rent us a hall. This meant tremendous labor on the part of fine comrades and myself. But one of the toughest blows came a few weeks later when the *Leader* was denied the right to *receive* any kind of mail.[22]

[Sketch of returned letter bearing the words, "Mail to this address is undeliverable under the Espionage Act."]

First—no second class mailing rights. And now no right to receive any kind of mail.

How could we run a daily paper under those conditions? How could we? Every night I saw my husband pace the floor and plan and give it up and begin again to pace the floor. What sleepless nights we spent. Yet the fate of the Socialist Party and the cause we had taken upon our shoulders demanded that we continue. We borrowed money! We borrowed from Peter to pay Paul! We thought we had to close down the presses—but somehow each day the paper appeared on the streets and in the homes.

Contracts amounting to thousands of dollars were returned to the sender with the official stamp on the envelope. Of course our advertising contracts disappeared over night.

We thought of ways of circumventing the postal authorities by asking trusted comrades to receive our mail and bring it to us personally. This didn't work at all, because as soon as the letter carrier reported an undue amount of mail being delivered to our trusted friends, the carrier had to report that fact to the authorities, with the result that our comrades were called down to some representation of the government and were put through the third degree. With sad faces these friends reported to us that they could not act as our intermediary and please not put them on the spot.

We came to the conclusion that the mail-men were all Secret Service men. That conclusion however is our own and I cannot verify the fact.

[22] The *Milwaukee Leader* did not receive first-class mail from August 22, 1918, through June 1921.

Five days after we couldn't receive mail any longer—my husband was indicted three more times in three different courts in the state of Wisconsin.[23]

The day before he was to appear in the federal court in Milwaukee, I met a comrade and friend who stopped me to inquire as to whether or not we were provided with the necessary bond money. He saw I was scared and worried and when I told him we hadn't a cent pledged—he was most alarmed and asked me if I knew what the consequences would be if we didn't provide the necessary bond. Then he said—"I'll see what I can do this afternoon." This comrade is Morris Stern.[24] The next morning he appeared in court and signed the bond of $40,000 for the defendants. I think there were three. I was numb with worry and care. All my senses seemed quite dull to me. And it was under these circumstances and during those hysterical times that we endeavored to elect Victor Berger to Congress in the fall of 1918.

Sometimes I felt I couldn't go on. But after taking another deep breath and rolling up our sleeves we started in to prepare for the hottest, bitterest campaign in our history. The government was against us. All the befuddled 100 percent patriots were against us, and the press was most vicious in its attack. We could not rent halls, so again we checked over the poll lists to apportion our postage. We did not neglect the hostile sections of the city; for we figured it was far better to be attacked than to be ignored. Once we had a citizen of this town who aspired to the job of sheriff. He was ignorant but ambitious. His keen desire for success had made him make a plea to the press.

"Boys"—he said—"Write me right, write me wrong; but write me."

Those were good tactics in a campaign. We had to be blessed or damned, but we had to be talked about.

Therefore our literature went into every section of the district and we were talked about. Again my work was to get the literature out. Also the Socialist Party organized a bundle-brigade composed of volunteer workers who delivered a copy or serial copies of a paper called "The Voice of the People" on the door steps every Sunday morning between 4:00 A.M. and 5:00 A.M. Those who didn't get our message through the mail thus had a chance to get a Sunday morning "Voice of the People" with their Sunday morning paper.

Naturally a campaign of this sort sharpened the feeling of bitterness and hostility as well as loyalty as the case might be.

And here I wish to express my deep appreciation and thanks to the party organization for their tireless efforts in making their party strong, for their

---

[23] Victor Berger was indicted two more times, in Milwaukee on October 28, 1918, and in La Crosse, Wisconsin, on December 3, 1918.

[24] Morris Stern (1878–1959), a Milwaukee attorney and Socialist, served on the school board with Meta Berger from 1915 to 1921. In an October 29, 1918, letter to her daughters, Meta stated that Stern "got his brother to put up half of a $60,000 bond" (Stevens, ed., Family Letters, 244).

loyalty to the cause and for the undivided support they gave their standard bearer. It was the most heartening experience I ever had.

As the days went by, the final time had come to count the votes. It must be a peculiar trait of candidates that they are always certain of election during the campaign. Certainly this was true of Victor Berger. I, on the other hand, was always more or less skeptical of success and often I tried to tone down my husband's enthusiasm. I shall never forget the time he made a speech in which he gave credit to the Germans for the contribution they had made to science, music and literature—then he gave credit to the English because of their contribution to literature and the democratic ideals of government they had given to the world. It really was a good speech, an intelligent speech. But when he came to ask me what I thought of it—I said, "Oh! It was a good enough speech, but you may have lost the election with this speech!" And sure enough, the next morning the morning papers head-lined the story with "Berger loves the Germans!"

As usual we spent the night of election day at the headquarters where votes were counted. And as usual my husband on the way over [to] those headquarters was a block or two ahead of me, I following as fast as I could, panting for breath. It was 6:00 A.M., all districts had reported but Waukesha County; and the vote was exceedingly close. Mr. Berger's strongest opponent was Henry Cochems,[25] a liberal, a Bull Mooser and one who was well known in Wisconsin as the star football player of his day. He was a man of courage and fine principle. Well when Waukesha County reported we found that my husband won by plurality vote of 5,920 votes; a narrow yet safe margin.[26]

How exhausted we were, no one will ever know. Yet we were startled as if by electricity the next morning by the press, which reported that Speaker Dallinger[27]—Speaker of the House of Representatives—announced that he would not permit Victor Berger to take his seat in Congress. More of this later. During all these weeks my life and interests were divided too between my school board work and on the fight for woman's suffrage.

The suffrage movement had split into two factions. The National Woman's Suffrage Association was headed by Carrie Chapman Catt. This was the more conservative movement. The other—the Woman's Party of America, headed

[25] Henry Cochems (1875–1921), a progressive Republican and prominent Milwaukee attorney, was Victor Berger's opponent in the 1910 congressional election, not in 1918. Berger's opponents in this election were Democrat Joseph Carney and Republican incumbent William H. Stafford.

[26] Victor Berger received 17,920 votes, 44 percent of the total. Carney received 12,450 votes, and Stafford received 10,678.

[27] U.S. Representative Frederick William Dallinger (1871–1955) of Massachusetts was not Speaker of the House. Dallinger objected to Victor Berger's seating and served as chairman of the committee that investigated Berger's eligibility for office. A Republican, Dallinger served in Congress from 1915 to 1925, then filled a vacant seat in 1926 and served until 1932.

by Alice Paul, was by far the more courageous movement and went so far as to picket the White House, and those who were confined to jail for their drastic tactics went so far as to go on a hunger strike. Quite naturally, I fell into the latter group due to my endorsement of an anti-war movement called the People's Council. This organization was very quickly suppressed and speakers for it were arrested and not given any platform from which to speak. As a result of my endorsement of the People's Council I was read out of the Wisconsin Suffrage Association and consequently organized a branch of the Woman's Party in my home.

At this time Jeannette Rankin,[28] first congresswoman from Montana, was much in the public eye. Consequently she was to be the guest speaker at the annual convention of the Wisconsin Educational Association. And everyone in town and in the state waited to welcome Jeannette Rankin.

While working desperately in the *Leader* office to promote the campaign I received a telegram from Alice Paul asking me to introduce a suffrage resolution at the Wisconsin Educational Association. At first I hesitated, and then my conscience told me I was a poor suffragist if I didn't comply. So telephoning to the superintendent of schools, who was to act as chairman for the big meeting, I succeeded in getting three minutes in which to introduce the resolution. I did not at that time know that Mr. Potter, the superintendent, had refused any time whatsoever to the Wisconsin Suffrage Association. This did not make for friendlier relations. However, since I was a member of his board of education he granted me the three minutes.[29]

At these conventions every teacher in the state of Wisconsin was expected to attend. Of course the meeting was large—about 15,000 teachers were present.

[28] Jeannette Rankin (1880–1973), a Republican representative from Montana (1917–1919 and 1941–1943), was the first woman elected to the U.S. Congress. A pacifist, she voted against U.S. entry into both world wars.

[29] Virginia Arnold of the National Woman's Party in Washington, D.C., had received permission from the secretary of the Wisconsin Teachers' Association, Maxillian Bussewitz, to send a representative to the convention; Arnold asked Ada James to speak, and James in turn asked Meta Berger. See Virginia Arnold to Ada James, October 29, 1917, and Ada James to Meta Berger, October 31, 1917, roll 33, VLB Papers (microfilm). Meta's correspondence shows that Bussewitz, Potter, and Rankin granted Meta permission to introduce the resolution. When she secured permission, she was unaware that WWSA President Theodora Winton Youmans had planned to introduce a similar resolution the following day at the convention business meeting. Youmans and the WWSA women were likewise unaware that Meta represented the Woman's Party, and they assumed that Meta had unscrupulously claimed Youmans's authority as her own. Youmans attributed Meta's supposed behavior to her "German code of morals or immorals and German ruthlessness" (Meta Berger to her daughters, [November 3, 1917], in Stevens, ed., *Family Letters,* 229–232; Theodora Winton Youmans to Mrs. Frank J. Shuler, November 3, 1917; Meta Berger to Ada James, November 4, 1917; and Meta Berger to the Executive Board of the WWSA, November 8, 1917, all in WWSA Papers, State Historical Society of Wisconsin). Meta presented the suffrage resolution on the evening of November 2, 1917.

When the meeting was called to order, the chairman introduced the first speaker.[30] He was a Four Minute speaker and his job was to create enthusiasm for the war. Four Minute speakers flooded the country. This was part of the propaganda scheme worked out by the 100 percent for the war group. To my consternation and horror, he started a tirade against Senator La Follette and Victor Berger, telling these teachers that Wisconsin had two snakes in the grass, two men who ought to be taken out and shot at sunrise etc. etc. This Four Minute speaker was a criminal lawyer from Green Bay and knew how to use the English language to denounce and to convict.

My friends in the audience, and there were thousands of them, just gasped and gasped so loud that the speaker heard them. He went on to say, "I was only to speak four minutes, but I can see by your sympathies that you need forty minutes of patriotic lecture" and continued.

Miss Rankin knew what emotional strain I was suffering and leaned over to me to say, "Please, Mrs. B.—let me be the next speaker." This I could not do, knowing crowds as I did; I knew that as soon as she had finished the audience would leave and my suffrage resolution would never be introduced. So I insisted on going on next. Then the chairman stepped to the edge of the platform and in a very precise way said—"It now becomes my duty to present Mrs. *Victor* Berger," the emphasis being on the name of course. I didn't know how I ever reached the edge of that platform. My heart pounded, my knees trembled, my mind was a blank. But suddenly the great mass of people in the audience rose en masse and cheered and cheered and called bravo to me. I saw I was not alone and that the criminal lawyer had over reached himself. The audience were seated again and upon my first word of "Friends" once more they arose and cheered and waved handkerchiefs, and one man hoisted his hat high up in the air on his cane in his effort to show me some understanding of the situation. This man was an assistant superintendent of schools. I was over come with relief and gratitude and finally got the suffrage resolution passed unanimously. After the meeting a reception line lasting a long long time of friends came up to shake my hand.

This was a thrilling and satisfying experience, especially in view of all the attacks and poundings we had been receiving for weeks, and election day was the following Tuesday. And the strangest thing in news-reporting happened. Every newspaper in town blue-penciled that demonstration. No wonder! They couldn't afford to tell the story as it might elect my husband.

This incident reflected the feeling of the teachers of the state.

[30] Patrick Henry Martin (1862–1925) spoke for the Wisconsin Loyalty Legion at the convention. He was the second speaker.

But to go back to the turbulent year of 1918. My husband was congress-man elect; since November 5. On December 3—four weeks later—he was again indicted under the Espionage Act at La Crosse. Would persecution never stop?! Again his bond was placed at $5,000. What did the future hold for us? First of all the great honor bestowed upon him by the citizens of the Fifth District, every one of whom had cast a vote expressing his confidence in our stand on the war. Of this, they were well informed since the campaign was entirely based on literature sent to their homes. Secondly—there was always the threat to the life of the only English [socialist] daily in the country. Thirdly and to me most frightening—the numerous indictments and what they might bring to us—constitutional guarantees or prison sentences.

We had good reason to fear the latter, for had we not seen Eugene V. Debs go to prison?[31] Did not Kate Richards O'Hare go to prison?[32] Did not the poor devils in the IWW go to prison?[33] And numerous others who were not so outstanding? And finally—was this a democracy and was the vote of Berger's constituency to be respected or was representative government to be thrown out on a wave of war hysteria? Which?

[31] Meta Berger is probably referring to the prison term that Debs served after World War I. Debs was convicted under the Espionage Act in September 1918 and was imprisoned from April 1919 through December 25, 1921, when President Harding released him.

[32] Kate Richards O'Hare (Cunningham) (1876–1948), a Socialist lecturer, organizer, and editor, was the most prominent woman in the prewar Socialist Party and the first well-known political figure indicted under the Espionage Act. She entered prison in April 1919 and was released in May 1920. She later became a prison reformer.

[33] The Industrial Workers of the World (IWW), a radical labor organization for unskilled workers, used strikes and sabotage to achieve its ends. The IWW opposed U.S. participation in World War I. In September 1917, more than two hundred IWW leaders were arrested, and nearly one hundred were fined and sentenced to prison.

WHi(X3)48966

Meta Schlichting Berger, pictured about 1897,
the year she married Victor L. Berger.

WHi(X3)5594

Above: West Juneau Avenue (Chestnut Street), Milwaukee, c. 1890. **Below:** The hurlyburly of downtown, pictured about 1900 by *Milwaukee Journal* photographer Robert Taylor. In 1890 the city had a population of 204,000; ten years later, it had burgeoned to almost 289,000.

WHi(X3)28619

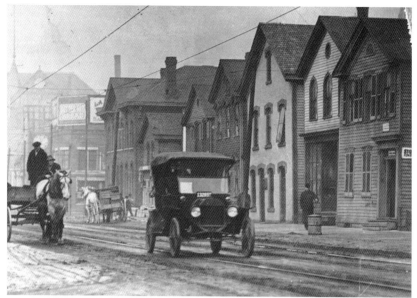

Milwaukee County Historical Society

Above: State Street, Milwaukee, c. 1914. The building second from the right housed the offices of Victor Berger's *Social-Democratic Herald*. **Below:** Berger (left) and socialist editor-politician Frederic Heath, 1897.

WHi(X3)12976

WHi(X3)48964

Above: The duplex at 1218–1220 Second Street, Milwaukee, where the Bergers lived from 1903 to 1912. **Below:** Victor in his study with his elder daughter, Doris, 1903.

At Home 1903

WHi(X3)49226

WHi(X3)48925

In 1910, Meta Berger was pictured as a sedate, conventional wife and mother. With her election to the Milwaukee school board in 1909, she entered the public arena and remained there the rest of her life. The *Milwaukee Leader* trumpeted her election as board president in 1915.

WHi(X3)49231

Above: Victor Berger's extended family, c. 1904. Meta and Victor are standing in the center of the back row. **Below:** The Berger family at the family cabin ("Kill Kare") in Shawano, Wisconsin, c. 1908. Jack Anderson, the boy to the left of Elsa and Doris, was the son of Meta's sister Paula, who died in 1902. He lived with the Bergers until about 1918.

WHi(X3)49228

Milwaukee County Historical Society

Above: Setting type and making up pages of the *Milwaukee Leader,* c. 1912.
Below: Campaigning for Frank Metcalfe, Socialist candidate for governor, in front of the *Leader* offices, c. 1930–1932.

Milwaukee County Historical Society

The staff of the Social-Democratic Publishing Company in front of Brisbane Hall, Milwaukee, c. 1912–1913. In the second row, beneath the word *Vorwaerts*, are Meta Berger and Victor Berger (in homburg hat).

Courtesy of the Milwaukee County Historical Society

Meta Berger Papers, SHSW

Portrait sketches made by Meta Berger during the trial of Victor and his four co-defendants for violation of the Espionage Act, December 1918–January 1919. Judge Kenesaw Mountain Landis (top left) presided; Victor Berger appears at the lower right.

WHi(X3)48915

Meta Berger in the 1920s, after weathering the storm of Victor's trial and his repudiation by the House of Representatives. In 1923, Victor returned to Congress; the following year, Meta was appointed to Robert M. La Follette's national presidential campaign committee.

WHi(X3)4799

Poster for Victor Berger's campaign for the U.S. Senate, 1918, measuring c. 6 x 8 feet. In the heat of wartime anti-German sentiment, many such posters were ripped down or vandalized; on some, Berger was given a Kaiser's upturned mustache and a spiked Prussian helmet.

WHi(X3)48960

In this photo taken in 1923, during their trip to Europe, Victor and Meta both show the effects of five years' unremitting political strife and anxiety over the future.

WHi(X3)48965

Above: The Bergers' daughters, Elsa Berger Edelman (left) and Doris Berger Welles, pictured about 1930. **Below:** Meta with her granddaughter Deborah Welles, c. 1928.

WHi(X3)48924

WHi(X3)48923

Meta about 1933, surrounded by (left to right) her cousin, Jennie Goessling; her granddaughters, Deborah and Polly Welles; and her daughters, Doris and Elsa.

WHi(X3)48914

Left: In her later years, Meta Berger was an outspoken advocate for unpopular causes. **Below:** Two artifacts of Meta's flirtation with Stalinism—a pamphlet depicting her as a stylish admirer of the Soviet experiment and a eulogy by Peggy Dennis of the Wisconsin Communist Party in the *Daily Worker*, 1944.

Courtesy of Michael E. Stevens

THE LATE META BERGER

Meta Berger-- Grand Old Lady

By PEGGY DENNIS

Page 4

Meta Berger Papers, SHSW microfilm

Chapter 8

The Chicago Trial

A nd now I must pause a moment. Even after nearly twenty-five years have passed, I am not yet calm enough to give a true picture of the nerve-strain, the anxiety and agony we went through during those fateful weeks when we had to appear in Judge K. M. Landis's court in Chicago. As I said before, my husband, who was sixty years old, was grouped with the office force of the national office of the Socialist Party. The next youngest person was Adolph Germer, twenty-eight, then Louis Engdahl, [Irwin] St. John Tucker—an Episcopal preacher—and William Kruse, all young men in their twenties. Again and again I asked myself, why only one member of the National Executive Committee of the Socialist Party, why not the whole committee? Not that it would have made it easier for us; now I think quite the contrary is true. However Victor Berger was the only member at that time who wielded political power in Wisconsin, and so I came to the conclusion that that was the reason for this particular grouping.

We were asked to appear December 9, 1918, at Judge Landis's court. It was my first experience with legal prosecution. I knew no other country, I loved America, I had great faith in the democratic processes of dispensing justice. I was very very naive and should not have been so after all the preceding events of the year 1918. Nevertheless I found it hard indeed to have all my ideas of loyalty to one's country abused and kicked around and it was indeed difficult to accept the disillusionment. It was my country, remember. I was born here. My husband had been a citizen for the past fifty years[1] and he was wholly identified with this country and all its institutions. His loyalty could

[1] Victor Berger became a U.S. citizen in 1886.

97

not be questioned except by those whose motives were indeed base. He was a prolific reader, keeping the English, German, French, Hungarian papers to get his European news. He was so well posted that at a glance at maps he knew the reports printed in the kept press were not based on facts; and as a result he tried to give the true picture of events in the *Leader,* often resorting to the blue-pencil when our staff only used the scissors. I mention this because two of our trusted Socialist writers were the ones who reported this news to the federal authorities.

So with anxiety and misgivings we tried to prepare our case. Our staff of attorneys were fine men. There was Seymour Stedman, William [A.] Cunnea, [Swan M.] Johnson and finally Henry [F.] Cochems of Milwaukee.[2] Henry Cochems was the big foot-ball player and liberal whom my husband defeated. I wish now to pay tribute to Mr. Cochems's sense of justice, fair play, courage and liberalism. He came voluntarily to our office and offered his services to defend Victor Berger.

My husband came into the outer office with his eyes shining to tell me of Henry Cochems's offer. We didn't have any funds for his legal services and were on the point of declining them. When I said, "No! By all means accept them. We will get the money somehow."

After that came the problem of raising money for the defense. The Chicago lawyers were taken care of by the Socialist Party, but we here had actually employed a Milwaukee attorney. We felt justified in that since a Milwaukee man, knowing the Milwaukee situation better than anyone else, might be of tremendous use to us. And how right we were!

Now it was up to me to raise money. After much deliberation I hit upon the idea of sending an appeal to each member of the Socialist Party throughout the nation, asking them to send a least one dollar to keep Victor Berger out of the prison and to fight to keep his voice heard in the halls of Congress. The response was fine. Sometimes their replies contained ten cents, sometimes twenty-five cents, more often a dollar and frequently as much as five; seldom more. But we did raise enough to feel comfortable about having engaged Henry Cochems.

It is needless to say that before going to Chicago to face Judge Landis we did all that we knew how to do to prepare for the case. My husband's life was at stake. It is true a ten year or twenty year sentence is not always a death sentence, but any prison sentence takes a fearful toll out of the remainder of a man's life.

Then too, there is a difference in a man's temperament. Eugene V. Debs, for instance, was made of the stuff that martyrs are made of. His calm angelic

---

[2] Charles H. Soelke also served as a defense attorney.

disposition enabled him to go to prison, conform to prison routine, encourage other unfortunates behind gray prison walls and become a beloved leader even under those trying circumstances. Even he did not long survive his experience after he was released.[3]

I couldn't imagine my husband taking prison discipline with any kind of equanimity. He would be irritable, smart under orders, resent discipline, chafe under prison routine. Debs accepted the situation and tried to do good even behind prison walls. I feared my husband with his temper would spend most of his time in solitary confinement, if indeed he survived.

So we made up our minds to use every avenue open to us to try to keep [him] out of a federal prison.

The federal government was building up its case too. They came into the *Leader* office, confiscated our bound copies of the year's edition of the *Leader* and other papers and documents which they thought might be valuable. The agents also went through my husband's office and desk, taking with them any letters to or copies of letters from him.

Also the district attorney[4] of the federal court in Chicago went on an investigating trip to the federal prison at Leavenworth where Carl Haessler[5] was confined as a conscientious objector.

And here—let me say a word about Carl Haessler. Carl was one of Wisconsin's brilliant students. He won a Rhodes scholarship and went to Oxford and Cambridge, England, to continue his studies. It was while he was in England that he became a socialist. As soon as the First World War loomed on the horizon, Carl returned to the U.S. and secured a position in the university at Urbana, Illinois. The conscription act requiring all young men in the country to register was passed by Congress in the early part of June 1917. This registration card also reached Carl to sign. This Carl did but declared on his card that he would not fight in what he considered an imperialist war. The result was that he lost his position and came back to Milwaukee. At about this time my husband and I met Mrs. Haessler[6]—Carl's mother—who asked that since Carl espoused the same cause as did my husband, she thought Victor Berger might give him a position on the *Leader*. This my husband agreed to do and thus Carl Haessler became one of the *Leader*'s staff. While working on the

---

[3] President Harding released Debs from prison on Christmas Day 1921; Debs died in 1926 at age seventy.

[4] Charles F. Clyne (1877–1965) served as U.S. district attorney for northern Illinois from 1914 to 1923.

[5] Carl Haessler (1888–1972) was arrested, court-martialed, and sentenced to twelve years at Fort Leavenworth in 1918. He was transferred to Alcatraz a year later for leading a prison strike. After his release in 1920 he worked for and eventually directed the Federated Press, a labor news wire service.

[6] Lina Haessler (1864–1952). Carl Haessler testified at the trial that his parents and the Bergers knew each other before his birth.

Leader it was Carl's job to read the foreign newspapers since he was familiar with foreign languages. In due time Carl was called in the draft. He came down to bid us "Good-bye," saying at the same time he would not put on the uniform. My husband cautioned him, even advising him to put on the uniform or else face a court-martial. Carl preferred to do this and subsequently was court-martialed and sentenced to ten years in Fort Leavenworth federal prison.

It was while the government was gathering evidence against us and while Carl was an inmate of the prison, that I received a carefully written letter from Carl talking about family matters and that, to his surprise, Uncle Charlie had come to visit him. I was puzzled and for days did not get the full meaning of the carefully worded warning. Then suddenly we discovered the district attorney's name was Charles Clyne. Then we realized why Charles Clyne had gone to Fort Leavenworth. He questioned Carl on his association with us, whether or not Victor Berger was responsible for his socialism, for his conscientious objector's stand. I cite this incident because we could not foresee what use District Attorney Clyne would make of his interview with Carl Haessler.

The time between the excitement of a successful election and the time when the Chicago trial began December 9 was about five weeks, and five busy weeks they were.

Several days before the opening we went to Chicago to confer with our attorneys and to line up our defense. Seymour Stedman had just returned from the East where he participated in the defense of five Socialist assemblymen-elect and whose seats were challenged.[7] I had ardently hoped too that Morris Hillquit would come to Chicago to help in our case. However he had a complete breakdown in health and had proceeded to Saranac Lake for a rest and recuperation. I was disappointed.

At any rate we had no choice now but to obey the summons and go on trial.

The charge was briefly "Conspiring to obstruct enlistment." And now for the first time I learned that "to conspire" in legal interpretation was to hold the same opinion on any matter. You need never to have conferred with anyone, met anyone or agreed with anyone no matter where that person might be, whether in San Francisco, Chicago, Miami Beach or Timbuktu. If you held the same opinions or agreed on a philosophy you were guilty of conspiracy. And in this case the so-called conspiracy was alleged to have been to obstruct enlistment.

---

[7] The New York Assembly refused to seat five Socialists thirteen months after Victor Berger's trial, in January 1920 rather than December 1918.

At Chicago the first thing we did was to have conferences with our legal staff [for] hours on end. I do not think we ever got to bed before 3:00 A.M. Naturally all our defense material had to be organized and marked Exhibit A and B and C etc. Then too we had to anticipate what line of attack the district attorney would take. In general, being wholly ignorant of court procedure, legal attacks, attacks built upon emotion, on patriotism, and on the charge of conspiracy etc., we were at the mercy of the prejudices of the times and the victims of a war psychology. We were bewildered.

Each night after the trial began, there were more conferences to see where our side had failed and to wonder at the clever tactics of the district attorney and the amount of office information he possessed.

Our first day in a federal court didn't help to instill respect for the U.S. federal procedure. Judge K. M. Landis was more responsible for our disillusionment than any one other phase of our experience during those tragic days. Perhaps it was my fault. Had I not read about his prejudices? Had I not known of his cruel sentences on victims before our case? Anyway I went into that courtroom with fear in my heart, with the knowledge that here we would not be given a fair trial! It was not the general physical appearance of the judge that startled me [so much] as the fact that his attitude was one of cold antagonism. His face was bitten and hard and full of hatred. He always had a huge cud of tobacco in his mouth and cheek. His cuspidor was some eight or ten feet away. But in his expert practice he hardly ever failed to hit the center with accuracy, [a] procedure which I'm certain he had practiced for years.

Then too, I had a definite idea of the dignity of a court. Therefore I thought it most undignified to see this white-haired federal judge call his clerk, give him the shoes off his feet and sit upon the bench in stocking feet. Later the clerk returned the shoes and the judge put them on his feet. I was disillusioned to say the least.

Oh dear! How can I put in cold words the agony of those days! Not until twenty-five years later have I attempted to relive those days. I have always tried to dismiss the memory of those harrowing days as a dreadful nightmare. I find it most difficult.

The attorneys on both sides were selecting the jury. From the very first juror interviewed to the last one, there seemed to be something strange and foreboding. Then it was generally talked about that every one on the panel from which our jury was to be selected had first to be OK'd by the Defense Council of those days. That meant that the government was pretty sure of its case.

Our defense really had nothing to hope for. Many months, almost a year after the trial closed, a police-officer conducting traffic on State Street in

Chicago stopped me one day to shake hands with me. I was surprised, for to my knowledge I had never seen the officer before. He then told me he was stationed at the door of the courtroom and didn't I remember him? No—I didn't. "Well Mrs. B.—I felt so sorry for you throughout those days. But let me tell you that never—at no time—did you folks have a chance. Your goose was cooked long before your trial opened."

All of which indicates that there was plenty of reason why we were so very apprehensive! And now I also see how terribly naive we were. But we had to put up the best legal fight we could and we did.

After the jury was accepted the crucifixion began. Day after day from 9:00 A.M. to 6:00 P.M., with an hour off for luncheon, I heard the D.A. denounce, attack [and] try to trap our young comrades and defendants. How glad I was that none of them tried to evade the responsibility of their party work. To me those young men became heroes, for they stood their ground under the severest cross-examination.

Day after day for three weeks the grueling went on. I didn't realize how much I was affected until I lost my appetite and the sight of food made me violently sick.

The first half of the trial was devoted to persecuting the four younger men. They took it very well. My husband was the last defendant to take the stand. As one might have expected, the court-room became electrified.

The judge gave my husband plenty of time. I suppose he thought the more time he got, the more he would hang himself.

During the first term Victor Berger served in Congress way back in 1910–1912—he had the courage and the decency to impeach a corrupt federal judge, Judge Hanford of Seattle.[8] When therefore he took the stand on one occasion, Judge K. M. Landis over-ruled the objection of the counsel on both sides [and] said, "Permit Mr. Berger to take the stand. I want to see the man who had the courage (temerity) to impeach a federal judge." Even that attitude on the part of our own judge boded no goodwill towards us.

During the days while we were in court, we heard persistent rumors that the jury was being talked to or tampered with. The stories always pointed towards hostility on the part of jurors and later it developed that the bailiff in charge of the jury was constantly talking about those "God damn traitors and the lying Dutchman."[9]

---

[8] Victor Berger called for the impeachment of Judge Cornelius H. Hanford (1829–1926), a federal judge from 1890 to 1912, on June 7, 1912. Hanford subsequently resigned.

[9] One of the jurors, Thomas Nixon, submitted an affidavit following the trial on January 25, 1919. In

As the trial progressed, the D.A. was trying very hard to accuse my husband of, not only conspiracy to obstruct enlistment, but of trying to make the young men with whom he came in contact of becoming conscientious objectors. When this happened we knew why "Uncle Charlie" (the D.A.) had visited Fort Leavenworth prison to interview Carl Haessler.

Henry Cochems, who was a liberal Republican, therefore asked Judge Landis to subpoena Carl Haessler and bring him up from the federal prison to testify that he (Carl) had taken his C.O. position, not because of what Victor Berger had advised, but in spite of it. I had always been a friend of Carl's parents and, thinking they would like to see their son again, telephoned them, asking them to come to Chicago if they wished. Mrs. Haessler was most grateful, saying she certainly would come as she could not and would not see her son behind the gray walls of a prison. So on the day we expected Carl to arrive from Fort Leavenworth, the mother and father and youngest and favorite sister and his young wife came to the courtroom.[10] About 11:00 A.M. the door opened and Carl appeared, both hands hand-cuffed together and with a guard. I was almost frozen with horror. My prayer was that Carl's parents didn't see their brilliant son in cuffs. Henry Cochems at once appealed to the court to remove the cuffs and as a result both Carl and his guard were turned over to Cochems for the day. That night Carl was interned in the Cook County jail. However, after a most trying day during which Carl testified as to Mr. B.'s advice, we took Carl, the guard and the family for an excellent meal, giving him everything from soup to nuts. I shall always remember that party, with the cloud of the law hanging over us and with the fact that I would literally have choked on food had I tried to eat any. When we arose from the table Carl had taken some of his food—such as fruit, cakes, nuts etc. with him. Of course we thought he was taking it with him to eat on his dreary ride back to prison. But this was not the case. Those good things were given to the colored victim who shared the same cell with Carl at the county jail.

I do not quite know why this incident has remained so vividly in my mind, but I include it in this story to indicate the psychology of the times and the length [to which] the authorities went to make an impression on us as well as on everyone else.

---

it he cited examples of bias against the defendants by other jurors and especially by Bailiff Streeter, who, Nixon claimed, compared the defendants to Benedict Arnold and made remarks such as "Berger is a damn lying Dutchman and ought to be in Hell."

[10] Carl Haessler's father was Herman Haessler (b. 1864); Carl's youngest sister was Dorothy Haessler (Todd) (1899–1975); and his wife was Mildred Haessler (b. 1890). Mildred, a teacher, testified at the trial.

The trial itself and the conduct of it were after all the important thing, as the lives and freedom of five fine men were at stake.

We also discovered where the D.A. got so much information about the Socialist Party. Months before the opening of the trial, the government had succeeded in getting Adolph Germer, the national secretary of the party, to employ a stenographer[11] and who acted as a stooge for the government.

Well as the trial proceeded, the attorneys for the defense could only build a legal case which might be appealed. That was the procedure after we all discovered there was no hope for fairness and since the war hysteria and psychology had influenced the press, the courts and even the Supreme Court, as evidenced by the Eugene V. Debs case.[12]

We were also told that Judge K. M. Landis rarely agreed to appealing a case because he maintained that anyone who was tried in his court had had a fair trial.

However Christmas Eve came along. We were in court all day long. In the evening as we emerged we saw the holiday decorations and the red, blue and green lights everywhere. I must say for the first time in my life I felt resentment at the efforts for a gay holiday season.

And then something very beautiful happened. We—the party being tried by K. M. Landis—received an invitation to dinner by Jane Addams in her private apartment. I was overwhelmed by the kindness, the thoughtfulness and the courage of Jane Addams. I had known her slightly before as any liberal or radical did who was welcomed on occasion at Hull House. But to know Jane Addams as I did this Christmas Eve, to admire her as we all did and to love her devotedly for her kindly deed—was indeed the bright spot in those dreary agonizing days. We spent a quiet evening with her at Hull House. Naturally no one felt holidayish or jolly. We were all too sober for that, but dear Jane Addams did her best to give us a great deal of cheer and comfort. As long as I live I shall eternally be grateful to her. Our paths crossed again years later when we both worked for peace, and with the years my devotion to her increased.

The trial was drawing to a close; in fact both sides rested their case. The jury received its instruction from the judge and retired to its headquarters under the charge of Bailiff Streeter, the bailiff who cussed and damned the defendants throughout the deliberations.

The court took a recess, so the court room was cleared. We—who were so terribly miserable and who had put every ounce of our energy into keeping

---

[11] Bessie Oxenhandler, Germer's former stenographer, testified at the trial.
[12] The Supreme Court upheld Debs's conviction on March 10, 1919.

up with the proceedings for weeks, had only the corridor of the federal building to stay in. Naturally we did not move from the spot. Then suddenly the clerk of the court, I think his name was Sullivan, asked me as the eldest woman to come into his office where I could sit down. There I waited for four hours when word came that the jury had reached a decision.

Mr. Sullivan, the clerk of the court, exclaimed, "Oh that's not so good for you, Mrs. B. But before we go back into the court room I must tell you that I think your husband is a brave man and the finest patriot I ever met." This after that fearful trial and from the clerk of the court. It was a little comforting but couldn't help much.

The jury found all the defendants guilty.

Then came the fateful day for the judge to pronounce sentence. First the four younger defendants were asked if they had anything to say before sentence was pronounced. I wish the world could have been there to witness the bravery of those young comrades. They defended their stand and gave the judge a lesson on imperialistic wars and socialism etc. I believe now that the judge was not only surprised but angered.

Noon hour came! We recessed for lunch. My husband came to me and said, "Mama—do you want to eat?" Of course I didn't and neither did he. So we took our noon-hour and did what he liked best to do—which was to browse around in the big book shops. And for the first time in my married life I was comforted to see him spend money for books he had long wanted.

As the court convened for the afternoon session, Victor Berger was asked if he had anything to say before sentence was pronounced. As I sat there in my nervous and terrified state, I didn't quite hear what my husband said. Only after the proceedings were printed was I able to read it. The speeches of all five defendants were later printed in pamphlet form and are worth reading even today.[13]

Then silence! The worst silence I ever endured before the judge finally pronounced a sentence of twenty years in the federal penitentiary at Fort Leavenworth, the sentence to begin at once.

I don't know what a brain storm is—but if there is such a thing—I suffered from it, for I was too stunned to see, hear, think or move. And of course the defendants at once were put into the care of a U.S. marshal and disappeared. Oh! It was cruel! Cruel! Cruel!

---

[13] The defendants' speeches appear in the pamphlet *100 Years—For What? Being the Addresses of Victor L. Berger, Adolph Germer, J. Louis Engdahl, William F. Kruse, and Irwin St. John Tucker to the Court That Sentenced Them to Serve 100 Years in Prison* (Chicago: National Office, Socialist Party, [1919]).

Fortunately for us, our attorneys had arranged with Judge Alschuler[14] that he would honor an appeal.

Mrs. Seymour Stedman came to me, shook me by the arm and said, "You cannot stand there like this. You have work to do. You will have to help raise the bond to keep these boys from going to Fort Leavenworth tonight."

By this time the "Extras!" appeared and, as might have been expected, the head-lines in bold two to three inch type read, "*Berger* sentenced to twenty years in the penitentiary." Somehow that head line spurred me to action. My husband with the other four defendants were now in reality victims of the law—technical prisoners in [the] charge of the U.S. marshal—and had disappeared somewhere in the federal building. Our attorneys then advised me that we had until 9:30 P.M. to raise the necessary bond to keep these men free. However when we appeared before the bonding-clerk—a Mr. O'Brian—we were told that the D.A. had now changed the amount of bond necessary to keep my husband and the four young men out of the prison. He (the D.A.) placed the first bond at $25,000 which he required must be doubled—or $50,000—and [required] that the surety bond of $25,000 also had to be doubled. That meant a bond of $100,000 must be raised for each defendant or $500,000 in all before 9:30 P.M., when Judge Alschuler agreed to accept the bond if we could raise it. However the government would not accept liberty bonds or cash. The security had to be in unencumbered real-estate.

I asked permission to raise $100,000 in Wisconsin, as my husband was a Wisconsin resident and well known. But I was told—"Nothing doing. You must raise this amount in Illinois." Oh! I was desperate, and again Irene Stedman told me, "Don't stand there and stare. You have work to do."

We began at once to telephone friends and known liberals. Three women, Irene Stedman, Nan Howe and I commandeered three telephones. As might be expected, I had to do most of the talking since all of Chicago was now aware of the sentences. So I had to call up perfect strangers and say something like this: "I am Mrs. Victor Berger, my husband was sentenced to twenty years in the penitentiary"—but before I could go any farther in my plea I usually heard a surprised or distressed, "Oh! Please wait until I call my husband!" Usually the wife had answered the telephone call. Then when the man of the house came to the phone I would repeat—"I am the wife of Victor Berger who was sentenced to serve twenty years in the penitentiary. My husband and the four other defendants must go to prison tonight unless we can raise the sum of $500,000 in unencumbered real-estate. I am told that possibly you would

---

[14] Samuel Alschuler (1859–1939) served as a judge on the U.S. Circuit Court of Appeals (1915–1936).

be willing to sign for part of the bond. Will you? Will you keep five men out of prison, pending an appeal of the case?" There was usually a pause and a, "Wait one moment, I'd like to talk with my wife." I waited. And God bless them the answer was always, "Yes, I'll be down tomorrow." "Oh no! You must come tonight by 9:30 or they leave for Fort Leavenworth." "I'll be there," came the answer.

And so I stood from 3:00 P.M. to 7:30 P.M., calling and explaining and waiting most anxiously for each reply. Once only was I refused. This was by a nurse who told me the lady I was trying to reach was on her death bed.

I have forgotten to mention that William Bross Lloyd had gone on the first $150,000 of the bond. But there is a fearful stretch to cover between $150,000 and $500,000, especially since all our known and unknown friends were not in the moneyed class. But a dear friend of Jane Addams's, a Mrs. Uri,[15] pledged $30,000, and a good Socialist lawyer, Peter Sissman,[16] pledged $19,000. I remember these two big figures because they were a substantial lift.

About 7:30 P.M. I expressed a wish to see my husband if possible. So I was taken upstairs in the federal building and shown into a very large room. Before I could see my husband I noticed two huge iron cages with pad-locked doors in this room presided over by the U.S. marshal. Again I was frozen to the spot and couldn't move. Finally through a lot of smoke in the far corner of this large room I saw the five defendants. Adolph Germer came up to ask what progress we had made thus far in raising the money. He saw my distress and put his arms around me and said, "Dear Mrs. Berger, don't grieve and don't worry so much. We young fellows have decided to put the first $100,000 on Victor's bond. He will go free tonight." How generous and fine were these comrades. But that generosity had to be met. It was a challenge to us. And since we were more than $100,000 short of the $500,000 needed, Germer gave me the list of unions which were holding their regular meetings on this night and asked me to go to these meetings, tell the story, and proceed to the next meeting. An Irish school teacher, Miss O'Reilly,[17] volunteered to go with me. So, taking a taxi, we set out to cover the labor meetings in Chicago. I had not realized the great distances we had to cover. Miles and miles we traveled over icy and slushy pavements, skidding much of the way.

Fortunately labor was aroused by the news in the papers. We were admitted at once. Briefly we told our story and asked for help. We did not wait to hear the results as we had to go on to place after place. But we did notice

---

[15] Either Meta Berger or Miriam Frink added here: "A Quaker, husband an officer in Navy—."
[16] Peter Sissman (b. 1868) was a Russian-born attorney and Chicago Socialist.
[17] Probably Mary O'Reilly (1874?–1950), who helped found the Chicago Teachers' Federation.

individual members of the union we were addressing putting on coats and leaving. Later in the evening we discovered why—to get the deed to his home and to bring it to the federal building.

We finally got back to the office of the bonding clerk to discover the room filled with people, the legal looking deeds to their property held in their hands or protruding from their pockets. Mr. O'Brian, looking at me in the midst of his duties of listing the people and registering their certificates—said, "Oh Madam! You are ill. Please let me open a window. Here—sit here and get some fresh air." It was an act of kindness and I appreciated it.

The hour was midnight. Judge Alschuler had not yet appeared. He was attending some banquet. This gave us the necessary time.

A long distance telephone call came for me. It was from my daughter, Doris, then a student at the University of Wisconsin. She was brave as was Elsa throughout the trial, and you can imagine that my girls did not have an easy time at college. This however was Doris. She had been out all evening trying to raise her father's bond and had something like $20,000 which she could send on. I was deeply touched and saddened to tell her the money was no good in Illinois. But I have never forgotten it.

As Mr. O'Brian finished his work it was close to 2:00 A.M. He totaled up the amount and we found we had more than enough. Can you imagine the relief? Men are boys and never seem to grow up. They laughed and suddenly were hungry and everybody had to go out to get something to eat. How could they? I still was keyed up, too strained to appreciate a man's relaxed feeling and that eating was the way out. But I went with the entire group and watched them eat. It was near 5:00 A.M. when we finally reached our hotel room. On the table was a magnificent basket of fruit from Jane Addams. Then for the first time I broke and wept hysterically and couldn't stop weeping for some time. This time my husband couldn't understand why I was weeping when everything so far had turned out so well.

The next day—we gathered up our documents and papers and things and started for home. Not until I got back to Milwaukee had I noticed how gray or rather white my hair had gotten in Chicago.

The first night of our return home, the Socialist Party had called a big mass meeting to welcome us back and to hear our story. More than 22,000 people turned out. The main hall, all the four or five other halls, the West Side Turner Hall and overflow meetings on the street greeted us joyously. The contrast between our treatment in Chicago and our welcome home in Milwaukee was [unfinished]

CHAPTER 9

"Fighting, Fighting, Fighting"

To be in Milwaukee again after those harrowing days in Chicago was comforting. But I must confess that our emotions, so strained during the trial, were dulled so much so that today after twenty-five years I still think of the fact that it was impossible to enter into the spirit of a temporary triumph which all our friends felt for us.

I cannot exactly remember what we did right after our return. My husband no doubt was terribly busy trying to keep the paper going. I turned to our home, and I believe I tried to wear off the nervous strain by plunging into the house-wifely task of cleaning our house with its huge library. Hard physical labor often helps to bring one back to a normal life. We had perhaps the largest private library of its kind in the state of Wisconsin. These books had to come off the shelves twice a year for a thorough dusting. This was always my task. Our library was devoted to history, economics, and social problems and the international relationship of our present day civilization. Fiction was not in evidence to any degree. However the Greek classics as well as the best present day literature was on the shelves. Often my husband found relaxation and fun reading the Greek classics. It was a working library for him. He knew where every book was and what was in the book. I remember that once while he was confined to his bed for several weeks due to illness, he would ask me to go into the library and go to the south wall of shelves; on the fifth shelves, the third or fourth volume from the left hand side, I would find such and such a book. Would I please get it for him? And not once did I fail to bring the required book.

On the long center table would be the new and latest books which did not find a home on the shelves until the contents were familiar to my husband.

So my job was to keep the library in order and never to throw anything written or printed away, as it might be valuable.

While I was thus busy, often the telephone would ring. My husband calling me to come down town to lunch with him. If I already had had my lunch— he would say—"Come anyway and just sit with me."

The fact that I was needed showed me that he was extremely burdened or nervous or unhappy. I never failed to respond. Each difficulty and each new problem brought us closer together. It was throughout these weeks and months that I received what was more than an equivalent of a college education.

The month between the second of February, that memorable day of the twenty-year sentence which was always alluded to by us as our croix de guerre, and the time for us to go to Washington, D.C., to claim the congressional seat of the Fifth District of Wisconsin passed all too quickly. Henry Cochems was to represent us in Washington, so there were conferences and still more conferences.

Fortunately for me personally, my very efficient maid Josie [Rudkowsky] took all burden of household duties off my shoulders. And Elizabeth H. Thomas, that remarkable and learned woman, carried the great burden of the *Milwaukee Leader* for my husband while he was fighting for representative government.

In due time we arrived in Washington. Through the effort of the proper person we secured the use of an office in the House Office Building. There was some doubt for a few hours whether or not we would be allowed the use of this office. But discretion overcame hostility and we were assigned to an office, pending the decision of the House of Representatives.

Again we prepared to go on trial—this time a political trial if there ever was one. We had had plenty of warning through the press of the country that my husband would not be seated. Nevertheless we owed it to our Fifth District to be there and claim the seat.

So on the morning of the opening of the first session of the Sixty-sixth Congress [in] March,[1] the day the House of Representatives was to swear in the new members and to organize itself for the business of Congress, my husband also appeared.

Of course we were excited and a bit nervous too before going over to the House of Representatives. Not only was a great democratic principle at stake, the importance of which we realized, but we did not realize that we were really making history, since never before in the history of the United States had a similar incident occurred.

[1] The first session of the Sixty-sixth Congress began on May 19, 1919.

Just before leaving the hotel, the telephone rang. Mrs. William Kent[2] of California was on the phone asking me for the privilege of accompanying me during the morning session. She—the wife of a man on the Tariff Commission, an official of high rank; she the wife of a millionaire, had the humane feeling that possibly she might be of some comfort to me at this critical period. How I blessed her for her thoughtfulness and her kindness. My voice broke a little when I told her that of course I'd love to have her go with me but warned her that the whole affair might be very painful. She called for me at the Congress Hall Hotel and together we went up into the public gallery. The gallery reserved for members' family was denied me.

Naturally the House was full as well as all the galleries.

As I witnessed the procedure on the floor of the House, [and as] I saw my husband stand aside and then leave for his office, I must have sat very rigid with hands tightly clasped when suddenly Mrs. Kent put her hand over mine and said, "My God! It's great to have grit." I shall never forget her as long as I live.

As everyone knows, the Speaker of the House administers the oath of office to the members-elect. He takes them in blocks—i.e., those whose names begin with A and through to those whose names begin with G and so on. Since our name began with B, my husband arose with others in his group. At this moment the Speaker, before administering the oath of office to anyone, asked Mr. Berger to step aside, not take the oath and to await further developments. I saw him leave the floor of the House.

As soon as I could I rushed over to the office building to join my husband. As I entered I found he was not alone. Three gentlemen came to see him and express their indignation and disgust at the happenings of the morning. One was Mr. Milholland, the father of beautiful Inez Milholland, who took such a leading part in the fight for suffrage.[3] Mr. Milholland was not a Socialist, had very little in common with us, since he was extremely rich and was the builder of New York subways. But he loved his daughter, and since she had joined the Socialist Party, he came to express himself most sympathetically. The second gentleman was Frederic C. Howe,[4] scholar, writer and immigration commis-

[2] Elizabeth Thacher Kent (b. 1868) of Kentfield, California, was active in women's clubs and charitable and suffrage organizations. Her husband, William Kent, served as a U.S. representative (1911–1917) and as a member of the U.S. Tariff Commission (1917–1920).

[3] John E. Milholland (1860–1925) was a New York newspaper reporter, editorial writer, and businessman who built underground systems for carrying mail. He supported social reform. His daughter, Inez Milholland Boissevain (1886–1916), an attorney, was active in socialist, labor, and suffrage movements. In 1916 she collapsed after a speaking tour for the National Woman's Party and died ten weeks later.

[4] As commissioner of immigration, Howe supported free speech and resisted the deportations of aliens

sioner of the Port at New York. We had known Mr. Howe for some years and were friends and had read many of his liberal writings and loved him through the years for his courage. The third gentleman in the office was Mr. Theodore Lunde,[5] a Norwegian by birth, a resident of Chicago and a member of the International Chamber of Commerce, representing Norway in this country. Mr. Lunde had been sympathetic to us and to our cause, as was his daughter, a lecturer and platform speaker.

As I shook hands with these friends, dear Mr. Lunde kissed the palm of my hands while tears flowed down his cheeks. He was emotionally overcome, as were all of us.

However, I said—"Oh! I think you all need a drink," to which they all responded with great alacrity. Then followed a steak dinner after which we all felt renewed. There was nothing else for us to do for the time being, so as quickly as we could we took the train for home. I left Washington a very disillusioned person and took a dislike for that beautiful city. After all, it was the spirit in the political life of the capital which caused my dislike. I could still admire the gardens, the beautiful magnolia trees, the cherry-blossoms and the cold white marble buildings which nearly blinded one when the sun-shone. Yet my love for the whole setting had received a shock from which I suffered for many years. I recalled with what pride I first saw the big dome of the Capitol with the stars and stripes fluttering in the breeze; I remembered with what joy I took my children to see the sights, [to] explain to them the meaning of the House, the Senate, the Supreme Court, where I always visited with a feeling of awe. I thought back to the days when I proudly took them around the White House grounds and through the White House. I still felt the thrill of climbing the Washington Monument, visiting the park along the Potomac River and the beautiful setting of Mount Vernon. It had been a very great pleasure and privilege to show my children the wonderful city way back in 1910. And now I was leaving it with bitterness and disappointment. Naturally Washington lost some of the glamour and rich beauty with which I had adorned it. And to this day much of the idealism I felt about Washington has suffered.

We arrived home as quickly as possible, only to begin our hard task of keeping the *Leader* alive. My husband plunged into the problem of meeting the finances of the paper, which had no credit at the banks, no second class mailing rights, no advertising accounts which usually pay for a paper, no right to even receive any mail. What to do? We borrowed from Peter to pay Paul

during the 1919 Red Scare. He became the subject of harassment and a congressional investigation and resigned in September 1919.

[5] Theodore H. Lunde, a peace activist, was president of Chicago's American Industrial Company.

and then borrowed from Paul to pay Peter. Elizabeth Thomas did much of the borrowing for the publishing company.

If it had not been for our very dear friend Oscar Ameringer I believe we might have had to close shop. However the ingenious Oscar came to the rescue. He volunteered to cover the state of Wisconsin selling freedom bonds. Everyone had had to buy liberty bonds from the government in support of the war. But no one had ever heard of freedom bonds before. Oscar made only one condition, that a percent of the money he secured for these freedom bonds, which was to tide us over the most difficult period, was to be set aside for the purchase of another socialist paper down in Oklahoma City. So during these dreadful times, he sold enough freedom bonds to keep the *Milwaukee Leader* alive and to purchase land, build a plant fully equipped, and establish the *Oklahoma Leader,* which while nominally a branch of the *Milwaukee Leader* was later under the direct supervision of our friend Oscar.

Of course the money received from these freedom bonds was a second mortgage on our own paper. But the paper appeared every day throughout those hysterical days. I must say that the job was terrific and the energy exerted tremendous.

I, in the meantime, now had a desk and office at the *Leader* and was useful in my small way by keeping up the morale of the place, listening to any and all grievances, getting the confidence of the business manager, the cashier and the book-keeper. Many a time, people would come to me when they couldn't get the attention of my husband on a matter of policy or on any other difficulty. It was my job, then, to await the time when I could get my husband to listen and to give his final OK on whatever problem it may have been.

Fortunately, my children, who were at the university, were fine healthy girls, wrote me almost daily, keeping me informed of their life at college. Not once during those years did I have a single worry about my family. I was grateful indeed.

Affairs at home also were in capable hands.

Then one day we received word that a committee on elections had been appointed by the Speaker of the House of Representatives to try my husband's right to his seat. Now—since the House of Representatives is the sole judge of the eligibility of its members, it in reality was trying the eligibility of a man who was not a member, since it had refused to submit the oath of office to him. We knew that, at the time, but did not raise the point as it would have done no good. Furthermore, Mr. Joseph Carney,[6] the man who ran in the same

---

[6] Joseph P. Carney (1871–1941), a printer and proofreader for the *Milwaukee Sentinel,* served on the Milwaukee Common Council (1908–1912, 1918–1922, and 1924–1932) and as city treasurer (1912–1916).

election but was some five or six thousand votes behind my husband, was now asking the House of Representatives to seat him, since he too felt my husband was not eligible. So we had a double trial. However no one took Mr. Carney's request for the seat seriously, although he appeared in Washington at the proper time with his attorney, Mr. Harry McLogan.[7]

The committee on elections was called to meet June 11. Naturally we arrived in Washington a few days before that, so that we might get our material in order and be prepared. Henry Cochems and we worked late every night, marking the exhibits and putting everything in order, so that Mr. Cochems would have no difficulty in presenting our case.

Naturally, we needed advice too. So one of the first and I believe the only one we called upon was Senator La Follette. We believed that since "Old Bob" had taken a very similar position on the war and on the entrance of the U.S. in the conflict in Europe that we would find a sympathetic friend, especially since both men were from Wisconsin, and of course we also believed Wisconsin stood solidly behind us. Also Senator La Follette had a good chance of losing his seat in the Senate due to a speech he made in St. Paul and to his attitude on the war in general.

Senator La Follette was visibly made uncomfortable by our visit to him. He was unable to suggest anything that we might do to help us. He was at a loss to suggest anything at all but said he'd like to think it over and would call me at 6:00 P.M. that evening. True to his word, he called and said over the telephone, "I've thought it over and am asking you *not* to talk to a single Wisconsin representative but to leave the entire Wisconsin delegation entirely to me. I'll see what I can do." Well—that was something. So of course we did not approach any Wisconsin man.

We lived at the Congress Hall Hotel, which was just across the street from the House Office Building. The hotel no longer exists. But at that time it was considered a good second class hotel with prices not too high. We signed up for the American plan, which meant taking our meals in the large general dining room, and the meals were not a la carte. We soon discovered that some seventy or eighty congressmen and senators lived there also—with their wives. My reason for alluding to this situation is that not a soul would bid us the time of day; the ladies seemed to me to draw their skirts tighter for fear I'd get too close to them. Also as I looked the men over, I thought they had rather pleasant faces, calm and untroubled. It is possible that I imagined much of this, but I don't think so.

---

[7] Harry R. McLogan (1881–1939), a Milwaukee attorney and Eagles Club leader, served as justice of the peace (1910–1918), circuit court commissioner (1921–1933), and state industrial commissioner (1933–1939), in which role he chaired the state pension department (1935–1939).

However, there was one courageous woman in this hotel who was not afraid of contamination, who always spoke to me, often putting her arm through mine and walking down the center aisle of that dining hall. Frequently she left her table to come and sit with us. This lady was none other than Mrs. Champ Clark, whose husband was then the Speaker of the House.[8] Mrs. Clark did much more than give me public and moral support. She spent hours and days in the congressional library looking up the history of the U.S., trying to find a precedent which might be of value to our case. Frequently she sent her maid to our room with delicious fruit from her home state [Missouri] and a note saying that so far she had been unsuccessful in her efforts at the library.

To me, who was wounded to the core, who needed some friendly companionship, Mrs. Clark was a god-send. She helped me during those troubled days more than I can say. I shall always be eternally grateful to her.

The committee on elections appointed by the Speaker of the House called for the first meeting on June 11, 1919. As might be expected, Mr. Cochems and Mr. B. and I were on time. As we entered the committee room, we saw various clerks arranging papers, documents, pencils etc. at the place of each member of the committee. The table was somewhat raised and was sort of semi circle in shape.

Among the documents was a suspicious looking volume that made us fear it was verbatim a copy of the Chicago trial. Our doubts were soon allayed [confirmed] when members of the committee began to stroll into the room and to our dismay, the district attorney of Chicago, Charles F. Clyne, came with them.[9] He seemed to be on very friendly terms with these members. We at once concluded that he had had sessions with the committee and that we would now be tried again on the basis of the developments at Chicago, but this time not only would the legal aspects be considered, but that the political aspects were to be brought forward most prominently. And after all—what could we expect from a political committee in the year 1919 when the war hysteria was still raging throughout the country? Sanity had not yet returned.

The committee consisted of nine members.[10] They were members of either the Republican or Democratic Party. Their names—well it doesn't matter now what their names were. Suffice it to say—all were reactionaries, most of them uninformed on any really fundamental philosophy of life or on a future pro-

---

[8] Genevieve Bennett Clark (1856–1937) promoted women's suffrage and progressive labor legislation, among other causes. Her husband, James Beauchamp "Champ" Clark, a Democratic representative from Missouri (1893–1895 and 1897–1921), had been Speaker of the House during the previous four Congresses. In 1919, however, the Speaker was Frederick H. Gillett.

[9] Clyne testified before the committee on September 15–16, 1919.

[10] The committee members were Frederick W. Dallinger (R-Mass.) (chairman), R. Clinton Cole (R-Ohio), Joe H. Eagle (D-Tex.), Oscar R. Luhring (R-Ind.), Clifford E. Randall (R-Wis.), Leonidas D. Robinson (D-N.C.), William A. Rodenberg (R-Ill.), John M. Rose (R-Pa.), and Benjamin F. Welty (D-Ohio).

gram for the country, none were returned to Congress,[11] and at least one, the one who was most vicious in his questioning and his comments, served a jail sentence shortly after my husband was refused the right to take the oath of office. This gentleman—who was so patriotic, was sentenced to jail for having charged soldiers an exorbitant price for legal advice—which violated a law to protect the rights of soldiers.[12]

I have the names before me but prefer to blot them out of my memory, all except one, who seemed to be fairer or more intelligent than the others. This man was Mr. W. A. Rodenberg[13] of [Illinois].

On the first morning three of the ladies from our hotel were prompted by interest or curiosity to come to the hearing. I do not know how they felt for I never got acquainted with them. However they had the grace to leave and never appear again. For this I was grateful.

And now began the most grueling search of the committee to find reasons enough so they could justify the exclusion of my husband from the House of Representatives. The story is a long one. It fills two great volumes of the *Congressional Record* of this special committee. Only recently I read the evidence and the proceedings again. And I found I couldn't take it even after twenty-four years. I went to bed ill and wept throughout the night even in my sleep. That didn't happen to me during the hearings. Then, I knew we all had our backs to the wall and were fighting, fighting, fighting. We were fighting for our honor, for the great democratic principle of representative government. For the second time within a year, trials were held which involved life, freedom and democracy. My emotions were torn asunder with the deepest sympathies for my brave husband who had already endured so very much, and a terrific indignation against these smug and self-righteous members of Congress who were out for the kill.

My part in this whole sordid affair was to help Henry Cochems arrange and assort the mass of evidence he had prepared, sometimes working through-out the night. Then I was called upon frequently during the hearings to read to the committee the material we desired introduced, and since Cochems's voice was not in good form and since my husband was not a good reader, I was asked to help out. But the hardest and most heartrending task I had to perform was to be an understanding person, to listen by the hour and by the

[11] Dallinger, Cole, Luhring, Rodenberg, and Rose were reelected to the Sixty-seventh Congress.

[12] Benjamin F. Welty (1870–1962), an attorney and Democratic representative from Ohio (1917–1921), was convicted on October 16, 1923, of accepting an excessive fee for obtaining government compensation for a war veteran. He was sentenced to one year in prison and fined five hundred dollars. The conviction was reversed on appeal on November 3, 1924.

[13] William August Rodenberg (1865–1937) served as a Republican representative from Illinois (1899–1901, 1903–1913, and 1915–1923).

day to Mr. B. when he lost his temper over the stupidity or the intellectual dishonesty of the members of this committee. To realize that his highly strung nervous system had often reached the breaking point and to soothe him and comfort him as best I could. His whole being was hurt, his soul was bruised. And who knew it better than I did?

The committee started out by reading the resolution introduced into the House of Representatives and which caused the creation of this special committee on election. Then the chairman announced that the committee would consider the second question, i.e., the right of J. P. Carney to the seat in question, simultaneously with the question of eligibility of my husband so as to save the time of the members sitting in judgment.

Then began the Chicago trial all over again. All the overt acts[14] of that trial were introduced as evidence and Mr. Carney's attorney showing a state of mind had always existed in Mr. B. which made him a disloyal member of the U.S. In fact Mr. Carney went as far back as 1909 to show the committee that editorials written by my husband were not in line with whatever administration was then in power. And of course it is true a socialist program could not by the wildest stretch of the imagination coincide with the Democratic or Republican Party programs.

The story of the hearings in Washington lasted weeks. It is a story that belongs to a carefully written history of the Socialist Party and its difficulties during the times which indeed tried men's souls.[15]

To me it was inconceivable that persecution of this kind could take place in my own native land, the land that meant so much to me. It was inconceivable that persecution of this type could happen to my husband, who had voluntarily given up a life of ease and culture to be of service to the common man. He gave up every opportunity to serve the economic masters of the country, such as refusing an offer of Mr. Arthur Brisbane,[16] then and always a Hearst man, back in 1909 of $10,000 a year with a contract for ten years. It was a tempting offer to the struggling school teacher and dramatic critic and Socialist teacher.[17] But not for a moment did he hesitate in his loyalty to the Socialist Party with

[14] Meta Berger indicated that she intended to append these acts. For a copy of both the special committee record and the trial transcript, see *Hearings before the Special Committee Appointed under the Authority of House Resolution No. 6 Concerning the Right of Victor L. Berger to Be Sworn in as a Member of the Sixty-sixth Congress,* 2 vols. (Washington, D.C.: Government Printing Office, 1919).

[15] Meta Berger deleted the following sentence: "But for the benefit of my reader I should like to incorporate one or two comments made by the district attorney, Clyne, who mind you was not a member of the committee but who was invited to sum up the final arguments in this hearing."

[16] Arthur Brisbane (1864–1936), son of social reformer Albert Brisbane, was the managing editor of the *New York Journal,* owned by William Randolph Hearst, and a popular columnist. Brisbane supported the *Milwaukee Leader* with loans and stock purchases.

[17] By 1909 Victor Berger was a newspaper editor.

all of its birth-pains, all of its struggling for a foot-hold in American politics.

To get the full import of the great struggle, one has to read the defense-appeal before the appellate court. There you will get the story of not only the American but also the struggle of the European socialist movements.

If you have never been before a district attorney whose job is to convict, you just cannot imagine the tactics he used before this committee. By clever innuendoes, insinuations, denunciations, falsehoods and implications he appealed to the members of this congressional committee, playing on their highest and most patriotic emotions. The whole hearing was so dreadful, that it [is] hard to believe such things could have happened in these United States.

Our attorney, Henry Cochems, was superb. He did not spare himself in his defense of my husband. In vain had he dug into history to cite the words of Lloyd George during the Boer War, Lincoln, Webster, Clay during the Mexican War, La Follette and Borah[18] and others besides dozens of congressmen speaking against our entrance into the war. Editorials and cartoons of non-socialist papers were quoted and introduced. The complete history of my husband's past was gone over with searching eyes. But nothing—nothing made a dent on the committee. They were bound to crucify and crucify they did.

The hearings ended about the last half of September so again we returned to Milwaukee to await the findings of the committee.

Back in Milwaukee, we gave our best energy, energy that was left us during these difficult weeks in Washington, to the task of holding the *Leader,* and the family, together.

The family didn't worry me much. The girls at the university had learned to "take it" with us. And right now I wish to say that no one can be as cruel as the young immature college student, who believes he is right and with the majority.

Fortunately for us and the girls we were able to keep them in college due to the fact that Mr. Berger's sisters, who lived in Connecticut but who didn't understand or comprehend our whole situation, but who trusted and loved their brother, sent us each month one hundred dollars so that the children could stay in Madison, Wisconsin. Also I want to pay tribute here and now to several of the professors in Madison who were kind and gentle to the girls and whose home was open to them. Then, too, whenever prominent people who knew us and believed in us came to Madison, they did not fail to seek out my daughters. Jane Addams was one of these.

---

[18] William Edgar Borah (1865–1940), a Republican senator from Idaho (1907–1940), voted in favor of U.S. entry into World War I but opposed war measures such as the Espionage Act. In later years he regretted his vote for the war. He is best known for preventing U.S. participation in the League of Nations and the World Court.

In the meantime, even though our burdens were great, it was good to be back in Milwaukee. Here at least we met warm friends, pleasant and encouraging greetings. The relief was great even though the final word had not yet come from Washington and that fearful committee.

No matter what later developments led to my severing my relationship with the Socialist Party, I shall eternally be grateful for the loyal support during those hellish days. And I did not mis-interpret that loyalty. It was as much and more devoted to the cause as it was to a personality. The Socialist Party, standing solidly behind us, gave us strength to carry on.

Finally the word flashed across the country. Victor Berger was unfit to have a seat in the House of Representatives. That was the recommendation of the committee. This on October 24. The vote was eight for the majority report, one for a minority report signed by Mr. William A. Rodenberg. Mr. Rodenberg's report was weak, did not come to the defense of my husband, but asked the House of Representatives to withhold a decision until the courts had reached a final decision.

Then began the second wait for the House to act. On November 10, 1919, the House passed the resolution denying my husband's seat.

It is a matter of course, that for this dramatic and painful situation we both were again in Washington. And again, while my husband was on the floor of the House to make his defense speech, I sat in the gallery.

I did not hear all of the speeches made by members of Congress against admitting my husband as a member. Perhaps I was too emotionally stirred, but I do remember with what amazement I saw the faces of those who spoke and who lived in the same hotel where we lived. Formerly, I noticed how genial, calm and self-righteous they appeared in the dining hall. How smug they were and how pleasant to each other. This day, these same pleasant calm faces were distorted when they spoke with the zeal of the fanatic. They were making patriotic speeches for home consumption and were leaning over backward in their efforts to convince their constituents that the welfare of the country depended upon them, and that the way to do it was to exclude Victor Berger. I was amazed at their transformation.

The morning was long—interminably long. Finally—the Speaker of the House asked Mr. B. what he had to say in defense of himself and why he should be permitted to become a member of Congress.

Appended is his speech.[19] You will notice that at no time did my husband retract a single thing which had brought about the numerous indictments, the

---

[19] Victor Berger's speech appears in the *Congressional Record*, 66th Cong., 1st sess., 58, pt. 8:8223–8233.

verdict and sentence of twenty years in Leavenworth and now finally his exclusion.

When the roll call was finished, with one exception all members voted to bar Mr. B. from the House. That one exception was Congressman Voigt of Sheboygan County, Wisconsin.[20] It took a good deal of courage for Congressman Voigt to cast his vote to seat Mr. B. The roll call is called in alphabetical order, and since V came at the end of the roll call, Mr. Voigt had the opportunity to know the feeling of his co-workers. And then he voted "For" instead of "Against." At that time we were grateful to him. Both men are dead now, but it is to the everlasting credit that at least one man had courage.

I saw my husband [leave] the House and I hurried over to our temporary office. To my surprise he said, "Well Mama, the fight for representative government has just begun." He did not seem too downcast at all. We needed food to calm us down, so instead of going into the big dining hall, he thoughtfully suggested we go into the smaller European dining room which no one ever frequented. This was done I know to make it easier for me.

As we entered, over in the far corner sat Mrs. Champ Clark, the only person who had been so considerate of us and who had tried so arduously to find a precedent for our case. She was with two young people—a gentleman and a lady. These three people looked so inexpressibly sad that I couldn't resist the temptation to go to speak to them. Then, upon introduction to Mrs. Clark's daughter and her young husband, I found that they had just come to Washington from the burial of their young daughter. No wonder they were sad. My heart went out to them.

As I returned to my corner table, I told my husband that our disappointment was as nothing compared to the poignant grief suffered by those young parents. How grateful we ought to be that our family was well and healthy.

We left Washington immediately of course. Upon our return to Milwaukee the following day, November 11, the Socialist Party had again nominated Victor L. Berger as a candidate for the Fifth District of Wisconsin to Congress.

The press of the nation was excited and not a bit sympathetic. Editorials and cartoons were printed, all of them denouncing the Socialist candidate and the Socialist Party.

Wisconsin at that time was governed by a conservative legislature with Governor Emanuel L. Philipp[21] at the head of the administration. Governor

---

[20] Edward Voigt (1873–1934), a German-born Republican politician and lawyer, served as a U.S. representative from 1917 to 1927 and as a Wisconsin circuit court judge from 1929 to 1934.

[21] Emanuel L. Philipp (1861–1925), a Republican businessman, served as governor of Wisconsin from 1915 to 1921. He appointed Meta Berger to the Wisconsin Board of Education in 1917.

Philipp was a wealthy man, had no sympathy for the Socialist Party, but was able and honest. He immediately called for a special election to fill the vacancy in the Fifth District of Wisconsin.

Once again we got ready for a bitter campaign. This time the two parties (Democratic and Republican Parties) decided to pool their interests on a candidate which both could support and which would make Victor Berger strive for a majority vote instead of a plurality vote. Henry L. Bodenstab[22] was their choice. The campaign was bitterly fought. And again we could not get halls, and the radio was not yet popular enough, besides it was too expensive. Therefore our only means of reaching our voters was through the mail. So once more we sent circulars, cards, pamphlets to as many homes as funds permitted us to send. The postal clerks at the federal building were sympathetic too and often called me at 1:00 A.M. or 2:00 A.M. to say, "Mrs. B., get your stuff down here before the gang goes home. We want to be sure it gets out in time." So all night long until three or four in the morning I and all those good volunteers worked. This was the mechanical side of campaigning. The literature of course was written by my husband and others before we saw it.

We were so busy we didn't have time to worry and when we did get home were too exhausted to speak to each other.

The election day finally arrived. Now there was nothing to do but wait until the votes were tabulated. This sort of waiting day seemed hardest of all.

In the early morning of December 20, 1919, we heard the results. Victor Berger was re-elected over Henry L. Bodenstab by a majority vote of 4,806.[23]

We were so relieved, but not elated, for we didn't know what next would happen. The press of the country was as vicious as ever and the *New York Times* quoted Chairman Dallinger of the special committee on elections as saying that "if Victor Berger again presents himself to be sworn as a member of the House I shall then object, as I did the previous time. The facts in the case are exactly the same. . . . His ineligibility is just as great as when he first presented himself . . . and action will again be taken the second time."[24]

It was not until January 10, 1920, that the seat was refused a second time. This time I did not go with my husband, as we were given to understand that the action of refusal would be formal and no speeches would be made by anyone. So on January 20, 1920, the House again voted to refuse my husband's

[22] Henry H. Bodenstab (1874–1948), a Republican, served as a Wisconsin state senator (1909–1913), Milwaukee assistant district attorney (1913–1914), and Milwaukee County court commissioner (1934–1941).

[23] Victor Berger received 24,367 votes, and Bodenstab received 19,561.

[24] "Berger Elected by 4,806 Majority," *New York Times,* December 20, 1919.

seat, but this time there were really six courageous members who dared to vote on our side.[25]

On the same day—the Socialist Party again nominated him to run for the office a third time. That was loyal and courageous on the part of our party.

However Governor E. L. Philipp notified my husband that he was loathe to call another special election, thus spending the people's money, and asked if it would not be all right for my husband to wait now for the regular congressional election the following fall.

We appreciated the governor's position and said that we would take our chances in the fall.

---

[25] In addition to Voigt, the representatives who voted to seat Victor Berger on January 10, 1920, were Anthony J. Griffin (D-N.Y.), John W. Harreld (R-Okla.), James R. Mann (R-Ill.), Isaac R. Sherwood (D-Ohio), and Thomas U. Sisson (D-Miss.).

CHAPTER 10

"The Philippine Islands"

So we settled down to live a normal life, although the times and conditions were still somewhat abnormal. I went to the office of the *Leader* daily; since it seemed to be my job to answer nonessential correspondence, to keep the morale of the women workers up, to listen to the tales of unhappy men who were soliciting advertisements for the paper, to lend a sympathetic ear to the harassed business manager, to smooth down a ruffled temper when things got too bad for even my husband to take. So it was that I became a cog in the wheel of the struggling paper and both its circulation and financial difficulties.

But it was comforting to feel and know that we had the sympathetic respect of Milwaukee's citizens, even those who [never] under any circumstances would have voted the Socialist ticket. Personally we were surrounded with friends.

In the meantime, my two daughters at the university weathered the storms and made good in their studies. And now, for the first time, my oldest daughter had written me to tell me she was bringing a young college student home for the week-end. Of course we were glad to have her bring her friend. This was the very first time she had ever accepted the friendship of a gentleman and the first time she wanted to bring him home. And so it was that Colin G. Welles[1] came into our house. He was a nice lovable person whose sympathies on the conditions of the time were with us. I feel almost certain that his friendship for Doris during the years while the girl was ostracized by many students was the basis for a budding romance. Naturally I was glad for both young people.

---

[1] Colin Welles (1896–1962) taught at the University of the Philippines from 1921 to 1922 and completed a doctorate in botany at the University of Wisconsin in 1923. From 1925 to 1950 he taught at the Milwaukee Vocational School.

Also it made both my husband and myself wonder a little about the future. We did not need to speculate long because at the end of the college year 1920—both came home with the announcement of their engagement. We thought both were too young for marriage, but our objections were over-ruled and so before the summer was over they were married.[2] Colin had made application to teach in foreign parts, and shortly after their marriage he accepted a position to teach in the University of the Philippines at the College of Agriculture at Los Baños. Before leaving her home, her parents and her native land, Doris had some misgivings and so came to me with a pledge written in legal form, asking me to sign it. This document pledged me to appear at the Welles shack in the Philippine Islands one year from date. I signed it. Both my husband and I trembled a little at the thought of our daughter going so far from home, but we had made up our minds not to interfere with their plans and their start in married life.

I'll admit my heart gave a fearful turn as I bade the children good-bye. He was twenty-one, she just twenty[3]—so children they were still to us. Of course we waited most anxiously for letters, and Doris was most faithful in writing.

At home we applied ourselves to the work at hand and again prepared to enter the next congressional campaign. We were aware that the hysteria about the war was letting up somewhat by the fact that the federal postal authorities restored our right to receive mail again. That was a hopeful sign. During the fall campaign we were opposed by William H. Stafford,[4] a stalwart Republican. Mr. Stafford had served in Congress a number of terms, knew the ropes well, and since our district had always been a strong Republican district, we put up a strong campaign. To our surprise, however, Mr. Stafford won the election. Either the people had had short memories, or we put up a poor campaign. Anyway we lost and a most conservative man represented the Fifth Congressional District of Wisconsin. Of course we were disappointed.

Early the next spring—March 15, 1921—the *Milwaukee Leader* received a check from the federal government for excess postage we had to pay during the period in which we were deprived of our second class mailing rights. Things were brightening up for us. And again on May 31, 1921, the *Leader* had its second class mailing rights restored.

Also all indictments against my husband were dropped in the Milwaukee federal courts.

---

[2] Doris Berger and Colin Welles married on July 17, 1920. They had two daughters, Deborah and Polly.

[3] Doris was twenty-two and Colin twenty-four when they left for the Philippines in December 1920.

[4] William H. Stafford (1869–1957), a Republican, served several terms as a U.S. representative (1903–1911, 1913–1919, 1921–1923, and 1929–1933); he was Victor Berger's perennial opponent.

But we heard nothing from the court of appeals in the Chicago case for some time. Then either through our attorneys or the press—I do not remember from whom, we heard that the Supreme Court of the United States remanded the case for a new trial on the technical point that Judge Landis—the judge of the U.S. district court—was without jurisdiction to decide a motion asking for a change of venue and alleging as a reason [for the denial] therefore the judge's own prejudice.[5] That was indeed good news, even though we had no idea about the next step the Department of Justice might take. But we had another respite and that was good.

Then too, the *Leader* had restored to it the second class mail rights. All these events were indicative of a changed psychology on the part of the federal government and as effort of a return to normalcy.

During the summer of 1921—I made up my mind that now I must prepare to keep my promise to Doris and visit her in the Philippine Islands. So I talked up the matter of going soon. One evening my husband put down his paper and said, "Aren't you getting tired of talking about a trip to the Philippine Islands?" "Oh no!" said I—"I promised and so I am going." "Well, you have never asked for much and I'd like to see you go—but good God! Where shall I get the money—just tell me that!" You see our legal troubles and expenses had bankrupted us. The costs ran into many thousands of dollars. I really did feel a bit guilty but was nevertheless determined to go. So I said, "Oh! I won't ask you for a penny. I have it all planned. I shall sign over for three years my small income from my mother's estate. My friends have already agreed to loan me the money. So please don't worry about finances, just make a reservation for me on a steamer sailing for Manila." He was surprised, and yet pleased that I was so determined and promised to send me more money as soon as he had it.

The librarian of the *Leader*—Alma Jacobus[6]—a young beautiful and intelligent girl, wanted to go with me. So it was arranged. And on the appointed day[7] Alma and I started out for San Francisco, where we had to get the necessary visas for China and Japan. The British government declined to give us a visa due to trouble in India.

As the day came for boarding the ship I was torn between a desire to return to Wisconsin and the anticipated joy of seeing my girl again. The Chamber of Commerce of San Francisco had chartered the boat on which we were sailing, so the send-off was particularly gay and lavish, with crowds of people

---

[5] The U.S. Supreme Court overturned the conviction of the five defendants on January 31, 1921.

[6] Alma Jacobus (b. 1892?) worked as librarian's assistant at the Milwaukee Public Library and as librarian for the *Milwaukee Journal* before joining the *Milwaukee Leader* staff.

[7] Meta Berger left Milwaukee in late September 1921. She returned to the United States in April 1922.

on the pier, air-planes circling above dropping huge bouquets of roses and flowers, confetti filling the air and everyone so very jolly and gay. As I stood at the railing of the boat as it slowly pulled away from the pier, the band played the "Star Spangled Banner." That was too much for my struggling emotions and I broke and wept and wept. I am still sorry about this as I didn't get a final look at the Golden Gate and the beautiful setting.

The next thing I knew I had a baby in my lap and one hanging on to my skirt. They were the children of Mr. and Mrs. Frank Eldridge, who were passengers going to Japan. Mr. Eldridge representing President Hoover on some commercial alliance. Mrs. Eldridge became sea-sick early in the trip, so I had volunteered to take care of the Eldridge babies while the parents went below deck. So for three days I took care of my two little charges until Mrs. Eldridge was better. Often I have thought how much those children did to calm an emotional storm within me. They certainly helped to bridge over the terrible feeling of homesickness I experienced on leaving my husband and Elsa, who now was a student at the medical school at the University of Pennsylvania.

I saw too how bitterly opposed those California people on the boat were to the Japanese. More than once I heard them refer to the Japs as yellow-bellied devils. It was my first contact with prejudice of this type.

The voyage was otherwise pleasant. At Honolulu I stayed two weeks, making use of the opportunity of a stop-over on the steamship ticket. Of course the Hawaiian Islands are beautiful beyond description and here surely the East and West met. In the light of present day history (1943) I could readily understand that in the thickly settled Japanese quarters, fifth columnists may have existed in great numbers.

After two delightful weeks in the islands, I boarded the next steamer for Japan. Upon arriving in Yokohama, I was met by a former companion on the first trip—a Mr. Mayer[8]—who also was sent by President Hoover on a commercial diplomatic tour to Vladivostok [in southeast Russia]. Mr. Mayer was most pleasant, had dinner ready for us and expressed his delight in meeting us again. It was so nice to be met in a foreign part by an American citizen. Japan was a surprise to us. It was tiny, businesslike, very cultivated and the entire island—even the rice fields and huts—electrically lighted. One must have seen the Japan of those days to appreciate it, with its colorful temples, its imposing Buddhas, its lama priests and its cherry blossoms and chrysanthemums. I felt like Alice in Wonderland. The civilization was so entirely different. But even in 1921 we noticed the growing militarism, as exemplified by

---

[8] Probably Ferdinand L. Mayer (1887–1986), who was posted by the U.S. State Department to Beijing on March 8, 1923. He was on detail in Tokyo from September 12 through October 8, 1923.

the youthful military garb on the school children. However, hotel managers and clerks were extremely cordial and did everything to make our stay pleasant. There was one aftermath of World War I noticeable. Every hotel required a guest to register [with] the police. This I found out later had a distinct advantage for me because a wire-less message from Manila was addressed to me as "somewhere in Japan." It found me in the city of Kobe. I was so happy to get it from my children.

Leaving Japan, we crossed the channel for Korea. Here we saw the first evidence of what a conquered nation had to endure. Our guide in Seoul, who was a student of the YMCA, spoke English fluently. With a great deal of indignation and resentment he told us of Japan's conquering Korea. How the schools were taken over, the press had to print the news in Japanese, the yen became the money for Korea. It seemed Japan had conquered everything but the spirit of the people. And an unhappy people they were.

We made our way up through Manchuria; visited the city of Mukden [Shenyang] (now [in] Manchukuo) and again saw Japan's military ambitions quite plainly. In the city of Mukden Japan had purchased huge tracts of land which were laid out as a military drill field. Little did we think then that a Second World War would put this place to use. Little did I then know that eleven years later I would be present in Geneva, Switzerland, while attending the one and only disarmament conference, [and] that I would witness the dramatic scene at which the Chinese delegate to the [Women's International] League [for Peace and Freedom] placed China's case against Japan's aggression in taking and holding Manchuria. More of that later.

While waiting at the railroad station to take the train to Peking [Beijing], a gentleman approached us to ask if there was anything he could do for us. After some pleasant remarks he gave me his card. He was from Chicago and on his way to Korea to help build railroads. I exchanged cards with him and upon reading my name he exclaimed, "Well! Well! How is the congressman?" You can imagine my surprise at meeting someone in Mukden who knew of my husband. It seemed that he had followed our trials at Judge Landis's court and was quite familiar with our case and not altogether unsympathetic. That chance meeting brought the fact that after-all, the world is getting smaller and closer. But it was a really pleasant surprise.

We finally got the train for Peking. Many other and better writers have written about the Orient and about Peking. But I venture to say that everyone was as thrilled as I was at the walled city, the beauties of Chinese temples, [especially?] the Temple of Heaven, [and] the great broad dusty main thoroughfare through the city, with its coolies, ox-teams, automobiles, rickshaws and camels coming down the street to meet you. The effect was kaleidoscopic to say the least.

We stopped at the Hôtel de Pékin; a very first class hotel with good food, excellent music and wonderful entertainment each evening in the lobby. Of course we were anxious to do a little shopping, but an American school-teacher living in Peking advised us to wait until just before leaving the city before buying anything. So we took her advice and found it good. The Chinese like all Orientals asked exorbitant prices in the beginning. But once they realize that their customers are preparing to leave, they come running to you with their goods and you really can get bargains.

Of the trips I shall always be happy I made was climbing the Great Wall of China and going to visit the Ming Tombs being carried in sedan chairs. By this time too, I had accepted the rickshaw. At the beginning I was humiliated by being drawn by a fellow human being.

We spent two weeks at Peking and then made our way to Shanghai, getting there several days before our boat was to sail for Manila.

On the way down to Shanghai I had volunteered to take two children of a Mrs. Hodgeson with me to Manila where they were to meet their father. A boy of nine or ten and a girl of eleven or twelve. Mrs. Hodgeson was confined to the Rockefeller Hospital in Peking due to an infection caused by vaccination for small-pox. The children were charming and well-behaved and it was fun to have them in my charge.

We arrived in Shanghai on Thanksgiving Day. Naturally we stopped at the Astor Hotel on the Bund [neighborhood], which served the foreigners who traveled that way. The Thanksgiving dinner at the hotel was the typical American dinner with turkey and cranberries down to pumpkin pie. When we had finished the little Hodgeson boy was visibly disappointed, and upon inquiry he said—"I haven't got that stretched feeling I have at home." So I called the waiter and asked him to serve another complete dinner for the young gentleman. That did the trick and our little friend was completely satisfied.

During the three remaining days before the boat sailed for Manila, I had a fur coat made from sow skins I had purchased up north. It was a Russian cat coat and cost the sum of thirty-five dollars.

While in Shanghai I met Mrs. J. Cudahy of Milwaukee who was visiting her daughter Mrs. Lansing Hoyt and her husband.[9] I got the impression that Mr. Hoyt also was on some sort of a mission for the Hoover administration. These American friends were extremely nice to us and did what they could to make our stay pleasant. (Mr. Hoyt is now the head of the America First Com-

[9] Meta Berger is either referring to Katharine Reed Cudahy, the wife of John Cudahy and the sister-in-law of Josephine Cudahy Hoyt, or to John and Josephine's mother, Anna (Mrs. Patrick) Cudahy. Josephine and Lansing Hoyt moved to Milwaukee in the late 1930s, and Lansing served as chairman of the Republican Party and worked as a metallurgical engineer.

mittee[10] in Wisconsin.) I haven't seen them since our very pleasant time in Shanghai. But I still smile at our little incident which happened on the boat. I am no bridge player. Since however partners are few on boats, I was asked to take the fourth hand. Now I did know enough to follow suit, but to bid—well that was another matter. So holding four aces in my hand, which I later discovered scored one hundred points, I passed. When the hand was played and Mr. Hoyt, who [was] my partner, discovered my four aces—I was given a polite but stern lesson on playing bridge. The game went on to the next round. Again I held four aces and this time bid according to instructions. Then said Mr. Hoyt—"Are you sure you have four aces?" I am not yet a bridge player but sort of enjoy the post-mortems held after each hand.

The hours dragged now. I was so very anxious to arrive at Manila and see my daughter. Finally the happy moment came when we steamed into Manila Bay and came to a stop waiting for the medical inspection and quarantine officials.

I know now that I lost the beauty of the bay and Corregidor, because I was watching so intently for the quarantine launch to come up along the side of our big boat.

Finally, at long last, a tiny launch came across the blue bay and headed for our steamer. Naturally all passengers lined the railing waiting so patiently. While I too was waiting and looking at the tiny boat, I suddenly saw the hand of a lady resting on the side. This hand wore the blue turquoise ring I had given Doris. Then I knew through some way she had gotten permission to meet me on the boat. Now the minutes seemed like hours. She was still in the launch while all doctors and officials were already on the boat going through the routine of inspection. Then why—why was she still way down there waiting? Later I found out that only upon agreeing to wait until the work of quarantine officers was finished was she permitted to come on board ship.

Oh! Such a happy re-union. How glad we all were to be together once more and how warm was the greeting. I have always lived in happy thought at that memory of our reunion.

It did not take us long to pass through the Manila customs house where I paid a slight duty on the few things I had bought in Japan and China. Soon I was introduced to Dio Gracius! Dio Gracius was an old battered Ford car which the children bought and which they said "ran by the grace of God." It was very disreputable in appearance and must have had a history of abuse. But miraculously it ran. We proceeded to the Manila hotel for our luncheon.

[10] The America First Committee was an organization founded in 1940 to prevent U.S. involvement in World War II. The committee disbanded after the December 1941 Japanese attack on Pearl Harbor.

This hotel with its circular large dining room, without windows of any kind to obstruct the view on Manila Bay and Corregidor, has always remained to me as a very lovely spot; cool, delightful, spacious even though tropical. I noticed however that no where in the entire hotel were there any carpets. Upon inquiry I was told that the bare floors were a sanitary measure; as no Filipino wore shoes and as almost all suffered from some foot disease, it was considered necessary to protect tourists and others against this.

We had a most jolly time at luncheon, but the best part of course was the happiness of the children at my being with them. In due time we again got into Dio Gracius to go to Los Baños—some forty miles away—where the College of Agriculture was located and where Mr. Welles was teaching. Riding along that dusty highway, passing the crowded buses, which stopped when necessary to relieve native passengers etc., I knew why our crazy little Ford with its top tied to the car with ropes had been purchased by the children.

The way was interesting to me. I was fascinated by the primitive native houses built high up on stilts, with the pigs and chickens sharing the abode with the natives, with the water-buffalo and with the colorful vegetation all along the way.

The villages were small and the stalls for the sale of foods very crude and primitive. But the dress of the Philippine girls was charming, with great airy-puffed sleeves, rather slenderizing skirts but most lovely in color.

Finally we arrived at Los Baños and the College of Agriculture. Here the faculty lived in little two-room houses, thatched roof, swallie or bamboo sidings, with great openings for windows. However there was no glass for window-panes, only shutters made of sea-shells which were only shoved into place in case of heavy rains. Otherwise the space for the big windows was open. Bats, lizards, geckos, rats, cockroaches, ants, mosquitoes and what-not shared the house with us. However we soon got used to most of these vermin; all but the rats. They more or less terrified me, when in the evening they came down from the ceiling and visited us.

But the surroundings and the campus were beautiful. Palms, banana trees, hibiscus and other flowering shrubbery made the whole situation very attractive.

Life at the Welles shack was pleasant and lazy. During the daytime it got to be very hot, the temperature hovering between ninety-eight degrees and one hundred degrees, but the evenings were always delightfully cool, and for the first time I realized how white and beautiful the southern moon was.

Occasionally we would go in to Manila for some function, such as the reception given for General Leonard Wood, then the governor-general of the islands;[11] or perhaps the president of the University of the Philippines[12] asked us to dinner.

One of the characters who was especially interesting was Dr. Baker, in charge of the School of Agriculture. He was a brother of Ray Stannard Baker.[13] Dr. Baker had been in the islands for many years, loved the natives and devoted his entire life to helping them.

During our stay we of course were warned about tropical diseases and about boiling our drinking water and never to eat any uncooked vegetables such as celery, radishes, lettuce etc. as tropical dysentery was to be avoided at all cost. Now too I understood why the white people were indolent or lazy. Most of them couldn't take the constant heat.

During the Christmas holidays my children had rented a cottage at Baguio, a so-called summer resort high up in the mountains where the climate was much like that of Wisconsin and where pine trees and spruce dotted the mountain side. Baguio was just the right place to go to get away from the tropical low-lands.

The trip to Baguio was a long climb up the mountain sides. The road was mostly too narrow for two vehicles to pass each other. So the government had placed gateways at proper places with a Philippine boy to close the gate when one car or bull cart had passed so that no other vehicle could come up while those that were on the road were coming down. The stations or gateways were in telephonic communication so that each guardian of a gate would be notified if the road was clear.

We started for Baguio but lost our way and as it was our luck had a flat tire. When going to the tool-chest we found it empty. The garage man had forgotten to replace our tools. So after scurrying around, Mr. Welles found a wrench in a village which he thought he could use. Somehow, I have always felt that Ford cars were wonderful. If you couldn't find Ford parts you could find a wrench which would do.

All this delayed our progress very much. After finding the right road for the climb up the mountains, night had fallen, but the glorious southern moon came out and shed its benediction on us. Our climb up the narrow road was

[11] Leonard Wood (1860–1927) served as chief of staff of the U.S. Army (1910–1914) and as governor-general of the Philippine Islands (1921–1927).

[12] Guy Potter Benton (1865–1927) served as the third president of the University of the Philippines from 1921 to October 1923. Benton, the last American president of the university, was succeeded by Rafael V. Palma, who served until 1933.

[13] Charles Fuller Baker (1872–1927), a zoologist, was appointed professor of agronomy at the University of the Philippines in 1912. His brother, Ray Stannard Baker (1870–1946), was a reform journalist and author.

interrupted several times. The Ford car just chucked along until it finally stopped. Then when the cold night air had cooled the engine it started again and went a few more kilometers, only to stop again to cool off. This made us very late. It was long after mid-night and the gate-men had gone home. As we moved laboriously up the steep-incline and around a curve, a bull-cart came down to meet us and fell right over the Ford car. After much shouting and noise, the covered cart was finally righted, with no one hurt. Again we climbed only to have the car stop once again. This time Alma Jacobus and I decided we really could walk to the next gateway—when we heard again the welcoming chucking of the car. It came along beautifully this time, so we motioned the children to proceed as we could now see a light or two which we felt might be Baguio. It was. It was also 2:00 A.M. and beastly cold. However in a very short time a car came down to pick us up and take us to our cottage. To say we were glad is putting it mildly.

We hastily made our beds, ate chocolate candy for our dinner and went to bed. The next morning we felt amply repaid for our experience of the night before.

Lee—the Chinese cook—followed on the train. So we were well taken care of.

Those two weeks at Baguio are never-to-be-forgotten. Naturally, since we were back in a climate which was more invigorating, we hunted for things to do. And so one of the things to do was to take a horse-back ride to the top of the mountain, where we were told we could find ice almost any night.

After the ride up with Dio Gracius, I couldn't think of anything harder or more exciting. So I was eager to ride up the mountain on a horse. I, who had never been on a horse in all my life! How could I know what was in store for me? So happily we started out. The first difficulty I had was to mount the pony, which seemed so awfully big to me. I couldn't get up. So Colin tried to help; Doris tried to help and still I could [not] get on that horse. Finally we found a fence which I climbed and from the fence I got on to the horse. At last! But how could I know the horse's back was as wide? But this time I decided to be stoical and not say a word. We finally started the climb. The path was so very narrow that one foot scraped the mountain side while the other extended way over the precipice. All I could do was to watch the narrow path ahead, praying that it would not get narrower. To glance over the valley or precipice was too terrifying. Soon, too soon, I ached and wished I could get off that horse. But pride they say comes before a fall. Well pride made me stick and groan.

After a while, pride fled and I yelled for help to take me off the horse. Upon reaching the ground I couldn't stand but just doubled up. We laughed and I almost cried. Then I made up my mind that the young folks could climb to the top, but that I would spend the night at a half-way house placed there for weary riders. The little house had nothing in it but two bamboo cots. Here I determined to stay. But both Doris and Colin took pity on me and decided to stay with me while Alma proceeded to the top of the mountain. We were to wait for her return the next day. I still have a feeling that my children also were glad to get off their steeds and rest, although this they never admitted.

The next day going down to Baguio I saw the scenery. I saw the scenery because I could not get on the horse again and so walked him down the steep path. Now we began to feel the warmth of the tropical sun. The walk down the mountain took us until late afternoon. Naturally I was exhausted after walking eight or ten kilometers and was anxious to get under a shower bath. Showers were rather primitive. True, the water which came from nearby streams was piped into the cottage and was moderately warmed from the sun. But the fixture itself consisted of a tin pail hung on the pipe. The bottom of the pail had holes pounded through with nails. Nevertheless—we had a shower, which was something to be grateful for.

No sooner had I got under the shower when my back began to sting as though hundreds of bees had stung me. Upon investigation I discovered I was fearfully sun-burned, the burns following the daisy pattern of the open-work of my blouse. Great blisters had formed and had filled up. Ah! Me! I had to go to bed I was so miserable. Then I thought with a bit of humor—what price vacationing! However, I soon was able to enjoy life again.

Our food was mostly imported. The butter and canned milk coming from Holland. Meat consisted largely of poultry. But Lee—the Chinese cook who had received his training in an American army—was an excellent cook.

The culture and civilization of the islanders was primitive except on the coastal towns. There occidental influence had made quite a dent. Manila was a big city, with buses, streetcars, stores, shops and churches and a Rockefeller Hospital. I know that every government-sent Philippine student that had been sent to the States or elsewhere brought back some of the advantages he had learned to enjoy elsewhere. Not so much could be said of the villages off the beaten path. A U.S. Army post was located a few miles from Los Baños. This army post furnished us with ice.

The college buildings were attractive and gleamed white against the luscious green background.

There was much talk in the United States at the time of the approaching independence for the islands. However while there we found only the coastal towns and especially the politicos who were interested in independence. All the other natives had no conception of independence and were quite indifferent. I saw more Igorots, the head-hunters, than any of the other tribes. The Igorots lived in the mountains mostly, were completely naked except for the G-string and were shorter and beautifully built. I still remember with what admiration I saw them climb the steepest cliffs with apparently no great effort.

As soon as we returned to Manila [and] Los Baños, both of the children came down with dengue fever which put both children into beds. So I turned into nurse which had some disadvantages, since all things used had to be made sterile by baking everything in the oven of a wood-burning stove. Also our Chinese cook Lee had to go to China to visit his Chinese wife, who "had to catch him boy."

My little friend and traveling companion Alma was getting restless and wished to return to the States before I could possibly leave the children. So she left soon after. That meant that I too had to return home alone which was also a new experience for me. So after another two months my children accompanied me to Shanghai by way of Hong Kong and Canton [Guangzhou]. It was a happy trip except for the gnawing feeling that soon we would be parted again.

I was very much impressed by Hong Kong and its mixed population. Canton was most interesting too. There I did some more shopping which was real fun. I bought silk by the bolt, since the Chinese would not cut the material into yards but just threw the bolts of silk on-to a scale and weighed it. Also dozens of pairs of Chinese embroidered slippers and a couple of silver mesh-bags which at that time were quite fashionable. I have always hoped and declared that sometime in the future I would go back to China to finish my shopping. Just what, if anything, can be left after this catastrophic global war is difficult to imagine.

At Shanghai I said "Good-bye" to my beloved children and for three days out on the ocean I was still weeping at our parting.

The trip home was interesting, largely because the majority of the passengers were returning missionaries who had plenty to tell us of their experiences in the Far East. However these missionaries objected to dancing on the boat and appealed to the captain to bar that pleasure. Since there also were young people and others returning to America who very much wanted to dance, the captain compromised by ordering no dancing before 9:00 P.M. So by 9:00 P.M. all missionaries retired and the rest of the guests on the boat enjoyed dancing.

There were several passengers on the steamer who interested me very much. There were Mr. and Mrs. Loeb[14] of the Kuhn, Loeb Bank of New York.

---

[14] James Loeb (1867–1933) was a banker, classical scholar, and philanthropist. His wife was Marie Antonie Hambuechen Loeb (1865?–1933).

Mrs. Loeb was charming and knew how to enter into the life of the boat and make everyone feel much at home. She was just finishing a round-the-world trip and was loaded with the things she had purchased from every country she had visited, from needle-point bags to Japanese kimonos, Chinese wall-hangings and things to Indian prints. She had dozens of large hampers full of things she brought into the U.S. I was so impressed, not only by her wealth but by her charm and simplicity.

The other lady who interested me had been visiting her sister in Japan when she received word of her husband's death. Her name was Ida Schmelkes. Ida was a refined well dressed lady who was very much alone on the boat. She was a resident of Prague, Czechoslovakia and was on her way home. She was somewhat worried for fear her late husband—who was the recipient of her dowry—might have willed it away to his people and thus leave her penniless. Such was the law of her country. I was sorry for her and interested too. The result was we became good friends and have been ever since, although I have no idea of what became of her and her estate when the Germans took the Sudetenland.

We were approaching the USA. I shall never never forget the magnificent sight as the snow-capped mountains hove into view. Everyone was spell-bound and breathless at the wondrous view.

We met the boat-train at Seattle and were on our way across the continent. It was great to drink good water again and to eat celery and lettuce and greens.

My husband met me at the train. After a seven months glorious vacation, full of experiences, miles of travel into foreign lands, never forgotten scenery, it was grand to arrive at the dingy old Milwaukee railroad station and be at home.

It did not take twenty minutes before I was told that I must get ready that afternoon to accompany my husband to some eastern city to attend another Socialist convention or meeting of the Socialist executive committee. So I came back into the old routine at once. It was not too easy to get into the turmoil of the political life of a minority party. Then too I found my husband different. I couldn't quite put my finger on what the difference was except the fact that my long absence had made him quite independent of me. The old comradeship had somehow weakened. My husband seemed indifferent to his personal appearance. His coat collars were never in place, one side up and the other side down. His hats, formerly so correctly creased, were knocked into all kinds of shape and were never on his head at the proper angle. I looked at him and wondered. Finally I came to the conclusion that I had been away too long and that I must work my way back again to the place I had occupied before I left for the Orient. Time would tell. My job now was to make myself indispensable again to my husband and his works.

Events were shaping themselves fast.

The *Leader's* right to receive mail had been restored. A check from the federal government for excess postage was received some time before. As was the right to again enjoy second class mailing rights. Now in May of 1922— the federal indictments in Milwaukee were dropped against Mr. B. and the other Wisconsin men. Surely the future was brightening for us.

We were now preparing for the fall congressional campaign. Again Mr. Stafford was our main opponent. We made the best campaign we could. Our method was to circularize our district with literature, which work always fell to me.

On November 7, 1922, Mr. Stafford was defeated and Victor Berger became the congressman elect. Naturally we were elated. It was so important to have a member of a minority party in the House of Representatives. Important for us as well as for the whole country.

The federal indictments issued at La Crosse were dropped November 16, 1922.[15]

As soon as the election returns were certified, we received word through the hostile press of the city that the federal case in Chicago against Victor Berger, et al. had also been dismissed by U.S. District Attorney Olson in Washington the previous May.[16] This fact was a complete surprise to us as the papers here had not given us this joyful news, hoping by keeping it secret that the fall election would thereby be lost to us.

Personally, I think the suppression of that news was about as contemptible an act as any I know of. We had to win the election against the great odds of a twenty year sentence still hanging over us.

Such were politics during the Great World War. And now we could write finis to the stormiest period of [Victor Berger's] career!

———

But we had work to do. The financial condition of the *Leader* was pitiful. Advertising accounts were hopelessly small and couldn't possibly support the paper. Our personal finances were well-nigh catastrophic. There were still legal obligations to be met.

Nevertheless, so far as was possible we put our house in order in preparation of claiming the congressional seat, twice denied to my husband.

[15] The *Milwaukee Leader* reported on November 17, 1922, that the La Crosse indictments would be dismissed within a few days.

[16] Victor Berger learned in late February 1923 that the Chicago case had been dismissed the previous month. He also learned that Charles F. Clyne, the prosecutor for the Chicago case, had been ordered to drop the case as early as September 1922 (Stevens, ed., *Family Letters,* 313–315).

CHAPTER 11

Washington, the Beautiful!

That's what everyone said. I too tried to make myself see the beauty that was there. I'll admit the city was well planned with its wide avenues, its circles and parks and magnolia trees. Its outward dress, especially in the springtime, was very beautiful and colorful. And marble buildings galore with the sunlight blinding you with their glare. There were places that gave me a real emotional thrill too. Mount Vernon I adored, as I did the Potomac basin, the Lincoln Memorial and Rock Creek Park.

But Washington meant something more to me than its physical appearance. There were people there, people of so-called importance, who were to do the job of representing the folks back home and the welfare of the country at large. I hunted for a spiritual up-lift. I couldn't find it. It just wasn't there. Perhaps my experience of six years before embittered me, and my perspective was all wrong. But I really did try to find the worth-while things I was looking for. But congressmen, I soon learned, were good rabble-rousers on the home front and quite unprepared to cope with the vital important problems confronting the nation during the period of reconstruction after the First World War. How could I find leadership in a man like John C. Schafer from the Fourth District of Wisconsin! Or Blanton of Texas. Or Snell of New York.[1] Yes—even from the leaders of the two entrenched old parties.

But I must not get ahead of my story. Upon arriving in Washington, we found the atmosphere most friendly. The clerk of the House immediately as-

[1] John Charles Schafer (1893–1962) was a Republican representative from Wisconsin (1923–1933 and 1939–1941). Thomas Lindsay Blanton (1872–1957) was a Democratic representative from Texas (1917–1929 and 1930–1937). Bertrand Hollis Snell (1870–1958) was a Republican representative from New York (1915–1939).

signed my husband an office in the House Office Building, and then [we] found an apartment in which to live. We awaited the day for the opening of the session of Congress with a feeling of trepidation. It is true we heard nothing, either in the press or through gossip, that my husband's right to take the oath of office would be challenged. Yet we were a little bit nervous nevertheless. But we went ahead as though everything would be perfectly all right. Mr. Berger even secured a secretary, a gentle lovable patient but intelligent young man by the name of Marx Lewis[2] who had graduated from the George Washington University as a lawyer but who was also a member of the Socialist Party. How very fortunate we were to have Marx work with us. He could be trusted to do research work so necessary sometimes, he worked tirelessly because he believed in our cause, and his devotion to Victor Berger was unquestionable and beautiful. I shall always remember Marx with love and gratitude.

The fourth of March finally came. When the Speaker of the House administered the oath of office to the members-elect, Mr. Berger was *not* asked to stand aside as happened the other time; he presented himself to be sworn in, with all the rest. Oh! What a relief! In a few moments that auspicious occasion was over and my husband was again a member of the House of Representatives. The occasion called for a celebration. But we had not prepared to celebrate and didn't quite know how to proceed.

As soon as the House adjourned for the day we proceeded to the office, there to have a so-called gab-fest over the events of the day. We laughed and I sometimes cried because the burden of years had some-how lifted. In the midst of our exchange of views and emotions, callers, members of the House, came to shake the hand of their new colleague. It was all very pleasant.

Throughout the day I could feel the strain on my husband. He was "raring" to begin his campaign and to organize his office in a more efficient manner. There were reference books, government bulletins by the thousand, books from the congressional library, any book on history, economics or international relationship to be placed. Was he not a great student on these matters? Also there were files of the big newspapers of the country from the East, West, South and North. Our home-paper files also were of great importance to us. Soon our office became a reference room for many many members of Congress.

As I indicated before, many colleagues were hopelessly ignorant of national and international affairs. They no doubt knew what their respective districts wanted but little beyond that. So many came most frequently to get information

---

[2] Marx Lewis (1897–1990) served as secretary to Socialist congressman Meyer London of New York (1917–1919 and 1921–1923) before working with Victor Berger from 1923 to 1929. After 1929 Lewis became a labor organizer.

or translations or what-not. The office became a bureau of information.

I spent a good deal of my time in my husband's office, learning and watching the procedure. One of the big problems confronting us at the time was how to get the message from the lone-Socialist congressman before the public.

The only district interested in his activities was the Fifth District of Wisconsin. But the importance of having the voice of Victor Berger heard throughout the nation was great, since he felt he represented the socialist point of view for the whole nation.

So before long we added to our staff a news correspondent who agreed to send out to the thirty-four or thirty-five papers he represented a daily statement from the Socialist congressman. Thus a message went out daily on some current topic. Of course not all papers printed it. That was hoping for too much. But if the message was striking enough, interesting enough or controversial enough, many couldn't resist the temptation to print it. Thus we soon got quite a good deal of publicity for the work done in Washington.

We soon found the office staff had increased way beyond the number or the amount for services allotted by the government. That meant the extra amounts came out of Victor Berger's salary. But it certainly was worth it.

As for me, I spent much of my time in the office, helping here and there, or in the galleries listening to discussions and watching the unruly House. It never seemed to me to carry the dignity of a great legislative body of a great nation. Only occasionally, when the rumor got out that some prominent member was to speak, did the members of Congress file into the House chamber from the cloak-rooms to listen.

Sometimes the older members gave very creditable speeches and these made the impression that they knew what they were talking about. One such speech still lingers in my memory. That speech was fiery, beautiful and extemporaneous. It was made by Fiorello La Guardia.[3] He brought down the House, which burst into tumultuous applause. But for most of the rest—enough said.

We had rented an apartment in the same building and right next door to that of Congressman Voigt of Sheboygan, Wisconsin. Mr. Voigt was the one member who had dared alone to vote to seat my husband four years before.

Mr. Voigt shared many of our opinions on the character of the Congress and its members. It was very pleasant indeed to have him and his family as neighbors. Often I would [go to the] market for big juicy steaks and have [the Voigts] in for dinner. It was fun to see those two men enjoy a home cooked dinner, and it was relaxing, too, to find such agreement between them.

---

[3] Fiorello Henry La Guardia (1882–1947) served as a Republican representative from New York (1917–1919 and 1923–1933) and mayor of New York City (1934–1945).

I had determined not to enter the routine of the social swirl, such as calling on Mondays on the hill, Tuesdays on the judiciary, Wednesday on another part of hostesses and Thursday on others. I was no longer interested in the superficial chatter and formalities, but found time to go to lectures, meetings, musicals and so forth. My time in Washington seemed to be ineffectively used and therefore wasted. There was such a contrast between life in Washington and life in Milwaukee, where I was kept so busy attending to my work in the school board and all its attending demands. Not a moment in Milwaukee was wasted, which was not the case in Washington, D.C.

Europe—1923

Soon after we were settled in Washington, my husband and I made preparations to attend the first congress of the Second International to meet after war.[4] Mr. Berger, Morris Hillquit, Morris Berman[5] and others whose names I do not now recall at this moment were delegates representing the American socialist movement. This congress was to meet in Hamburg, Germany, about May 1. The Socialists of the world were trying to salvage their international movement.

Furthermore, my husband was most anxious to study the economic breakdown which was going from bad to worse in Germany. Inflation—they called it. I guess few people fully appreciated just what inflation is, or what the complete economic breakdown of a country meant in all its ramifications and disastrous results. My husband wished to study the conditions in central Europe, and through his connections he was able to get first hand reports on the results of the food-blockade, a war measure, and the accompanying results.

The first effect of inflation came to us as we entered Hamburg and got 40,000 marks for one American dollar. So in exchanging a five dollar bill we received 200,000 marks. It was quite an experience to handle so much money and to quickly translate either into marks or dollars everything we did, whether it was the price of our room or the price of a meal. But more of that later. Today I can understand the desperate efforts made by President Roosevelt and

---

[4] After the war, the Second International split into the Third International (or Comintern) and two social-democratic groups that joined in Hamburg, May 21–25, 1923, under the name Labor and Socialist International.

[5] Morris Berman (1866–1945) was a Russian-born Socialist businessman (retired 1919) who served on several boards of directors and was a candidate for public office in New York. From 1929 to 1945 he served as president of the People's Educational Camp Society.

the administration of today to ward off inflation after this war of 1944.

The congress was thrilling. I had attended many U.S. national conventions, but never an international congress. This was new to me. I had a difficult time, sometimes, to listen to the different languages and the English interpretation of each speech. And all delegates seemed to be practiced orators. Most European delegates could understand two and three languages. Thus the English members were well versed in French or Italian or German. We of America were somewhat handicapped, as we in this country are victims of one language usually.

I was deeply impressed by the ability and the scholarliness of the British. There were Beatrice and Sidney Webb, [Henry Noel] Brailsford, Arthur Henderson and dozens more.[6] Among the French the one who impressed me as the most able and the most fiery orator was Léon Blum, who [a] short time ago was the chief of the French government during the period of the United Front [and] who failed the cause by refusing aid to the Spanish republic and by supporting the embargo to aid Spain.[7]

The German delegates were quiet and subdued and all other members of the congress did their best to make them feel less uncomfortable. One outstanding Italian delegate made a deep impression on me. He was a heavy set man with a long beard by the name of Modigliani[8] who later became a victim of Mussolini's persecution. Oh! There were others who commanded admiration and respect. Among these was Breitscheid, Paul Löbe, a Russian Menshevik Abramovitch, Scheidemann, Hilferding, Braun and many others.[9] Kautsky and

---

[6] Beatrice (1858–1943) and Sidney (1859–1947) Webb were English socialist economists and historians who organized numerous institutions and strongly influenced British social policies and thought. Arthur Henderson (1863–1935) served as secretary of the British Labour Party (1911–1934) and as a member of Parliament (1903–1931).

[7] Léon Blum (1872–1950) served in the French Chamber of Deputies (1919–1928, 1929–1940) and as the first Socialist premier of France (1936–1937, 1938, 1946–1947). Blum's government followed a policy of nonintervention in the Spanish Civil War. The United Front was a Soviet policy of cooperation with socialist and liberal groups from 1921 to 1928; it was revived under the name Popular Front in 1935 in opposition to fascism.

[8] Giuseppe E. Modigliani (1872–1947) was a Socialist member of the Italian Parliament (1913–1924), a pacifist, and a leader in the antifascist movement. Forced to leave Italy in 1925, he lived in exile in France and Switzerland until October 1944.

[9] Rudolf Breitscheid (1874–1944) was a German Social Democratic politician who served as Prussian interior minister (1918–1919) and as a member of the Reichstag (1920–1933). He opposed World War I and was a member of the minority Independent Social Democratic Party from its establishment in 1917 until 1922, when its remaining members rejoined the majority Social Democrats. Paul Löbe (1875–1967) served as a German Social Democratic member of the Reichstag (1920–1933) and as Reichstag president almost continuously from 1920 to 1932. Raphael Rein Abramovitch (b. 1880) was a Russian Menshevik (non-Leninist) exile and author. Philipp Scheidemann (1865–1939), Rudolf Hilferding (1877–1941), and Otto Braun (1872–1955) were German Social Democratic politicians. Scheidemann served as a member of the Reichstag (1903–1918 and 1920–1933), as the first prime minister of the Weimar

Bernstein were not delegates.[10] Then there was Vandervelde from Belgium, Hysman—Holland, Branting—Sweden and others.[11] In fact there were about six hundred delegates and the gathering was a very impressive gathering.

But to our astonishment we found that the international executive committee had gone over the important questions, which should have been discussed before the whole congress, and had brought in the entire program cut and dried with recommendations which the congress adopted without debate. Oh! There were some formalities observed. I recall that Victor Berger was on the committee on reparations. He did not agree with the committee's report and was preparing a minority report. But pressure was used to prevent him from introducing his minority report. Breitscheid was most vociferous against the report. We could not then and have not since understood his attitude since all we wanted was a fairer and more workable program on reparations toward Germany. We have always felt that the appeasement policy of Breitscheid and the French and Belgian comrades was wrong.

The congress lasted one week and wound up with a huge mass meeting on the Moor Weide (field) with 100,000 people in attendance. Thirteen wagons placed in a circle in the center of the field furnished the platforms. The last demonstration was a huge parade through the city of Hamburg. To the consternation of the Socialists of the congress, the Communists had also organized a parade on the same day and over the same route. So one branch of the minority groups marched down the right side of the street while the other group passed them on the other side of the street. Fortunately it all went off without disturbances. One thing the Communists did, however, was to impress the Socialists by their strength and numbers, as their parade was as long if not longer.

Republic (February–June 1919) under President Friedrich Ebert, and as mayor of Kassel (1920–1925). Hilferding, a former Independent Social Democrat, served as a member of the Reichstag (1924–1933) and as finance minister (1923 and 1928–1929). Braun was a member of the Reichstag (1920–1933) and Prussian prime minister almost continuously from 1920 to 1933.

[10] Karl Kautsky (1854–1938) was the German Social Democratic Party's leading Marxist theorist before World War I and editor of the journal *Die Neue Zeit* (1883–1917). Eduard Bernstein (1850–1932) was a German Social Democratic politician and theorist who advocated an evolutionary socialism, a position eventually adopted by his party. He served as a member of the Reichstag (1902–1907, 1912–1918, and 1920–1928). Both Kautsky and Bernstein opposed the war and joined the Independent Social Democrats in 1917. Bernstein rejoined the majority Social Democrats in 1919, Kautsky in 1922.

[11] Émile Vandervelde (1866–1938) held positions in Belgian coalition governments from 1914 to 1937 and played a leading role in the Second International. Meta Berger is probably referring to Belgian politician Camille Huysmans (1871–1968), who lived in the Netherlands during World War I. He served as secretary of the Second International (1905–1922) and as prime minister of Belgium (1946–1947). K. Hjalmar Branting (1860–1925) edited the *Social-Demokraten* (1886–1892, 1896–1908, and 1911–1917) and served in the Swedish Riksdag (1896–1925) and as prime minister of Sweden three times between 1920 and 1925. In 1921 he was a co-recipient of the Nobel Peace Prize.

And now just a final word on the social life in Hamburg of the Socialists. The American Socialists and the British Socialists had invited the German Socialists to a dinner and had asked me to make up the menu. Not being familiar with the customs there, I appealed to the editors of the *Hamburger Echo,* the socialist paper. They were glad to help. Hesitating a little, they asked, "Could we start by having *Kirschwasser* (cherry brandy) to begin with?" "Of course." Then, "Could we wind up by having compote?" "Certainly." So it was arranged, and I believe for the first time these German comrades had a full meal since the war.

Here for the first time I saw wives of members of the Reichstag take the leavings of bread, wrap them up in clean handkerchiefs and tuck them into their bag. They did not apologize but merely said, we are taking this for members of the family who have little or nothing to eat. This I saw happen again and again while I was in Germany.

We left for Berlin. I had always heard of the cleanliness and the efficiency of German railroad. But to my surprise the trains were never on time, were over crowded and exceedingly dirty. The seats were disreputable and dirty with grease spots and filth. This I was told was due to the fact that all good and useful rolling stock was taken by the Allies, leaving only the miserable railroad cars we were then using. Thousands of cars, freight and passenger cars, were standing on the side-tracks. These cars were the [ones] Belgium had refused to take, demanding new cars for those destroyed during the war. We began to see the tangible effects of war, reparations and chaos in Germany proper.

Arriving at Berlin at dusk, we took a droshky [carriage] to our hotel, passing through the Tiergarten and its grotesque Siegesallee.[12] In the twilight this Siegesallee intrigued me. I made up my mind to see it in daylight. I am glad I did. It so thoroughly disillusioned me.

The first day in Berlin was of course devoted to a call upon Socialist headquarters, only to find it quite deserted. Next a visit to the Reichstag. Here—Herr Breitscheid again met us but again we were impressed with his somewhat aloof hospitality, telling us that there were no Socialists present that day on the floor of the Reichstag and that the man then speaking was a noisy Communist. I found the session of the Reichstag on a par with the House of Representatives in the U.S. as far as order and decorum was concerned.

The next day we met Guido Enderis, a Milwaukeean who had represented the Associated Press during World [War] I and who now I think represents

---

[12] The Tiergarten is a Berlin park. The Siegesallee, an avenue in the Tiergarten adorned with white plaster monuments of military figures, was destroyed during World War II.

the *New York Times*.[13] Guido was glad to see us and offered to do anything he could to help Mr. B. get facts and figures and meet people. So again we went to the Reichstag meeting and this time meeting many interesting folks, both from the press, the party and government officials. For the first time also we met Bernstorff, the former German ambassador to the U.S. and who was compelled to return to Germany during the World [War] I period.[14]

Mr. Berger soon connected up with representatives of the German press, labor leaders, party members, diplomats etc. Our best conferences were of course with party leaders who usually met us in some home or a quiet corner of the Rathskeller [lower-level bar/restaurant in the city hall]. We learned a lot of the bitterness left from the defeat of Germany. Particularly, these people resented the blockade which had caused malnutrition and starvation. They arranged for me to visit the schools of Berlin and observe the Quakers at work feeding the undernourished children. But by the time 1923 had arrived even the Friends were inadequate, not in the desire to help, but there really was no food for them to give the children. I remember a little girl I thought was five years old, and when I asked her how old she was, she said twelve years old. She never had a chance to grow. Really those children were a pitiful sight to see and I was heart-sick by the end of the day.

We got most of the inside information about Germany from the private gatherings in the homes of trusted friends and comrades. Such was the case when we were guests of President Fritz Ebert, the first president of the Third Reich (?).[15] President Ebert lived in the palace of Prince von Eulenburg,[16] who had fled. The palace was on Wilhelm Strasse quite near the government buildings and near the American embassy. It was a dignified building, quite richly but plainly furnished. Our dinner with President Ebert was very simple, but the Rhine wine served was excellent. And that reminds me that a fine bottle of Rhine wine could be had anywhere for the price of ten cents, due to the

---

[13] Guido Enderis (1874–1948), brother of Dorothy Enderis, wrote for Milwaukee newspapers before becoming a foreign correspondent in Germany in 1916. In 1917 he joined the Associated Press in Berlin, and he stayed in that city during the war, though he was unable to send reports. In 1929 he became director of the Berlin bureau of the *New York Times*. After the United States entered World War II, Enderis moved to Bern, Switzerland, and reported from there.

[14] Johann-Heinrich Bernstorff (1862–1939) served as German ambassador to the United States from 1908 to 1917. He returned to Germany when the United States declared war on that country.

[15] Friedrich Ebert (1871–1925) led the German Social Democratic Party and helped establish the Weimar constitution. He served as a member of the Reichstag (1912–1918) and as the first president of the Weimar Republic (1919–1925).

[16] Philipp zu Eulenburg (1847–1921) was a German diplomat and an adviser to Kaiser Wilhelm II. Eulenburg's career ended in 1906, when he was accused of homosexuality. His residence, Liebenberg, was just north of Berlin.

inflation which was going from bad to worse daily. The mark had now dropped to 800,000 marks for one dollar.

There were no goods to be had. Stores were almost bare of consumption goods. Food was bought up each day for fear that the next day the same goods would have increased in value in marks. The workers of Germany were desperate. Wages didn't keep pace with the ever increasing price rise and the hunger of their children. Also the people resented the fact that at the borders were citizens of surrounding countries waiting with their visas ready to cross into Germany to buy what goods that were left before the merchant had time to adjust prices according to the increased fall of the mark. I never saw a more desperate or unhappy people in my life.

We, who were tourists, finally refused to be seated in a restaurant window, where hungry women and children could see food served us. It was too painful and we were ashamed.

All the four months I was in Germany I never saw fruit, except one dried up moldy lemon. Merchants had nothing to sell, either food, socks, shirts or anything else. Sometimes the display in the window was a pitiful try to induce folks into the shops, only to be disappointed. No wonder the beer halls and cafés were crowded every night. There at least over a glass of beer or a cup of coffee these miserable people could exchange views, or forget momentarily.

Finally, the mark fell to one million marks for the dollar. Then the printers who printed this worthless money went on strike and refused to print any more of the worthless stuff. The result was hunger strikes. I witnessed one of these strikes. I shall never forget it. Children crying for food, women walking the streets with staring eyes—mumbling about a cup of coffee. The owners of shops boarded up their windows for fear of rocks and riots. No one would or could exchange our money. Even the American consul said he himself had to sign an IOU for his food when he got it.

In the meantime my husband was busy with party-leaders, newspapermen and labor leaders. One of the men he met was a Herr von Raumer,[17] who belonged to the aristocracy and was therefore a conservative. Herr von Raumer invited us to come to dinner to his home to meet some of the other industrialists for a conference. Present at this dinner was the big industrialist Hugo Stinnes.[18] At this meeting the hostess carefully kept me out of the conference and tried to entertain me herself, a woman in whom I had not the slightest

---

[17] Hans von Raumer (1870–1965) of the German People's Party served as a member of the Reichstag (1920–1930), minister of the treasury (1920–1921), and minister of economics (1923). His wife, the former Stephanie zu Putlitz, probably served as hostess at the dinner the Bergers attended.

[18] Hugo Stinnes (1870–1924) was Germany's leading industrialist after World War I.

interest. So I sat there a whole evening listening to the lady with one ear and trying to learn a little of what was going [on] in the other room with the other ear. It was [a] miserable evening!

Finally the conference broke up. No sooner when we got by ourselves I asked my husband to tell me all about it. "Well," said my husband, "I gave them my word of honor that I would not divulge what was said in that room. But I will say, they are the goddamnedest SOBs I ever met. They do not know what patriotism is. All the while while Germany was at war with the Allies, they were doing a flourishing business with the French, selling coal and steel with which to carry on the war against the nation, just so they could continue pocketing profits." And that's all I got out of that conference.

Before leaving Berlin we had a few more conferences, one of which was again with President Ebert, who made an urgent plea that if anyone in America could provide potatoes and coal for the most destitute in Hamburg and Berlin. Then and there I resolved to see what I could do.

We left Berlin gladly and proceeded to Cologne and the Ruhr district which was then occupied by the French army. Here we ran into considerable red-tape. Permission had to be obtained from the commander of the French army of occupation, which permission we finally secured. The American consul in Cologne[19] warned us that we could not travel by train as it was too dangerous, since only inexperienced Frenchmen were in charge of running the trains. Finally, Mr. Sauer, the American consul, provided us with an automobile and more necessary papers before we could cross the Rhine River and go to Düsseldorf, in the Ruhr.[20]

Our trip through the occupied district was dismal and somewhat harrowing. Here was the most densely populated district of Germany with its big iron industries and coal industries and its millions of sullen Germans who bitterly resented the occupation. Every hotel, church, school house, public building, store etc. had been taken over by the French army. The German citizens did what they could by passive resistance. During the ten days of our stay in the Ruhr I never saw a smile on a single person. Resentment, hatred, revenge were reflected everywhere. Certain restaurants were reserved for French officers. But there was one hotel only which was open to the traveling public with permits. This was the Essener Hof—formerly the private hotel for the Krupp industry.[21] This was used before World War I by Krupps to entertain their customers and salesmen. Here we found a room and food. But each menu card had printed

---

[19] Emil Sauer (1881–1949) was the U.S. consul in Cologne (1915–1917 and 1919–1925).

[20] The Bergers traveled by train to Cologne and then by car to Düsseldorf, Essen, and other towns in the occupied area.

[21] The Krupp family manufactured armaments.

on it a request that guests do not ask for seconds. The reason this hotel was not occupied was that the Allied commissioners made it its headquarters and did not wish to be disturbed.

We were glad to leave the occupied section for it was depressing in the extreme.

We finally got back to Cologne where I could feast my eyes on the loveliness and grandeur of the cathedral. We now traveled up the Rhine to Frankfurt and Mainz. Then over to Nürnberg and finally landed in Stuttgart where our good friend Carl Hildendorf took us in hand. From Stuttgart we traveled through the Black Forest after which we went to Munich and from there to Innsbruck.

We left Germany to visit Vienna, the once gay city of central Europe. I was especially interested in the city of wine, women and song because it was there that my husband went to the university. But the visit to Vienna was spoiled by my getting sick, and very sick. So while I was waiting for [my] temperature to drop; I made up my mind that as soon as that happened we would be on our way to Budapest. Luck was with me for the next morning we were on a steamer going down the Danube. I have often wondered why it is called the blue Danube. It really was a broad yellow stream bordered on each side with somewhat barren hills and did not have the beauty of the Rhine or its old feudal castles. But Budapest! Oh! That was a sight to behold in the evening. Hotels, good hotels lined the water front. Flowering oleander trees decorated the front and gypsy music playing at all doorways of the big hotels. It was lovely and a great relief after dismal Germany and poor and dirty Vienna.

It was nearing time for our return home. So we took the night train to Switzerland. Gorgeous beauteous Switzerland with its snowcapped mountains and its clear blue lakes. Then on to Paris.

In Paris we found again the aftermath of the war. Every hotel furnished each room with graphic pictures of destruction of the war and the small amount of reparations made. The barkers on sightseeing buses used their opportunity to interpret history falsely in the light of the past war. Finally, I thought it best that my husband visit the book-shops and I went to the Louvre to see the great art gallery. A drive through the *bois* [woods] was delightful, and of course the other sights of which I had read made a great impression on me.

Then on to Belgium, Holland and back to Hamburg to catch the steamer for the U.S. and home.

Upon arriving in New York I was astonished and a little ashamed to see our food shops bursting with delicious foods and pastries. Meat markets full of hams, bacon, beef and lamb. And I had just come from a continent where food was scarce and people were starving. Surely we and they had not organized the lives of the people correctly. And today as I write, I believe in the Atlantic Charter and in the administration's programs to prevent inflation. Yes, give us subsidies if we need them. Don't let the whole economic system of the country break as it did after World War I.

And so back to Washington, D.C.

CHAPTER 12

"Hope and Despair"

After some weeks back in Washington, D.C., I discovered a very interesting group of liberals. They had formed the Penguin Club and had rented an old house not far from the White House on or near Seventeenth Street NW.[1] I was told the reason it was called the Penguin Club was that in hunting for an appropriate name, they looked through the dictionary to find the name of a queer bird, and since the penguin seemed the queerest and since the birds who were members of this liberal group were all queer, they had adopted the name Penguin Club. While I did not find any Socialist there, I did find quite a few left-liberals, who I am certain had there been a good organizer for the party would have corralled these left-liberals into the party as comrades. Here I found many pleasant associations.

News now came from the Philippine Islands that Colin Welles was stricken with malignant malaria, was confined in the Rockefeller Hospital and was told by the doctors there that he could not remain in the islands. So there was [not] much for Doris to do but to sell-out and come back to the States.[2]

In the meantime, my daughter Elsa had graduated from the Pennsylvania Medical University and was interning in the Emergency Hospital in Washington, D.C. It was a great joy to be in the same town with her where we could see each other as often as her work and ours permitted. Naturally her circle of friends came from the medical group. Elsa was a wholesome and quick witted girl who made friends easily and who was devoted to her work at the Emergency Hospital. She stayed on there until she became the resident doctor. After

[1] Meta Berger added here: "H Street."
[2] Doris and Colin Welles returned in July 1922.

her services were over there and through the influence of friends she decided to branch out into ear, eye and nose medicine. Consequently she took the internship at the Episcopal Hospital for ear, eyes and nose,[3] where she took the training until she became the resident doctor at that hospital. When her work there was drawing to the close, her father planned that she should prepare to go to Europe and study for a year at the Vienna Krankenhaus [hospital] and other medical centers of Europe.

In the meantime, political lines in Washington were being shaken by the fact that the progressives of the country were trying to form a new party to support old Bob La Follette, who had definitely broken with the Republican Party and who was willing to head a ticket on a third party.

So like other Socialists I wanted to help. I knew nothing so far as to how far the new organization had gone. So quite innocently I went to Mrs. J. C. [Elsie W.] Schafer to ask whether she would co-operate in organizing the progressives. This was a very confidential meeting, and Mrs. Schafer agreed to co-operate. However, the next morning a newspaper item publicized the fact that Mrs. J. C. Schafer was busy trying to organize the progressives of the nation. To say I was surprised put it mildly. But the publication brought really good results.

There was a knock at the office door and in came a gorgeous creature, young, beautiful, with a crown of two braids of auburn hair topping her head, and introduced herself as Isabelle Kendig.[4] [She] brought the newspaper clipping with her and asked me what we were intending to do, organize another progressive group? And didn't we know that an office force was already at work doing the identical thing that I myself had proposed.

After some conversation with Isabelle—Sally for short—I went with her to her office and from that moment worked hard lining up the forces for the new effort behind Bob La Follette Sr. I was happy in Washington now. I had work to do and work which had the approval of Morris Hillquit, Victor Berger and the Socialist Party in general.

So we worked hard collecting money—which is always a hard job, sending out letters and circulars and preparing the progressives of the country to get ready for a conference to be held the next June in Cleveland.[5]

Our work and the work of others throughout the country bore fruit. The conference at Cleveland was a huge success. The two main forces being the Railroad Brotherhoods and the Socialist Party. Robert M. La Follette had agreed

[3] The Episcopal Eye, Ear, and Throat Hospital in Washington, D.C.
[4] Isabelle V. "Sally" Kendig (1889–1974) was active in feminist and peace movements. She later became a psychologist.
[5] The Conference for Progressive Political Action met in Cleveland on July 4–5, 1924.

to run for president of the U.S. with Burton K. Wheeler[6] as his mate running for vice-president. The difference between these two men was that Robert M. La Follette had definitely broken with the Republican Party—while Wheeler had not left the Democratic Party.

I recall sitting in the big hall in Cleveland waiting to hear Young Bob[7] read his father's speech. His father was a sick man and was unable to be present at this big conference. As I sat next to my very dear friend Ada James from Richland Center, Wisconsin, she leaned over to me to say, "Do you think all these nuts can hang on the same tree?" I wondered too. Later events showed that they couldn't.[8]

After La Follette and Wheeler were nominated the conference broke out in tremendous applause. There were many there who really believed a new era in political life was in the making.

Dear Zona Gale,[9] an ardent supporter of Robert La Follette, came up to us to shake our hand and to say—"Believe me, you Bergers, I know what a sacrifice you have made today!" Both my husband and I couldn't speak but went up to our room and for an hour or more we battled down our emotions so as to get into the spirit of the new political effort. We well knew that the Socialists, who were organized nationally and who had managed to get the election laws in many states permitting the Socialists a column on the ballot, had for this federal election to give the column to the new organization. As a matter of fact, in those states the Progressives ran in the Socialist column. They had to, or not appear on the ballot at all. Well, the up-shot of it all was, we furnished our party organization for the work, we furnished many many speakers and a good share of the financial support for that 1924 campaign. If my memory serves me right, La Follette was supported by more than five million votes.[10] A most auspicious beginning. Would all these nuts continue to hang on the tree? Oh! That remained to be seen.

During the autumn of 1924, my husband and I went to the Panama Canal zone. He was most interested in that project and took the trip in the line of

---

[6] Burton Kendall Wheeler (1882–1975), a Democrat from Montana, served four terms in the U.S. Senate (1923–1947).

[7] Robert M. La Follette Jr. (1895–1953) served as secretary and political adviser to his father (1919–1925). After his father's death, he became a U.S. senator (1925–1947) and a prominent progressive in his own right. He held office as a Republican and, after helping to found Wisconsin's Progressive Party in 1934, a Progressive.

[8] The organization did not create a third party, as Socialists had hoped, and disbanded entirely in February 1925.

[9] Zona Gale (1874–1938) of Portage, Wisconsin, was a novelist and social activist.

[10] La Follette received 4,826,471 popular votes in the 1924 presidential election, about 17 percent of the total.

duty, while I just went along for the vacation it would provide. We went on a little transport boat which carried freight mostly. But there were several very nice passengers on the boat. Two were wives of senators, and the other one which I remember most pleasantly was Miss Morrow, the sister of Dwight Morrow—later the ambassador to Mexico.[11] Miss Morrow tried her best to teach me mah-jongg, but I never mastered that game.

We finally arrived at Port-au-Prince, Haiti, and were met at the dock by two former members of Congress who had given up their political careers to go into sugar-cane raising. One of these men was Mr. Rodenberg, who in 1919 had signed the minority report on the question of denying my husband the right to take his oath of office in 1919.[12]

They took us around the Republic of Haiti, showed us the sugar plantations, the native schools and hospital and such other sites as might interest us. On leaving the same night for the canal district, they presented my husband with two bottles of Haitian rum. My husband was delighted to get their gift, but how was he to bring it into the States under the Prohibition Act? That question bothered him to such an extent that I advised him to throw the stuff over-board. He was shocked and of course refused to do this. The canal was most interesting to us. We saw the locks operate, steamers slowly going through the canal, and [we] were of course interested in the military forces stationed there. The old Panamanian city too fascinated us, as well as the efforts of our government to control malaria.

The time came to return home. And again those two bottles of Haitian rum began to plague us. Really I didn't know quite how Mr. Berger would manage. We had heard of all kinds of smuggling done by officials of the U.S. bringing in great quantities of liquor, and we were a bit nervous too.

However when we arrived, my husband said to the customs official— "Look here, my man—open everything, all the bags and the trunk, but don't open this small hand bag." The official laughed a little and said, "What have you there, Congressman?" "Well, I have a present in there of two bottles of Haitian rum." "Oh! Oho!" said the official, "Is that all?" And marked the bag for entrance. That's how we brought those two bottles into the country. My advice however is not to drink Haitian rum. It just about burns the lining of your stomach. I never saw that Haitian rum again.

[11] Alice Morrow (1871–1940), a teacher, served as trustee and resident director of the American Woman's College in Istanbul, Turkey, from 1928 to 1937. Her brother, Dwight Whitney Morrow (1873–1931), a lawyer, banker, and diplomat, served as U.S. ambassador to Mexico from 1927 to 1930.

[12] According to Meta Berger's February 14, 1925, letter to Doris and Colin Welles, Rodenberg did not meet the Bergers in Haiti, but a friend of his did (Stevens, ed., *Family Letters,* 353).

Back in Washington, life took on a new interest. I plunged right into the work of organizing the progressives of the nation with Isabelle Kendig. I have already mentioned the big conference in 1924 in Cleveland. Nevertheless there was much to do to circularize the nation, to collect the money for postage, rent for the office, salaries for the girls who helped. Isabelle and I went on a money raising campaign. If you have never raised money for a cause, try it sometime. You will soon find out about the difficulties in the way, the prejudices of people, the politeness and the gruffness of being dismissed. One has to have a pretty thick skin to do this kind of work. We would go into the respective offices expecting a contribution of five hundred dollars and come out with twenty-five or fifty dollars. Of course we were deflated somewhat but not at all daunted. I was not a novice at collecting money, but my appeal was always to workers who gave willingly to something they felt was benefiting their class. But to try to get it from the moneyed class—ah! That was different. While we were working in Washington, the Socialist Party was working tooth and nail in Chicago to make that Cleveland meeting a success.

The holidays were approaching and Congress was getting ready for the Christmas recess. We were glad of that as so much depended on my husband's being on the ground at home. In fact, I never knew a more harassed man in Congress. He was burdened so heavily with the financial condition of our daily newspaper. From week to week we never knew whether the pay-roll could be met. Often Elizabeth Thomas would borrow enough to cover the necessary shortage. Then my husband would have to see the advertisers and jolly them along not to cut their space but to increase it. Also we would have to [be] alert to what they called "key" advertisements. These key ads were different from ads placed in the other daily papers. As soon as we noticed these, we would immediately organize a buyers group to go to the respective stores to buy things. This job fell to me. Soon we had a good friend in every section of the city to whom we telephoned, she in turn would call up friends and they again call up more friends, thus forming a sort of chain of buyers. Unfortunately few of our friends had charge accounts. Therefore we asked them also to save their sales slips so we could show the advertiser that the *Leader* was a good medium in which to advertise. All this didn't help us greatly. Soon we noticed that the ad placed in our paper was for expensive furniture which after all is bought only once in many years. Those were some of the difficulties with the merchants in town.

Naturally there were other uncomfortable situations, such as a notification that a car-load of paper was at the freight-yards and please call for [it] at once. Car loads of newspapers cost money. Money had to be borrowed. Banks were not too willing and so the vicious circle went on and on. And well we knew that the life of the Socialist Party depended upon the maintenance of the daily press expressing the minority point of view.

In the meantime, our relaxation from the burdens of life came through the use of our car. Many times we would take a ride away from everything, exploring the countryside and especially the lake front. Thus it came about that we came upon the farm along the shores of Lake Michigan which I particularly loved.[13] This farm was in the hands of a friend of ours who very much wanted to get rid of it and therefore offered it to us. We had no money whatsoever except ten dollars in gold which I had once given to my husband as a Christmas present. Our friend said—"I'll take your gold-piece to bind the bargain." So we suddenly found ourselves the possessors of the farm and an increased mortgage on our house and the prayers that we might be able to hold the farm. Often when I worried about finances, he would say, "If the dear Father in Heaven permits me to live, I'll see to it that you need not worry about the future. I know that under the capitalist system this is necessary and that thus far I haven't done my share toward our old age. Maybe this farm is the best thing I've ever done." With that I had to get what consolation I could.

Just about this time, we received word from Doris that she and Colin were returning from the Philippine Islands, as Colin's malaria condition made it impossible for him to continue living in the tropics. So we awaited most anxiously for their return. No one will ever know how happy we were to greet them as they alighted from the train, minus breakfast, at the Milwaukee railroad station. They had just fifty cents in their pockets and therefore couldn't buy the breakfast on the train. But all that didn't spoil the joy of being together again. It really was a happy reunion.

After many exchanges of views and news, we finally drove them out to the farm to see our latest and what proved to be our best investment. There were two old farm houses on the place. One at the north end built by the farmer himself and one at the south end built by the son who was married and who desired to live and rear his family away from the parental roof. Both houses were sturdily built but just ordinary meager farm houses. The south farm house was vacant, so we offered to remodel it for Colin and Doris and make it habitable with their help. After some doubts and delays the little house was ready and the Welles family moved in.[14] They made it the gathering place for all their friends, and many a jolly time we spent there with the young people. The children did much to improve the place, tearing down an old

---

[13] The farm was located near Thiensville, north of Milwaukee in Ozaukee County. The Bergers bought the farm and adjoining land in 1921 and 1922.

[14] Doris and Colin Welles settled on the farm in 1924 and raised foxes for pelts.

barn, cleaning up the manure piles and the garbage places and beautifying the place as best they could. Also my husband, who loved trees and resented the fact that any farmer could so denude a place of trees for potatoes, began to work with the state forestry department and soon had planted thousands of trees native to the soil of Wisconsin. Now after twenty years we are surrounded by beautiful pine, elm, oak and maple trees. Acres of land thus went back into trees and were no longer in use for cultivation for farm products.

I must say that this farm project was a life-saver, for it took us away, momentarily anyway, from the cares of the paper and the affairs of the Socialist Party as well.

Christmas was spent at home and then plans were made for a return to Washington. If my memory serves me correctly, I did not return to Washington for the short session of Congress; but preferred to stay at home taking up my duties as a member of the school board and the home front. Needless to say, I enjoyed my children too. Later I was sorry I did not go back to Washington with my husband, since it was in the middle of February that he made his maiden speech after he was seated as a member of the House.[15]

The speech was well received. But from that time on Victor Berger's popularity in the House was increasing as time went on. Not that he made any converts to his economic philosophy, but at least his colleagues recognized an honest, sincere and well informed man. The result was that our office was the place for many many members to congregate and discuss the problems of the day and incidentally to know Victor Berger a little better. So life held many pleasant things for us.

The months rolled by, the children fixed up their little house on the farm, and so far the burdens of the past years seemed to be fading out somewhat, although my blond hair never came back. During those fearful days I had turned completely white.

The summer months rolled by all too quickly. With the fall, we made our plans to return to Washington and the winter session of Congress. My daughter Elsa was still at Emergency Hospital and it was good to see her again.

The only social life we had in Washington was an occasional attendance at a White House reception. These we attended just to let the politicians in the capital know that we too were of the official set. I was always pleasantly surprised however at the cordial way in which we were always greeted by each

---

[15] Meta Berger indicated that she might append the speech. Victor Berger spoke on February 16, 1924, against income-tax revision and in favor of measures to alleviate poverty (*Congressional Record*, 68th Cong., 1st sess., 65, pt. 3:2625–2631). This was not his first speech in Congress but the first speech after the denial of his seat in 1919. Victor gave his first speech on June 14, 1911 (*Congressional Record*, 62d Cong., 1st sess., 47, pt. 2:2026–2030).

president. Perhaps cordiality and pleasant and warm hand-shaking is a wonderful asset to have as a political asset. This quality applied to all, from President William H. Taft through silent Calvin Coolidge. The only one who couldn't unbend was Herbert Hoover.

Back in Washington, I renewed my friendship with Isabelle Kendig. By this time I found out that she was the wife of Howard Gill[16] and the mother of three lusty boys. Our friendship grew closer with time and trial. Howard was charming, bright and cordial and seemed to be the most devoted of husbands. However it was not long before he became too devoted an admirer of my daughter Doris. This troubled me greatly. It troubled Isabelle too. So my job, it seemed, was to stand by Isabelle, who was expecting her fourth baby, and to try to help Doris at the same time.

It was about this time that Sir Oswald Mosley[17] (the present fascist leader in England), then a devoted admirer of Ramsay MacDonald[18] and Socialist leader, came to Washington and got in touch with us. His mission in Washington was to study conditions here in the United States, to have an interview with the late Senator Borah,[19] [and] to meet Chief Justice William Howard Taft,[20] who it seems was present at the marriage with Lady Cynthia's mother and father, the late Lord and Lady Curzon, formerly the viceroy of India.[21] We did what we could to introduce the Mosleys and to see that they had a pleasant time while in Washington.

It so happened that my daughter Elsa, the doctor, had finished the internship in both hospitals, the Emergency and the Episcopal Ear, Eye and Nose Hospital, and was then preparing to go to Europe for a year of post graduate work at the Vienna Krankenhaus and in other European centers. So Doris came down to Washington for a farewell visit and thus also met the Mosleys. A sort of friendship began then with the result that the Mosleys, after a brief trip to

---

[16] Howard B. Gill (1889–1989) was an industrial consultant and later a prison reformer.

[17] Oswald Ernald Mosley (1896–1980) of Great Britain began his political career as a Conservative in 1918, became an Independent in 1923, joined the Labour Party in 1924, formed the leftist New Party in 1931, and organized the British Union of Fascists in 1932. He served in Parliament (1918–1924 and 1926–1931) and was a powerful speaker. He served three years in prison during World War II.

[18] James Ramsay MacDonald (1866–1937) served as a member of Parliament (1906–1918, 1922–1935, and 1936–1937) and as the first Labour Party prime minister of Great Britain (1924 and 1929–1935).

[19] Borah was chairman of the Senate Committee on Foreign Relations at this time.

[20] William Howard Taft, former president of the United States, was appointed chief justice by President Harding in 1921.

[21] Cynthia Blanche Curzon Mosley (1898–1933), Oswald Mosley's wife, served as a Labour member of Parliament from 1929 to 1931. She joined the New Party in 1931 (eight months before completing her term in Parliament) and the British Union of Fascists in 1932. Her parents, George Nathaniel Curzon (1859–1925) and Mary Victoria Leiter Curzon, married in April 1895 in Washington, D.C. Her father served as viceroy of India from 1898 to 1905 and as British foreign secretary from 1919 to 1924.

Florida, wished to come to Wisconsin to stop for a week-end with Doris and Colin at the farm. The one good result was that the infatuation for Howard Gill was knocked into a cocked hat.

Before leaving us, Sir Oswald and Lady Cynthia invited Doris and Colin to come to England as their guests to attend the English labor school that summer. So after they left—I began to make plans that both children should go to Europe. Elsa had already left and was in Vienna.

After a little time had elapsed I went to my husband and said, "I have never asked you for a specific sum of money, have I?" "No, indeed," was his reply—"But what is on your mind?" "Well—I now want five hundred dollars in one sum." "What? What is this! What in all the world do you want with so much money?" "Well, I'll tell you after you give me five hundred dollars." Needless to say—I got the money. It was to be used for a one-cabin steamship ticket to go to London. My husband was not opposed to the trip but couldn't understand my insistence for this trip to Europe. Many weeks later, I told him why it was necessary to give Doris a different and new out-look on life and the affairs of living.

Also I had always determined that my children must get to Europe some-how, ever since I had been there and had seen the art-galleries, the people of other lands etc. etc. So it was settled. Both children had a wonderful experi-ence—Doris meeting the members of the English Labour Party from Ramsay MacDonald down and participating in the labor school for that summer, Elsa in the meantime making friends with her professional friends and meeting some of our associates and comrades.

Finally word came to us that Doris had declined being the guest of the Mosleys any longer and had looked up Elsa, who was now in Paris. So both girls had the experience of living in Paris on very little money, Elsa having to share her allowance with Doris for the time being.

Word also came to us that Elsa had fallen in love with a young Dutchman. Naturally we were disturbed and cabled Doris to send us her opinion since she too had met Jan Edelman[22] in Paris. The answering cable had a short message: "Elsa lucky." And so we had to content ourselves with that.

Doris returned to the States some months earlier. Elsa still lingered on in Europe, spending her time in the clinics in Berlin, Frankfurt and Paris. I'm afraid she had rather a good time in Paris, where she had made French friends formerly attached to the French embassy in Washington and who were now

[22] Jan Edelman (1900–1963) of the Netherlands married Elsa Berger on February 1, 1927, at the Bergers' Milwaukee home. The couple settled in Milwaukee in 1930 and had no children. Jan studied at the University of Wisconsin and received a bachelor's degree in electrical engineering in 1935.

showing her Paris. In due time however she too came home in December, and a month later Jan followed. The result was that on February 1 of the next year Jan and Elsa were married. They made their home in Boston.

Upon my return to Washington, I joined the Women's International League for Peace and Freedom. This organization was the result of a conference called by the women of the countries at war during World War I at Amsterdam, Holland.[23] These good women met with the one purpose of ending that war if possible. These women were socially minded, sincere and serious about the task that confronted them. America had also sent women to that conference, the most prominent of whom was the renowned and beloved Jane Addams.

At the close of the conference a number of proposals was drawn up to be presented to the respective governments of the then warring nations. Jane Addams was the chosen one to present these proposals to Woodrow Wilson. There were fourteen proposals.

Upon arrival back in the U.S., Jane Addams presented her document to the president of the U.S., who politely accepted them and pocketed them. It was some months later when, according to Miss Addams, she was called to Washington for a conference with President Wilson. There Mr. Wilson pulled out her former proposals pretty much thumbed through! Later the famous fourteen points accepted by the president contained at least nine of the proposals of the declaration which was the result of the Amsterdam conference.

One of the constructive results also [of] that international conference was the formation of the Women's International League for Peace and Freedom, with headquarters in Geneva, Switzerland. Naturally the women could not again meet for some time.

Finally the American branch invited the European members of the league to a conference in Washington, offering to pay the expenses of those members of the Central Powers who were destitute due to the inflationary period and its terrible results.[24]

It was at this time, at this conference, that I became a member of the national executive committee of the WIL, as the league was generally called. Now I had the opportunity to know some of the finest women and the most courageous women of the world. They were idealists and certainly not in any sense subversive, as Mr. Dies[25] would have you believe. What they wanted was

[23] The International Congress of Women was held in The Hague, Netherlands, on April 28–May 1, 1915. Women from both neutral and warring countries established the Women's International League for Peace and Freedom (WILPF) at the conference.

[24] The WILPF's fourth international congress was held in Washington, D.C., on May 1–7, 1924.

[25] Martin Dies (1900–1972), a Democratic representative from Texas (1930–1945 and 1952–1959),

a war-less world and they wanted to achieve this by arbitration and by complete understanding. They knew all about imperialistic wars, but when it came to getting at the root of all causes—i.e., the economic struggle due to the internal causes which lead up to imperialism—well, they sort of soft-peddled the issues. Most of the women were Quakers or sympathizers. But they were fine and self-sacrificing and hard working. There was Mrs. William I. Hull, Mrs. Lucy Biddle [Lewis], Mildred Scott Olmsted, Mrs. Raymond Clapper and many others, including the wonderful beautiful and courageous Katherine Devereux Blake.[26] Katherine Blake was always an inspiration to me. She was not always tactful, but she was by far the most intelligent and hard working of all. And it was in Katherine Blake that I found a life-long and beloved friend. It was with Katherine Blake that years later I went to the disarmament conference held in Geneva in 1932. Dorothy Thompson spoke for us, as did Mary E. Woolley, who represented the U.S. at Geneva.[27] I pay tribute to Miss Woolley. I see her name signed to so many good causes on letter heads that come to me. She has courage besides position and intelligence.

I had never taken the absolutist pledge that I would never support a war. As a Socialist I had learned that as the development of our scheme of life on the economic field [progressed], that there may have to be a final conflict between those who work and those who exploit and if that time ever came, I would quite naturally take my place with my class. But in the meantime I would do my utmost to bring every possible effort to enlighten the world and to bring about the cessation of war and to bring to the attention of these good women the point of view of the working people and their endeavor to wring from the exploiters better working conditions and more freedom in their up-hill fight.

---

built his political career on anticommunism. In 1938 he proposed the establishment of the House Special Committee on Un-American Activities, which was called the Dies Committee while under his leadership (1938–1945).

[26] Hannah Clothier Hull (1872–1958), Lucy Biddle Lewis (1861–1941), Mildred Scott Olmsted (1890–1990), Olive Ewing Clapper (1896–1968), and Katherine Devereux Blake (1858–1950) served with Meta Berger on the national board of the WILPF's U.S. section. Hull headed the U.S. section (1924–1928 and 1933–1939) and chaired the national board (1929–1933). Lewis also headed the U.S. section (1922–1924) and chaired the budget and office committee. Olmsted served as national organization secretary (1934–1946), administrative secretary (1946–1964), and executive director (1964–1966); she also served on the international executive committee. Clapper was national treasurer (1933?–1936?); she later became a writer, a lecturer, and the director of a foreign relief agency. Blake, a reform-minded New York City public-school teacher and principal, chaired the WILPF's national committee on education.

[27] Dorothy Thompson (1893–1961) was a prominent journalist and outspoken Nazi critic. Mary Emma Woolley (1863–1947) was a college president and peace activist. Both served on the national advisory council of the WILPF's U.S. section.

For ten years, the constant aim of the WIL was for a war-less world with little attention paid to labor's struggle. I continued to work with these ladies until Hitler began his reign of terror and until the Republicans of Spain were fighting to maintain their efforts for democracy. Then I was voted out of the national committee of the WIL,[28] although the idol of the WIL, Gertrude Baer,[29] was an exile from Germany in this country and who took the same position I had taken on the international situation. This was sometime between 1934 and later. I was now determined to fight to abolish all the things that were in the way of peace in the world. That means fascism and Nazism and all the things which brought about World War II. The trouble is that most of these ladies belonged to the comfortable—even well-to-do—middle class.

It is queer too, that it was so difficult to get the money to carry on work against these evil forces. The people who were sympathetic to the cause had money but no courage to give. We had to resort to card parties, begging for prizes, rummage sales, and what not to work for our very small budget to carry on the work which meant so much to the world had we measured even a small progress.

Meanwhile, my children Doris and her husband were settled in the little house on the farm, Elsa and Jan were located in Boston, Elsa struggling to establish herself in medicine, and my husband making a very good record for himself in Congress. His colleagues came to respect him more and more and his office became a bureau of information. Without the faithful Marx Lewis this would have been more difficult than it was. But Marx was the most dependable secretary we could positively have had.

One of the great pleasures I had in Washington was to cook big juicy steaks for us and for Congressman Voigt of Sheboygan, the only man who had had the courage to cast his lonely vote to seat Mr. Berger at the first denial of his right to a seat in the House. It was fun to see the men race to finish their steak and to hear the unanimity of opinion on the questions of the day as well as on the character and ability of their colleagues in the House.

During all these months and years, I had always felt that the succeeding Congresses ought to clear the record and to make restitution to my husband for the action of denying him his seat. But I was always met by the response, "Not yet. Give me and them time. But as sure as I live, the time will come when the House will recognize the error that was made and will do something

---

[28] Meta Berger is still listed as a member of the national board in 1936 but is not listed subsequently.

[29] Gertrude Baer (1890–1981) was a leader in the German section of the WILPF and a member of the WILPF international executive committee. She served as co-chair of the international organization from 1929 to 1946. In 1933 she escaped Germany for Geneva and then New York (ca. 1939); after the war she returned to Geneva and served as the WILPF liaison to the United Nations.

to recognize representative government again. Just be patient!" So I had to be patient as he would do nothing about it.[30]

Then, another campaign loomed on the horizon. Once more we had to prepare ourselves and again William H. Stafford was our opponent. This was in the early fall of 1928. Unfortunately I was sent to bed with a bad heart and had to stay there during the entire campaign. I did what I could to suggest and help. My husband's over optimism scared me. He was so certain of re-election. My daughter Doris took part in the campaign and made a good record for herself as a speaker. At the last moment I did so want to have my husband send out another 5,000 postal cards giving Mr. Stafford's record on woman's suffrage but was laughed at, saying that was an unnecessary expenditure of money, as the election was as good as won. But it happened to be a presidential year and in order to vote for Victor Berger folks had to split their ticket. And to the surprise of everyone, even those who had intended to vote for Victor Berger, the election was lost to us. All the days following the days after election well-meaning people called us up to tell us how very sorry they were that they forgot to split their ticket. Of course we were disappointed—but not for long. Often I compared my husband to a rubber-ball—the harder you hit him; the higher he would bound.

Mr. B. went back to Washington to relinquish his office. His colleagues were fine. They were actually sorry to see him go. Many called at the office and some made speeches on the floor of the House. I am enclosing just one to show you a little—how changed was their attitude now from that of a few years ago when the nation was still gripped by the past war hysteria.[31]

I was sorry too—we had not yet started to straighten out the record—I was so anxious to have a clean slate for my husband and for representative government. He however always said, "Not yet. Give me time. The time will come!"

There was much to do and he began his work at once. The *Leader* took the major part of our energy.

We were interested in our children's new start in life. There was the farm and the planting of some 20,000 trees, and there still was the work on the board of education for me. Not only that, during the past years I had [had] the high privilege of serving on several other boards, such as the central Board

---

[30] Congress passed a bill making restitution to Victor Berger's heirs in 1934.

[31] Fiorello La Guardia, a Republican representative from New York, paid tribute to Victor Berger in a March 4, 1929, speech. La Guardia noted that Victor had been a pioneer, performing a necessary, though unenviable, task: "Many of the policies and principles he has advocated have been adopted and accepted and some of them do not appear so extreme and radical to-day" (*Congressional Record*, 70th Cong., 2d sess., 70, pt. 5:5236).

of Education, a year on the Board of Normal School Regents and six years on the Board of University Regents.[32] Serving on these various boards was an education for me in itself. I felt I got as much as I gave and I really did give all I had in the way of bringing a little democracy into the management of the institution.

During the following summer I spent a few days with my sister at her cottage on Shawano Lake. Our own cottage had been sold some years ago. The children felt they had out-grown our cottage and had other interests. I however always got a good rest and relaxation at the lake. So to relieve the strain at home I went on a short vacation. While there I was suddenly called to come back to Milwaukee at once. My husband had met with an accident and was injured. Not knowing the extent of the injury—we drove home only to find my husband unconscious at the Emergency Hospital. He had met with a street-car accident and had received a base-skull fracture in addition to other minor though also serious injuries. Everyone was exceedingly kind to me, but the fact that the reporters [were] hovering outside of the room in which my husband lay scared me no-end. I guess I was pretty naive about injuries for I hoped and prayed that that man with his fine constitution would recover. Elsa, my youngest daughter, was traveling around in Europe by car. I didn't quite know where she might be, but a member of the press said, "Don't worry, Mrs. Berger—we will find her." And find her they did. By evening of that first day I received a cable from her that she was boarding a steamer to return at once.

For three weeks, my husband hovered between life and death. The four doctors were hopeful at times and then again they told me it would be better for him if he did not recover. All I could do was to stand by in hope and despair. Finally on [August 7, 1929], I was called at 5:00 A.M. to come at once to the hospital. My husband died that morning. I should have been prepared for that event, but somehow I wasn't. I was overwhelmed with shock—too shocked to think of anything but my loss. I didn't then nor for months after realize what it meant to lose the mainstay of the family and the prop upon which I had leaned so long. I had lost my husband and my comrade.

Again everyone was kind. President Hoover sent messages, Governor Kohler[33] sent [a] message, the legislature of the state adjourned as a tribute, as did the Common Council of Milwaukee. I remember a slight surprise at these tributes because they came from the opposite political camp. But what did it matter now? I was so desolate, so unable to carry on, so alone!

---

[32] Meta Berger served on the Wisconsin Board of Education from 1917 to 1919, on the Wisconsin Board of Regents of Normal Schools from 1927 to 1928, and on the University of Wisconsin Board of Regents from 1928 to 1934.

[33] Walter J. Kohler (1875–1940), a Republican, served as governor of Wisconsin from 1929 to 1931.

A month later the thought came to me that like so many others, I could either sink completely, or I could pull myself up by my own boot-straps. And then I knew what my husband would have me do. So I tried to pick up life and work again. I then set about to find out how I stood financially and just what my interest in the *Milwaukee Leader* was. Then I found out that I held the majority of the out-standing stock. My next move was to take the train for New York where the National Executive Committee of the Socialist Party was meeting. I approached the committee, asking them to take over the management of the *Milwaukee Leader*—the only daily English socialist paper in the country. The committee had had sad experiences with papers and financing them and were therefore unwilling to take over. This in my humble [opinion] was a great mistake, but that was their decision. In place of taking over the *Leader,* they showed me the courtesy of electing me to the national committee to fill the vacancy caused by my husband's death. The news of that action found its way into the New York papers. As a result, the next morning I received a caller, Mr. Arthur Brisbane, who knew, loved and respected Victor Berger. After the usual condolence remarks, Mr. Brisbane inquired of me—who owned the *Milwaukee Leader*? When I told him I held the majority of the outstanding stock; he made me an offer to buy the paper, provided I pay all the debts first. This of course I could not do and I would not do in any event. I had visions of seeing Mr. Hearst merging the *Milwaukee Sentinel,* the *Evening Wisconsin News* and the *Milwaukee Leader* into one large Hearst merger.[34] And since we did not approve of Hearst and his policies, it was inconceivable to me to let our working class paper slip away from us and become a Hearst vehicle. That, indeed, would be selling out the working class for a mess of pottage. So I frankly told Mr. Brisbane. He was quite provoked with me saying, "Don't be a fool! You cannot run the paper, the workers cannot run a paper. I know what it means to run a daily newspaper." But I was firm and refused. I could never again face my comrades again.

So I left New York—came home and reported my conversation to Mr. Thomas Duncan,[35] who temporarily had taken over the business managership. None of us knew what the future held for us. But for the present we were hanging on. Fearful months lay ahead.

Then one January morning, a telegram came from Arthur Brisbane asking me to meet him at the Blackstone Hotel for a conference. Mr. Duncan said for

[34] In 1918 Brisbane had purchased Milwaukee's *Evening Wisconsin, Daily News,* and *Free Press,* which he merged into the *Wisconsin News* and then sold to Hearst in 1919.

[35] Thomas M. Duncan (1893–1959) served in the Wisconsin Assembly from 1923 to 1929 and in the Wisconsin Senate from 1929 to 1932. He was secretary to Mayor Daniel Hoan (1920–1929) and to Republican (later Progressive) Governor Philip F. La Follette (1931–1933 and 1935–1938).

me to go. Possibly we could salvage something for those faithful ones who had so loyally supported us with what little they had. So once again I met Arthur Brisbane. This time he went right to the point of his mission. He offered to buy my stock for $100,000, no questions asked, and that he would invest the $100,000 dollars with his own fortune at 5 percent interest annually. It was a flattering offer and I would never again have to worry about rent or bills. But of course I refused again. Not even for such comfort and security could I sell out the cause of the working class to Mr. Hearst. Naturally Mr. Brisbane was disappointed. I never saw him again, although I have reason to believe that he still had a very warm personal interest in Victor Berger's family.[36]

After my report back, I was asked to go out to raise funds for the maintenance of the paper. In a small, very small measure I was successful, but it was not long before I knew we couldn't hold on. It was while I was on one of these money raising trips that upon my return home, I found the *Milwaukee Leader* sold. I was told by Mr. Duncan that he was compelled to let it go because notes held by certain paper companies were going to foreclose.[37]

Fortunately for me, our friends on the *Jewish Daily Vorwärts* in New York had undertaken to take care of my stock at a very nominal price.[38]

My consternation and surprise knew no bounds. Our paper, the life of the Socialist Party of Wisconsin, the paper for which we had sacrificed so very much and over which we had spent so many harrowing and sleepless nights, was gone. The new purchaser, Mr. Paul Holmes,[39] who had formerly worked for the *Milwaukee Sentinel* and who had lost his job with that paper, became the new owner and manager. He not having the necessary funds to carry on, immediately formed a new corporation and began to sell stock for his paper. Well—that didn't last long either. But that's his story.

Meanwhile I did what I could to busy myself with school work, party work, club work, and what not.

[36] Doris Berger Hursley wrote in her unpublished biography of her father that "Brisbane and [Victor] Berger made a secret contract that if the revolution came before Brisbane and his family died, Berger would protect the wife and children. If capitalism survived Berger's death, Brisbane would do the same for Berger's family" (Roll 12, VLB Papers [microfilm]).

[37] The Socialists lost control of the *Milwaukee Leader* in June 1938 after the newspaper's debts became too great to bear. According to Frederick I. Olson, three unfriendly buyers of a *Leader* note forced the owners to foreclose when payment could not be made ("The Milwaukee Socialists, 1897–1941" [Ph.D. diss., Harvard University, 1952], 558).

[38] Meta Berger and Elizabeth Thomas recovered 75 percent of the value of their stock. Many others lost their investments in the newspaper.

[39] Paul Holmes, a lawyer, worked as city editor and executive editor for the *Milwaukee Sentinel* in the 1930s. In 1938 he became vice president of the Wisconsin Guardian Publishing Company and editor of the *New Milwaukee Leader*. He returned to his law practice in 1939.

In the spring of 1932, the great and only disarmament conference was called in Geneva, Switzerland. Possessed of a restless spirit, still interested in WIL work, I became one of the delegates from America to go to attend that conference. Katherine Devereux Blake and I were traveling companions. I was one of the luckiest persons in my fellow-travelers. Katherine, tall, slender as a reed, beautiful to look at, intelligent and full of courage, was an inspiration to me through the entire four months of our trip. She knew Europe well and could speak French and English while I [unfinished].

CHAPTER 13

Russia

Early in the year of 1935 I received a letter from the Friends of the Soviet Union inviting me to come to Russia as the guest of the trade unions of the USSR, asking only that I pay my own expenses to Russia and back and that I receive a credential from the Socialist Party of Wisconsin.

I was surprised of course. But since I was then a member of the executive committee of the Socialist Party of Wisconsin I thought I might try to secure that credential, although I knew perfectly well that our party was very hostile to the USSR.

I was also looking for an escape from my home conditions, since my daughter Doris had divorced her husband and since the divorce had naturally created some dissension in the family.[1] I had very foolishly tried to prevent that procedure, since I was fond of my son-in-law and I believed that the children (there were two little girls) might suffer. In this I was mistaken and it was not long before I realized the error of trying to influence or shape the lives of adult children. To this day I regret my opposition and the dissension it caused. One lives and learns. My old fashioned ideals were shot and I had to make my own re-adjustment.

So I naturally looked for an escape. And this invitation seemed to be the opportunity.

Consequently I requested the credentials from the party, only to be re-buffed by a "Ha! Ha! Try and get it." This put me on my mettle and I said,

[1] Doris and Colin Welles divorced in March 1935. A year later Doris married Frank M. Hursley (1902–1989), chairman of the English Department at the University of Wisconsin Extension Division in Milwaukee. The Hursleys moved to California in 1946 and worked as scriptwriters. They had one daughter, Bridget.

"You are very silly in your attitude about sending one of our people to find out about Russia. But since you refuse I will get my credentials from my own union." This was a surprise to my silly comrades and they inquired, "And what union do you belong to?" "To the Teachers' Union," I replied. "OK, get the paper from them." So I did.

So after much correspondence with the Friends of the Soviet Union, I finally sent to New York the money for a third class ticket on the *Ile de France* for Europe and Russia. When the day came to meet the other members of the delegation, I found I was one of twelve: a doctor from North Carolina; a steel worker from Pennsylvania; two coal miners from West Virginia; two textile workers from New Jersey and Massachusetts; an electrician from New York; two farmers, one from Wisconsin and one from Michigan; a librarian from New York; a colored man representing the colored students; and myself. We all met the night before the boat sailed.

This was my first experience traveling third class. My children were much concerned because I was a poor traveler at best, and they urged me to take another boat, travel in comfort, and meet the delegation in London. This however I declined to do, since I was representing labor too and didn't wish to enjoy any special privilege.

On the night we boarded the boat, which by the way was very comfortable, I was suddenly seized with panic and began to weep. I, who had always been so loyal to the Socialist Party, I, who had all the prejudices the party held against Russia, what was I doing now, breaking with my own party, violating the discipline of my own group? Oh! What a mistake I was making! I think if I could, I would have gone back on land. But the organizer of this expedition, Herbert Goldfrank,[2] saw me and came to embrace me and tell me not to regret my decision, since I would get the thrill of my life etc. etc. So he said!

I suddenly realized too, that to appraise the Soviet experiment pre-supposes a knowledge of the economic systems which motivated both the capitalistic profitmaking exploiting systems of individual enterprise and the attempt to organize and socialize industry and business and agriculture in the interest of the common good. To reach a fair judgment too, one had to know the Russia of the czars and the primitive millions who were little better than slaves and illiterates who comprised the vast majority of the Russian people.

Also I was fully aware of the evolutionary process the Socialist Party had adopted of educating the masses and getting through democratic parliamentary action the utopia we all hoped for.[3] A revolution such as that which the Rus-

---

[2] Herbert Goldfrank was national secretary of the Friends of the Soviet Union, U.S. Section.

[3] Miriam Frink added here: "Victor Berger [said], 'A slow process but if it takes one hundred years I'd rather wait than go through such a slaughter as a revolution brings.' Meta Berger drilled in this idea."

sians had carried on was furthest from our thoughts. Also, we here in America were not quite familiar nor ready to adopt the Russian tactics because we couldn't put ourselves in the place of the starving freezing Russian workers who quite spontaneously revolted when their husbands, brothers and sweethearts were left without the material with which to carry on the war in 1917. So the workers at home started the revolution. Furthermore we Bergers in 1917 were in such deep trouble ourselves that I felt wholly incompetent.[4]

Anyway I went and for several days out on the ocean I was troubled. Then came a resolution that the least I could do was to be honest, honest with myself, honest with my party and honest about conditions in Russia. After that I felt better. Also I was under no obligation to speak for Russia or for the new economic system over there if I did not voluntarily choose to do so.

After we all got our sea-legs, we naturally got better acquainted. Then each of us pulled out of our pockets the numerous questions we all wanted to ask, for we were told to ask and ask, no matter how simple the questions might be; we were to ask them, and the answers were to be given us by the members of the Russian trade unions.

We soon found many duplications. So our librarian took all papers and organized our questions according to topics and typed them for us. When we reached Plymouth, each delegate was provided with neat typed pages of questions arranged according to topics, i.e., one [each] on divorce, religion, wages, cost of living, rents, housing, children, schools, education etc.

From Plymouth via third class coach we proceeded to London, where again the steam ship company took us to what I consider a third class hotel, near Russell Square.[5] This hotel was plain but clean and not used by the average tourists who quite naturally sought the bigger and better hotels in the downtown districts. Here the week-end guests from Wales or Scotland put up. Food was very simple and we had the same things to eat at every meal.

We spent two days in London. Those delegates who didn't know much about London or traveling spent much of their time buying post-cards from street vendors. I had been elected the treasurer for the delegates, and since each delegate had twenty-five dollars over and above their steam-ship tickets; they had to come to me for any spending money.

---

[4] Miriam Frink added here: "1917 facing Judge Landis. Had heard Anna Louise Strong, and stories of the famine." On the side Meta Berger or Miriam Frink added: "Looking ahead?" Miriam Frink also added on a separate sheet: "In reaching a judgment on Russia one must realize and recognize the tremendous effort Russians put in and what the revolution has accomplished. Not to go as a tourist—expecting all [medicines?] and luxuries of USA."

[5] Miriam Frink added here: "Meta Berger first time in England."

However Martha K.,[6] the librarian, and I were so anxious to see the Houses of Parliament, Big Ben, 10 Downing Street and Piccadilly Circus etc., that we shifted for ourselves and saw as much of London and vicinity, including Buckingham Palace and other notable places, as possible.

I have forgotten the day the bus came to take us to the 5,000 ton Russian steamer which was moored on the docks near the warehouses on the Lower Thames; but it is needless to say we were all curious and thrilled.

We soon left the Thames and were out in the North Sea. Our little Russian steamer looked tiny indeed and very simple after the luxury liner *Ile de France,* but it was comfortable. Most of the delegates were quartered in the lower part of the boat. But while I climbed down into the hold I fell and slipped down the steep stairway. I was only bruised, but promptly the captain of the boat assigned a stateroom to me on the main deck. Thus my age was recognized and I was most comfortable.

The boat boasted of very good staterooms, fine linens and blankets, a good dining room, and a salon where we gathered evenings around the piano, wrote letters or did anything we wished.

We discovered now that the rooms for the sailors, crew, deck-hands and stewardesses were the same as ours, the meals served to these people of the sea were the same meals served to us, and to our great surprise the seamen and crew had a lounge and library as large as the guest salon where the workers could rest, play games, read etc.

We were all invited to be the guests of the crew in their lounge. Here we had a most interesting evening listening to Russian music, seeing Russian dancing and drinking Russian tea. We discovered too that there was no class distinction whatsoever. Naturally we wanted to know who then was in control. The skipper was in control and his word was law while the ship was on the high seas, but every day a conference was held and complaints if there were any were submitted. If the skipper did not think the criticisms were justified, he governed. However if the crew wished to appeal from the decision made, then it had the right upon landing to appeal to a governing body.

The meals on the boat were excellent. Perhaps the smooth North Sea helped us to enjoy them also, for I had always heard that the North Sea did not always behave so well.

We were approaching the Kiel Canal. Some of the more leftish delegates wanted to sing Russian songs and the "Internationale" while passing through the canal, but upon entering that area, the captain of the ship sent word that while passing through foreign and not friendly territory there must be no

[6] Martha Koopman, a New York Socialist.

demonstration of any kind. So like good guests all passengers respected the command. It was exciting to go through the canal. Very nice neat little farms bordered each side of the canal. All houses were flying the swastika and one felt at once the power of the Nazi rule. We stopped twice for business or other reasons. At each stopping place German wine vendors or cigarette sellers offered their wares. And strange to say American cigarettes were cheaper at the Kiel Canal than in any American city. Some of our passengers indulged in wine and cigarettes. I couldn't bring myself to encourage even so little a trade with the Nazis.

Finally we entered the Baltic Sea and freezing temperature. The Baltic Sea impressed me as being beautiful and was dotted with islands every now and then. It was however much too cold to stay on the open deck long. Towards evening we entered the Gulf of Finland. The moon was full, the night icy cold, but our hearts beat a little faster for in the far distance we had seen the domes and spires of St. Peter and Paul glistening in the evening sunlight. We were about ready to retire for the night, expecting an early landing the next day, when our boat stopped. We discovered we were ice-bound in the Gulf of Finland and had to wait for the ice-breaker to come down from Leningrad to break a path for us. Of course no one went to bed. To be ice-bound in the Gulf of Finland is an experience in itself. So we waited, went out doors every now and then to look for the ice-breaker. About 2:00 A.M. it came and went to work. There was a crunching grinding sound and a booming off to the right and left as the ice buckled up, but a path was made and we began to proceed very slowly.

The next day we docked at a pier some distance from Leningrad in Russia. To my great surprise, as we came down the gangplank there was a little band of workers dressed up in caps and scarves and mittens and heavy overshoes and old worn coats, greeting us with American jazz. What I really expected to hear was the inspiring "Internationale"—certainly not American jazz. As soon as this music ceased, a worker stepped forward and in Russian greeted us. We did not of course understand one word of it; but just then an American girl who had formerly lived in New Jersey and who had gone to Russia after the revolution stepped forward as interpreter. The American delegation then asked me to reply to the welcoming speech.

This done, we proceeded to the customs house where the usual inspection took place. The officials were extremely strict. Finally, our bags having passed inspection, the customs official came upon our typed questionnaires. This was new to him, and since he couldn't read English he confiscated all our copies for fear that the material contained might be anti-Soviet propaganda. Our copy turned up much later during our visit while we were in Moscow.

While waiting our turn to pass the customs inspection we had a chance, our first chance, to see an Amtorg.[7] Here were gathered every conceivable article for sale. Beautiful oriental rugs, jewelry, fur coats, icons and whatnot to tempt the tourist. I myself wanted to buy a beautiful icon set in mother of pearl for a good friend of mine, but I checked my impulse, thinking, I will see many more in Russia and that it was foolish to spend $1,000 for the first icon I saw. So I resisted that temptation.

Finally, all formalities having been complied with, we got into a bus and rode miles and miles through lumber yards. Lumber cut and ready for shipment piled high on each side of the road. Upon arriving at the city proper we were taken to a hotel, not a first class hotel, but I believe a second class one judged by Russian standards. There were five women assigned to one room with a bath in the corridor outside of the room. But it was a bath, for which we were all duly grateful.

After a change of clothes, our interpreters were waiting for us to take us to dinner. As we approached the lobby and dining room we saw the "Red Corner" which every hotel has. The Red Corner is the library or reading room and contains a life-sized statue of Lenin, sometimes a bust of Stalin, and many pictures of pre-revolutionary Russia as well as maps, diagrams and pictures of reconstructed Russia. The Red Corner was always the meeting place for delegates and interpreters to plan each day's program.

After a sumptuous dinner in an attractive dining room, our guides took us to a late Russian theater. It was a good performance, but had it not been for the explanations the whole performance would have been lost.

After the theater, our guides bade us good night, saying—"Tomorrow, if you don't mind, we will treat you as regular tourists, for it is quite possible you won't know what to ask for; but after you have been here twenty-four or thirty-six hours, you will have gathered your thoughts and then you tell us just what you would like to see." That was very considerate and we were grateful. But the thought of going to bed was farthest from our thoughts. So we went out into the night to see Leningrad. And what a sight to see! Leningrad was as gay, as busy, as crowded at 2:00 A.M. as it was at 2:00 P.M. Then we discovered that Leningrad works twenty-four hours each day and that workers' shifts were changing all night as well as all day.

Two of our delegates didn't like being shown around by the interpreters. Their first reaction was—"We'll give them all day to see Russia, but by God the night belongs to us." I was a little shocked by this attitude, so Martha K.

---

[7] Amtorg Trading Company was founded in New York in 1924 for organizing trade with the Soviet Union; it was financed by Soviet foreign trade organizations.

and I decided to take these two youngsters under our personal supervision, and little chance did they have after that to carouse or visit Russian girls.

And now just a word about the type of people who were delegates. None of our group was a member of the Communist Party, but all had some union-labor experience. Only two or three had a knowledge of what the economic system over there meant, nor on what philosophy it was based. In fact my personal opinion was that more articulate, better informed delegates might have been sent. But I realize too, that the two trips twice a year were to educate the workers. Anyway we had to work with what we had, and I must say before our month was over every delegate was duly impressed and I believe better men with something constructive to think about.

The next morning, we met in the Red Corner to meet our guides who took us sightseeing, as per agreement. Thus we saw palaces, prison of St. Peter and Paul, churches, the University of Leningrad, the busy streets and over-crowded streetcars, the canals and parks. Also saw the homes of peasants and workers before the revolution which were left no doubt to compare them with the new yet still overcrowded apartment houses. It was all most interesting. And one can really appreciate that the workers who lived in a thatched roof hut with a mud floor some distance away from running water without lights are happier now that they live in well-lighted, albeit crowded, apartment houses, sharing the kitchen and bathrooms with other families. Only to touch a button to get light. Only to turn a faucet to get water. Yes these workers were happy now, even though luxury was not even in sight.

Poverty too was not yet abolished and clothes and shoes were scarce, as one could readily see by peasants who had come in with their feet still wrapped in burlap bags and rope. But these people were not aware of the things they didn't have. All, men and women, were only too happy to help their country with the reconstruction program.

The next morning we met our guides who thought that by this time we delegates had made up our minds as to what we wanted to see. Martha K. of course wanted to see the libraries, I was interested in the schools and the children and the kind of teachers they had. The coal miners wanted to see coal mines, the farmers desired to visit farms, the textile workers were anxious to see textile factories etc. So the guide said, "You shall see all, but since we haven't guides enough to do this all the first day, suppose we form groups. Those who wish to see farms and mines in one group, those who wish to see our cultural life and our factories in another group." We agreed of course. Now began the most intensive study and sightseeing I've ever done. To begin with, we dis-covered illiteracy was a thing of the past. Education was compulsory for every child up to fourteen years of age. All education was subsidized by the government. If a youth or girl desired to go beyond the regular grammar school, he or she was permitted to do so, all expenses paid by the government. If the youngsters desired to go into a factory, they were given a choice of work, and if, after having tried out certain machines or lathes, the worker desired to improve himself still further, the factory foreman sent him upstairs to the factory library to continue his studies along technical lines and so on until the youngster became a skilled worker. Each factory maintained a complete technical library and the youngster was paid his regular wage while learning his trade. It is little wonder that now during this World War II the Russian worker is able to accomplish so much.

Also in each factory, the workers maintained marvelous club houses[8] where lectures, concerts, movies, [and] drama were held besides the dance halls and the dining halls. Also each club house was equipped with a good sized library. The club houses created a spirit of camaraderie and provided a fine social life for the workers.

Wages were low, naturally, as Russia was pulling itself up by its bootstraps. So mostly the wives also worked to help out the family budget. Therefore the trade unions provided crèches or nurseries for the children of mothers who worked. These crèches were in [the] charge of trained teachers and nurses. There was a very decent medical department in each factory, with trained nurses present to assist the doctors.

You can imagine our surprise at the completeness of each factory unit. We were in Leningrad just after the completion of the first five year program which was entirely devoted to heavy industry, and by heavy industry I thought of dynamos, turbines, tractors, locomotives, rails etc. But these Russians even then feared attack from the outside and were bending all effort to provide the material needed for defense. The best material they had was the zeal and patriotism with which they worked to protect their home land.

The second five year plan provided for consumers' goods. I was gratified and amused too to see the textile factory reeling off thousands of yards of flowered cretonnes which could be used either for curtains or tablecloths. And I imagined what joy the women experienced when they had their first decorated curtain.

However the first of May was approaching and only half of us could be accommodated in Moscow. So we pulled straws as to who would remain in Leningrad and who was to go to Moscow. I was fortunate to be one of those to go to Moscow to see the big May Day celebration in the Red Square. So

---

[8] Miriam Frink added here: "Called House of Culture."

somewhat reluctantly I left half of my comrades in Leningrad and went on to Moscow.

I shall never forget all of the impressions I got from this city of four to five million souls.[9] There were factories employing 30,000 workers, club houses for their entertainment and convenience, the new apartment houses built so that all living rooms got sunshine some hours of the day, schools galore. We here in Milwaukee have somewhat of a difficult time building one or two schools a year. Moscow was building seventy-five new schools in the year 1935.

Then there were the cultural activities with the Bolshoi Opera House giving the finest of performances. And workers who received special merit for excellence in their work received a season ticket for the operas.

The Lenin Library—one of the largest in Russia, and I do not remember the number of books withdrawn each year, but it ran up to a million or more.

The Metro was opened for the first time and we were invited to be the first guests. The Moscow Metro put all other subways I have seen to shame. Architecturally and artistically it was almost unbelievably beautiful, and it was clean as could be. There was no gum which would stick to your shoes, no gum wrappers or cigarette butts, no spitting on the floor or walls. Here is a project which must be seen to believe!

We were entertained by the Red Army at their army club house, banqueted at the famous club at which the notables are entertained. We visited the workers in their limited apartments. There is still a shortage of houses in Moscow.

We saw working mothers call for their babies at the end of the day. Babies who had been in crèches all day, seeing the mothers only at nursing time, time off for nursing the babies being the rule in each factory.

Daily we saw teachers taking the children into the Red Square and into the tomb to view Lenin.

No one needs to tell me these people in Russia are not happy. They are happy and proud and zealous for their country. I think by now, during this Second World War, the critics and the skeptics in the world believe this.

Also I recall how eagerly the people lined up before the newspapers posted on the outside walls or bulletin board to get the news. Those who didn't get a chance to read the paper, got news through loud-speakers placed on street corner buildings and got the news from the broadcasting company.

There were three or four incidents or thrills in Moscow which I shall always remember and for which I am grateful.

I was invited to visit the home the Russian trade unions had bought and were maintaining for the widows and orphans of the Austrian Socialists who

---

[9] Moscow's population numbered about four million in 1940.

had lost their lives during the Dollfuss fascist storm in Vienna.[10] The Russian workers at once opened their arms for the unfortunate victims, maintained a home, [and] the mothers of the orphans cooked for the children. The school was maintained in which the German language was used for a number of years or until the children were old enough to take on the Russian language as an extra. I understand the same hospitality is being shown now for the victims of the Spanish Franco regime.[11] What other [country] has done likewise?

Then secondly—all delegates, 176 of them from all over the world (except Germany), were entertained by the Soviet officials of Moscow. About 1,000 people sat at long tables sipping tea and listened to speeches.

The main speaker was President Kalinin,[12] who stepped out before the loud speaker with two sheets of paper in his hand and he began, "I hold here in my hand two sheets of paper filled with the most asinine questions I have ever read. These questions come from the American delegates. Do these questions reflect the psychology of the American working class? What do they think we are! What do they want of us? Our houses—we haven't enough for ourselves, our shoes, we have but one pair?" etc. etc.

Here were the papers taken from us at the customs house.

I was humiliated, and angry too, for weren't we told to ask any questions and we [would] receive an answer? But instead we received a hard slap on the wrist. But Kalinin then went on to explain the revolution, the sweat and sacrifice that went into building their economic order etc., until I sat there perfectly satisfied that all and more that he said was true. I suppose only those who have fought a revolution followed by three years of civil war can ever appreciate all the fear, sacrifice and effort expended by the participants.[13]

As soon as he sat down and the applause had subsided, I was called to the platform to reply. A little of my first indignation returned and I was able to talk back a little on the humiliation but ended by giving the Russians full credit for the great things they had done.

Thirdly—the May Day celebration! Words can hardly do justice to the spectacular demonstration. More than two thousand[14] people passing through

---

[10] Chancellor Engelbert Dollfuss, the authoritarian (but anti-Nazi) leader of Austria who dismantled the Austrian Republic, squelched an uprising by Austrian Social Democrats in February 1934, sending them underground.

[11] General Francisco Franco's Nationalist army won the Spanish Civil War against the democratic Republican government in 1939. Franco remained head of the Spanish government until his death in 1975.

[12] Mikhail Ivanovich Kalinin (1875–1946) served as the president (formal head) of the Soviet Union from 1919 to 1946.

[13] Either Meta Berger or Miriam Frink added on the side: "Eloquent."

[14] Either Meta Berger or Miriam Frink crossed out "two thousand" and added "two million."

the Red Square. First the army with all its branches, then the navy, the motorized division [with] the airplanes and tanks, but what did surprise me was the dogs, the bicycle and the ski divisions. Somehow I had not expected this. And after the military display came the workers from farms and factories with colorful floats and pageantry.

Here I was, a pacifist admiring an army ready to defend its country. Since then I've become a belligerent pacifist. I am now ready to sweep any and everything out of my way to obtain a war-less world; this means Nazism, fascism and anything else that interferes with a democratic world.

I stood seven hours watching that parade and then another seven hours watching the young athletes in front of our hotel waiting for their turn to swing into the line of march. That night I also saw for the first time street-dancing on all corners, music coming from the loud-speakers and these sturdy young people having a happy time.

And now one more experience. I wanted very much to call on America's ambassador, William C. Bullitt,[15] who at that time and before had been very friendly towards the USSR. So I asked the interpreter to call the U.S. embassy and make an appointment for me. This my interpreter was most reluctant to do. Upon inquiring, she told me that trade relations between Russia and the U.S. had broken off and that an unfriendly feeling existed between the two countries. Also that Bullitt represented a capitalist country while I was representing labor. I was naive enough not to sense the political significance at the time. Nevertheless after a little discussion, she finally made the appointment for me.

So the next morning I went to the U.S. embassy and met Mr. Bullitt. He was most cordial and charming and made me feel quite at home. I understood at once what qualifications a diplomat must possess. He talked a little about Wisconsin, the La Follettes and my husband, when I said—"But I want to talk about Russia—tell me about this country and its government."

"All right. Then let me tell you that this government will endure while Jesus Christ (Lenin) lies over there in the tomb, and his twelve apostles."

And then Ambassador Bullitt proceeded to tell me that in his opinion, the twelve commissars in the Kremlin were the most intelligent and the most honest men he had encountered, that they had a well-defined constructive program for their country and that, if they were left alone—i.e., not attacked or prevented by outside forces—they would develop Russia and carry it far, and that they had work to do which would take them at least five hundred

[15] William C. Bullitt (1891–1967) was the first U.S. ambassador to the Soviet Union (1934–1936). He recommended recognition of the Soviet Union as early as 1919.

years. They had already done much to provide land and bread and peace. But the most outstanding accomplishment had been changing the USSR from a backward illiterate primitive land to one where illiteracy had almost disappeared. Mr. Bullitt was most enthusiastic about the leaders in Russia.

When I asked him about religion he said, "Oh well, the religion that you and I know is a thing of the past here. However, they have substituted a religion of their own, a so-called brotherhood of man, which they propagandize from the cradle up."

Then we talked of various other phases of life such as honesty among the people, since two of our delegates were victims of pick-pockets. Mr. Bullitt was of the opinion that the ethical code of honesty had not yet been achieved by every worker or peasant, saying—"They will do almost anything to get more room to live in, or an advancement in the factory." But this was understandable, since the entire mode of living had so suddenly changed.

My interview with Ambassador Bullitt was most pleasant, and in the light of our conversation I have been at a loss to understand his change of front in these later years, for today he is violently anti-Russian.

Another outstanding event was our interview with Madam Krupskaya, the widow of Lenin.[16] Before leaving Moscow, our interpreter asked me what I would best like to do, so immediately I said I'd like to meet and talk with Madam Krupskaya, since she was the head of educational work. So an interview was arranged. Madam received us in a large bare room and the usual tea and cakes were served. I think serving tea and cakes is a very nice thing, since the reserve is at once broken and one feels quite at ease.

Madam Krupskaya was charming and talked English perfectly. She related the difficulty she had when she and her husband were exiled and went to England to live. No matter how hard she studied English, whenever she went marketing and thought she knew what to ask for, the clerk invariably brought her a box of matches.

She told us of her work to educate and raise the standard of living and the standard for cleanliness among the poorest in Russia, how to take care of the babies and youngest children and many many things relating there-to. It was while we were in Russia that Madam K. joined with other famous women, Jane Addams representing the U.S., in an international broadcast in behalf of peace and a war-less world. I shall always remember Madam Krupskaya with gratitude and pleasure.

---

[16] Nadezhda Konstantinovna Krupskaya (1869–1939), Bolshevik founder and Lenin's wife, devoted herself to educational work after the Bolsheviks seized power in 1917. After Lenin's 1924 death and her initial opposition to Stalin, she dissociated herself from political struggles, and her influence waned.

But our time was getting short in Moscow. It was time to move on. So we were again given a choice of selecting our route. Some chose the Stalingrad route. We Americans chose the trip through the Ukraine, the Don coal mines, Kharkov, Kiev and south to the Black Sea. Kiev impressed me as a most beautiful city. Perhaps the blue lovely forget-me-nots planted in great circles around each tree on the main street of the town made me think it so beautiful.

Passing through the Ukraine we had a chance to see the vast, endless wheat fields and the natural snow fences of a double row of pine trees. Every peasant cottage which formerly no doubt had a mud-floor and was windowless had several new windows, and in each hut we saw a blooming geranium in the window. I couldn't help feeling that these peasant women cherished even the luxury and the beauty of a flower pot in the window of their home.

The task of collectivization of the farms must have been most terrific. In the first place the national government had to get food for the industrial workers in the towns where industry was growing by leaps and bounds. These workers were essential to complete the heavy industry five year program. Secondly, the kulaks or rich peasants couldn't or didn't understand the full program of the government and were very hostile to the new regime. Therefore, I was told, rather than give the necessary grain and cattle to the central government, they burned valuable crops, thus causing starvation not only among the city workers but also among the peasants who worked the land for the kulak. Famine resulted, causing the death of millions of people through starvation, malnutrition and disease. It was after these fearful famines that the government enforced the collective farms, taking the land from the kulaks by force, sending many obstinate kulaks to Siberia to start life over again but without the aid of peasant-slaves. That there were hardships goes without saying.

It was on my way to Simferopol [a city in the Crimea] that I was so unfortunate as to fall and break my ankle while visiting Eskonia Nova—a beautiful estate which was devoted to the study of science for better breeding stock. This meant I stayed in Simferopol while the rest crossed the mountains and went to the playground of the former czarist supporters and which was now the health resort and recreation centers for the workers who were on vacation.

After the doctor in Simferopol proudly showed me a brand new X-ray machine, I was told I had a fractured ankle and had to go to a hospital. I had no choice. The hospital was an old frame two story house turned into a hospital. Here I stayed eight days, knowing no one with whom I could converse. I finally, by sign language, got the nurse to bring me paper and pencil. Then by drawing a glass for water, a bed-pan or other thing I needed, I was comforted. The doctor of the hospital used to come in daily, sit on the foot end of the bed, smoke a cigarette and try to learn English from me. Those visits, my guide book and learning the Russian alphabet helped me pass the time.

After eight days, the doctor came in to put a plaster cast on my foot and told me that the next morning I was to meet my comrades who were returning from the Black Sea with the most glowing accounts of the Crimean playground. Fortunately my study of the guide book made me somewhat familiar with their accounts.

This just about finished my trip in Russia. But I do want to say how very very kind those Russians were to me, and how sympathetic. One worker, crippled during the revolution, was detailed to take care of me. So everywhere he ordered an automobile to show me the sights, and all the while this poor workman insisted on holding my hand in sympathy, since we could not converse at all.

The trip to Leningrad was most uncomfortable, but I just had to grin and bear it.

At Leningrad I was taken to their famous Leningrad Institute for Medical Science where the head of the surgery department wished to see me. Imagine my surprise when a frail and most beautiful woman came into my room which I shared with three other patients. She, this frail and beautiful woman, held the chair of surgery. I was more than curious and asked her whether she got her high position because she was a member of the Communist Party. She spoke German fluently. "No indeed! I am not a member of the party. I got this position because I know my business." Then she proceeded to put another cast on my ankle and said I was to get up and walk, which I did. She also said I could leave the next day for England since the ankle would permit it. Before leaving the Leningrad Institute for Medical Science, I learned that all doctors in the USSR who are serving in socialized medicine are required by law to return to some medical college every three years to take a refresher course, so that they may always get the information on the most advanced steps in medicine. Not a bad idea!

The trade union delegates asked me to go back to the Black Sea to recuperate and as their guest. This I declined with heartfelt thanks. They needed the bed and I needed to go to England where I could converse again. And now, before closing this chapter, I do wish to acknowledge my appreciation to my Russian friends and to those Americans who never left my side until they sailed for home, while I remained in England waiting to get my foot stronger as I didn't trust myself on a rolling ship with only one good leg.

I learned much on my visit to Russia. Never before had I realized that the whole nation was dedicated to the principle of "to each according to his needs, from each according to his ability." I realized what a social conscience was on a nationwide scale, and the pride each member of the society devoted to protect his fatherland and to provide for all the benefits of their economic order. I believe I was a better person because of my visit to that tremendous country and its pioneering experiment. You did not have to agree with their political philosophy. All you needed to do was to recognize the tremendous suffering, the excellent planning to organize that vast country, and to acknowledge the gallantry of the workers and peasants who had after long centuries finally found their fatherland. They will die to defend it as we witness this in the year 1943.[17]

[17] Meta Berger left the following notes at the end of this chapter. "This revolution was different in character and results than other revolutions. The Industrial Revolution was really an evolution from the feudal system to a capitalist system. The American Revolution caused a separation from the mother country. The French Revolution discarded the corrupt king and separated church from state. But the Russian Revolution changed the economic order from a capitalist society to a socialistic society; and [unfinished].

"I realize that my analysis of the Russian system can only be sketchy. I ardently wish I had had the opportunity that Hewlett Johnson had and could have written so comprehensive a study of [Russia as] this great scholar. Nevertheless, even I could see that low as the standard of living in Russia was, it was constantly rising. The bread and sugar cards were eliminated while I was there. Wages were on the upgrade and the youth of the country were certainly happy. I couldn't help but compare the society in Russia with our fumbling attempt to meet the depression in the U.S. with its ever increasing relief lists, its bread-lines, its back to work with shovel and pick, its effort to meet the food situation with limiting the pigs that were privileged to live, with plowing under every third row of cotton etc. And yet President Roosevelt had the foresight to attempt to meet the situation."

Afterword

by Kimberly Swanson

Meta Berger's relationship with Milwaukee Socialist Party leaders began to deteriorate soon after Victor Berger's death in 1929. In 1930 she contracted with nonunion labor to build an addition to her home near Thiensville, approximately fifteen miles north of Milwaukee in Ozaukee County. Predictably, unionists were outraged. Meta tried to justify her decision by pointing out that union workers from Milwaukee had always charged a transportation fee for jobs in Ozaukee County: "If and when the union is organized in Ozaukee county, I pledge myself to employ its members in preference to other workmen. But I am no longer able to make further financial sacrifices for organized labor, particularly when they seem unreasonable to me." Reasonable or not, overlooking the political repercussions of her decision was a mistake. Angry that her devotion to organized labor had been questioned, she worsened the situation by declaring, "No man or woman in the state has done as much for that cause as I have."[1] Why, then, did she fail to support the cause in this case? Most likely Meta's financial worries in the wake of Victor's death simply overwhelmed her usual political good sense. Her concern about finances was not new, of course, as money had always been in short supply in the Berger household. But with Victor gone she was especially fearful about the future, and she probably never expected anyone to notice this particular cost-saving measure.

Meta's explanation for hiring nonunion labor did not satisfy union leaders, and their dissatisfaction cost her the 1930 Socialist Party nomination to suc-

---

[1] Meta Berger to the Executive Board of the [Milwaukee] County Central Committee [of the Socialist Party], January 24, 1930, roll 34, VLB Papers (microfilm).

ceed Victor in Congress. Prior to Meta's conflict with the unions, Socialist
Mayor Daniel Hoan had encouraged her in strong terms to run for office: "You
are and will be the unanimous choice." But party leaders quietly withheld her
name from consideration, and James Sheehan, a union official, became the
Socialist nominee. Meta was furious that the party had excluded her name in
such a high-handed and undemocratic manner, but for the sake of party unity
she refrained from public discussion of her noncandidacy before the election.
She did ask National Executive Committee member Morris Hillquit to inter-
vene, couching her request in terms of the *Leader's* future rather than her own
ambition, but Hillquit merely exchanged a few telegrams with the responsible
leaders. Meta believed these leaders had purposely taken advantage of her
difficulty with the unions to thwart her candidacy. She posed no threat to them,
she maintained, but her election might have launched the political career of
her daughter, Doris, and thus "it was better to kill Bergerism now." Her assessment may have been correct, but it does not take into account the party's
need to avoid alienating union members. By 1932 Meta was no longer interested in running for office, and she withdrew her name from the vice presidential nominations at the national party convention.[2]

Meta's conflicts with local Socialist leaders became more pronounced as
she drifted to the left politically. In the fall of 1933 her commitment to peace
led her to travel to New York City and participate in the U.S. Congress Against
War. Three years later she accepted a position as vice chair of the organization
formed at that gathering, the American League Against War and Fascism, and
in 1938 she served as treasurer for the North American Committee to Aid
Spanish Democracy. These actions were serious breaches in party discipline.
The Socialists considered both groups communist-front organizations and for-
bade participation in communist-affiliated activity. The onset of the depression
had provided both the Socialist Party and the Communist Party with new
opportunities for growth. While Milwaukee's Socialist organization persisted
after World War I, the party faltered on a national level until Norman Thomas
revived it beginning with his 1928 presidential campaign. By 1932 membership had doubled and the popular Thomas won an impressive 800,000 votes

---

[2] Thomas Gavett, *Development of the Labor Movement in Milwaukee* (Madison and Milwaukee: University
of Wisconsin Press, 1965), 149; Daniel W. Hoan to Meta Berger, August 12, 1929, roll 34; Meta Berger,
"I Have Been a Socialist Too Long . . . ," [ca. 1930], roll 35; Meta Berger to Morris Hillquit [telegram
draft], [1930], roll 34; Morris Hillquit to Meta Berger, July 17, 1930, roll 34; Meta Berger to [Marx Lewis]
[incomplete], [ca. December 1930], roll 34; all in VLB Papers (microfilm); Peggy Dennis, "Meta Berger:
Milwaukee's Velvet-Fisted Radical," 1986, unpublished manuscript no. 138, Milwaukee County Historical
Society, 18–19.

for president. Conflicts within the party, centering in particular around a response to Roosevelt's New Deal (1933–1939), led to the Socialist Party's decline
just as the Communist Party experienced a resurgence. In the 1930s the Communists overcame the divisive infighting that had characterized their party in
the previous decade and adopted a new political realism. They formed alliances
with socialists and liberals; offered socially relevant critiques and programs,
especially in their efforts against racism; and began to work within the labor
movement in Milwaukee and other urban areas, with considerable success.
Socialists and Progressives responded by distancing themselves from communist activities and excluding communists from their ranks. Meta was by no
means the only Socialist to disregard party discipline by consorting with communists, but party leaders were more tolerant with Meta than with others,
many of whom the party expelled.[3]

Meta traveled to the Soviet Union in 1935. Although the trip itself was a
violation of party rules, she made an agreement with the trip organizer that "I
would speak upon my return only if and when I considered it wise, due to
the fact that I wished to abide as much as possible by rules of the Socialist
Party." Despite this arrangement, after returning she spoke frequently and with
admiration of what she had witnessed in the Soviet Union. Her experience
served to reinforce her new belief that the threat of fascism required united
action on the part of leftist organizations, and she became increasingly dissat-
isfied with the Socialist Party's resistance to cooperating with communists. In
1936 Hoan dropped her from his list of speakers during his reelection campaign. Meta had embarrassed Socialist candidates with her praise for the Soviet
Union, and she had alienated German-American groups with comments critical
of Nazi Germany. Meta responded to Hoan's snub in a speech to the Socialists
in which she accused him of placing election victories above principle. Two
years later, she made a public statement calling for collective action and criticized the party as a "faction-torn debating society." Party leaders still refrained
from reprimanding Meta, even blocking a motion to expel her in 1938, because
of the support that she enjoyed within the party and because of the negative
publicity that would inevitably result. However, in April 1940, national party
leaders finally warned her to cease participating in communist-front organizations at the risk of being expelled. Instead of appearing at party headquarters
in Milwaukee to explain her involvement, as requested, Meta resigned from

[3] Dennis, "Meta Berger: Milwaukee's Velvet-Fisted Radical," 19–20; *Proceedings, Third U.S. Congress Against War and Fascism* (New York: American League Against War and Fascism, 1936); Meta Berger to "All Unionists" [press telegram], November 3, 1938, roll 35, VLB Papers (microfilm); Gavett, *Development,* 176–197.

the party on May 2, 1940. In her statement she cited her wish to be free from restrictions, and she accused the party of red-baiting.[4]

Meta resigned in the same year that Mayor Hoan lost his reelection campaign, signaling the end of the Socialist Party's prominence in Milwaukee's political life. Two years later the Socialists split from the local Progressive Party, with whom they had formed a coalition in 1935, and returned to their own column on the ballot. At this juncture more members left the party. Depression-era reforms had encouraged labor leaders to influence the majority parties rather than work with the Socialists, so Milwaukee's long Socialist-labor alliance came to an end.[5]

Many Socialists viewed Meta's leftward turn in the last decade of her life with suspicion. Her affiliation with communists and her praise for the Soviet Union drew sharp criticism: "Her continuous preachment of the wonders of Russia is something that practically every Socialist resents," asserted Mayor Hoan. Longtime Socialist Frederic Heath believed that Meta had fallen under the "malevolent" influence of Eugene Dennis, district organizer for the Communist Party in the late 1930s. Heath believed that Meta was "trying to undo all that her husband had accomplished."[6]

Victor Berger had opposed communism throughout his life. His goal was to make socialism meaningful to American workers and to achieve reform through legal means. He denounced revolutionary tactics, contending that socialism would not work unless a majority supported it, and he battled ceaselessly with communists within the party before it divided in 1919. He made his position clear as early as 1901: "In America for the first time in history, we find an oppressed class with the same fundamental rights as the ruling class— the right of universal suffrage. It is then nonsense to talk of sudden bloody revolutions here, until the power to ballot has been at least tried." Eighteen years later he referred to the communism envisioned by American adherents as "a new form of *slavery*." Communists were equally dismissive of his views, considering piecemeal reforms to be insignificant goals, and the two groups, socialists and communists, were openly hostile to each other for decades.

[4] Meta Berger, Travel Notes, April 1935, roll 33; "Statement Read by Meta Berger before the Milwaukee County Central Committee," April 22, 1936, roll 35; "Motion to Expel Veteran Leader Is Blocked by Hoan," *Milwaukee Sentinel,* June 27, 1938, roll 33; Travers Clement and Arthur G. McDowell to Meta Berger, April 20, 1940, roll 35; Frank Zeidler to Meta Berger, April 29, 1940, roll 35; Meta Berger to Executive Committee, Socialist Party, Milwaukee, May 2, 1940, roll 35; "Mrs. Berger Quits Socialists," *Milwaukee Journal,* May 3, 1940, roll 33; and other newspaper clippings, rolls 33 and 35; all in VLB Papers (microfilm).

[5] Gavett, *Development,* 171–175.

[6] "Mrs. Berger Dies, Aged 71," *Milwaukee Journal,* June 17, 1944; Frederick I. Olson, statement appended to Dennis, "Meta Berger: Milwaukee's Velvet-Fisted Radical."

Meta's critics therefore pointed to Victor's opposition to revolution, his skepticism toward the Soviet Union, and the attacks he suffered from Communists, but she was unmoved.[7]

Meta considered her position to be principled. She explained in an interview with her daughter, Doris, "If I learned anything from Victor Berger it was that every new situation must be freshly examined in the light of one's purpose. And that explains why it is very easy for me, and entirely consistent as well, to take a stand on Russia or the United Front movement or any other subject, without feeling bound by any attitudes he took under different circumstances." She believed that the rise of fascism and the relative success of the Soviet Union had provided just such a new situation and required the rethinking of old beliefs and priorities. From this perspective she was open-minded and forward-looking. She was also confident enough to risk public disapproval. "I'm used to saying what I think and taking the consequences," she told Doris, but she admitted "there was lots more comfort in it and more joy when Mr. Berger and I took the consequences together."[8]

Meta's explanation for her unexpected political conversion is heartfelt and genuine, but it is not fully satisfactory. She had supported social-democratic tenets throughout her thirty-two-year marriage. What other motivations or circumstances could have influenced her to adopt a new philosophy so late in life? This question cannot be answered with any certainty, but several factors may have played a role in Meta's openness to communist ideas: the vitality of the communist movement itself; her reliance on the political judgment of others; and her belief, perhaps more pronounced after Victor's death, that ends do justify means.

Meta was not alone in her disenchantment with the postwar Socialist Party. The party's heyday was past, the early excitement of participating in a growing and influential movement long gone. After the war, membership dwindled, and enthusiasm for Socialist candidates gradually waned. Although the party revived for a short time under Thomas's direction, New Deal reforms met the public demand for change, and even in Milwaukee the Socialists began losing clout. According to Meta, after Victor's death the *Leader* became "innocuous and spineless," and local party officials thought less about socialist philosophy than about winning elections. Marx Lewis, Victor's former congressional secretary, concurred. He noted in 1935 that their party, especially the Wisconsin organization, now practiced the kind of "trickery and fraud that we used to

---

[7] Miller, *Victor Berger; Social-Democratic Herald,* October 12, 1901, quoted in Wachman, *History,* 73; Stevens, ed., *Family Letters,* 276; Hursley, interview.

[8] Hursley, interview, 1, 3.

condemn in the old [Republican and Democratic] parties."[9]

In this climate Meta took notice of the active communist movement. Although the communists continually battled the perception that they took direction from Moscow—later shown to be accurate—they thrived during the late depression years by loosening their ideological restrictions and participating vigorously in labor activity, antifascist campaigns, and other radical causes. They established connections with sympathetic socialists and liberals, including Meta, through organizations like the American League Against War and Fascism. The Milwaukee-based Communist Party organizers whom Meta befriended, Eugene and Peggy Dennis, were young, energetic, and charismatic. Perhaps with them Meta rediscovered the inspiration she had felt during her early embrace of socialism. She understood the obstacles the Dennises faced and identified with their plight: "You know those early days in the Socialist movement were not unlike the struggles of the Communists now. Socialists were anathema then and had no such soft and generally respected position in community life as they now enjoy. They were viewed with the same fear and violence as Communists are now." Meta never joined the Communist Party, but she did not shrink from affiliation. "I don't mind being called a Communist," she would say. "That doesn't hurt me."[10]

Meta visited the Soviet Union to judge the new society for herself. Peggy Dennis claimed in 1977 that her husband, Eugene, had encouraged Meta to go, but this statement is probably inaccurate. The Dennises arrived in Milwaukee only a month before Meta left, and much earlier Peggy had written, with a fresher memory, that they first met Meta shortly after her return. Early in the trip Meta was skeptical and noted that the only other Socialist in the delegation was rumored within the party to be a communist. Her later enthusiasm for the Soviet system was uncritical but based on real observations. She was particularly impressed with Soviet initiatives in fields of special interest to her: the care of children, education, and women's rights. She admired the efforts made to eliminate poverty, and her firsthand experience with Soviet medical care was positive. In chapter 13 and elsewhere she noted with approval the law requiring Soviet physicians to take regular refresher courses. Most importantly, Meta's enthusiasm was not dampened by accounts of abuse because she was convinced that the "capitalist press" distorted the reality of life in the Soviet Union. Her experience during World War I, when the press manipulated information to demonize Germany and German-Americans, had caused her to distrust much of what she read. She could dismiss disturbing reports about the Soviet

---

[9] Meta Berger to [Marx Lewis], [ca. December 1930]; Marx Lewis to Meta Berger, February 10, 1935, roll 35, VLB Papers (microfilm).

[10] Hursley, interview, 4; Frink Notes.

Union because she believed much of the news to be exaggerated or untrue.[11]

Although Meta maintained that she was "neither a fool nor a liar," her critics were probably at least partially correct when they accused the Dennises of manipulating her. In truth, Meta never developed a truly independent political viewpoint. She was certainly capable of independent action, and she excelled at advocacy, but she had always relied on Victor's analyses. As she so poignantly described in her autobiography, she was completely naive about world affairs when she married, and though she grew confident and knowledgeable, she never questioned the wisdom of Victor's political and economic views until after his death. "The difference between me and anybody else," she noted modestly but with some truth in 1936, "is Victor Berger. Except for him, I'd probably be interested exclusively in my grandchildren."[12]

The Dennises, articulate, intelligent, and intensely devoted to their work, may have filled a void created by Victor's death. Meta's relationship with them was likely mutually beneficial. She gained a renewed sense of purpose; they gained a prominent ally with intimate knowledge of local and state politics. The Dennises appreciated Meta and looked to her as a mentor, even a maternal figure. As Peggy wrote, "Meta Berger, a maverick Left Socialist, had taken us under her protective wing shortly after we came to Wisconsin." Meta introduced them to local community leaders and opened her home to them. The Dennises came to Thiensville for "a quiet weekend, a brief vacation, for acceptance into a family circle." Peggy recuperated at Meta's home after a botched abortion, and Eugene held at least one meeting there. Meta's irritation with Socialist Party inflexibility was not a pose; she undoubtedly wanted to remain on good terms with Socialists even as she took an interest in communism, but the political atmosphere in Milwaukee was so polarized that party leaders would accept nothing less than outright repudiation of communism. Peggy Dennis believed that Socialist leaders of the 1930s expected Meta to serve as symbolic widow of the party's founder, but Meta chafed against a ceremonial role. The Dennises offered her a different role, as the "radical conscience" of the Socialist Party, and she accepted it.[13]

Perhaps taking her cue from the official communist position, Meta reconsidered her longtime pacifism and even accepted the authoritarian nature of the Soviet regime. For her, the eradication of fascism became the worthiest of

[11] Peggy Dennis, *The Autobiography of an American Communist: A Personal View of a Political Life, 1925–1975* (Westport, Conn., and Berkeley: Lawrence Hill and Creative Arts Book Company, 1977), 108; Peggy Dennis, "Meta Berger—Grand Old Lady," *Daily Worker,* July 9, 1944; Meta Berger to family, April 12, 1935, roll 35, VLB Papers (microfilm); Mrs. Victor Berger, *I Saw Russia: Socialism in the Making* (New York: American Friends of the Soviet Union, n.d.).

[12] Berger, *I Saw Russia,* 3; Hursley, interview, 1.

[13] Dennis, *Autobiography,* 102, 107–108; Gavett, *Development,* 182; Dennis, "Meta Berger: Milwaukee's Velvet-Fisted Radical," 18.

goals, more important even than opposition to war. Remembering in 1943 how suffragist Theodora Youmans had called World War I a "holy war," Meta commented, "How could any war be a holy war? Except this one [World War II]." According to a friend, Meta "laughed at her inconsistency but meant it." Meta's adamant antifascism was no doubt highly principled. Still, viewed differently, it might be seen as a newfound tolerance for extreme measures. In chapter 10 she mentioned the likely presence of Japanese-American "fifth columnists" in Hawaii, suggesting that she did not object to their wartime internment. She seemed undisturbed by brutal aspects of Soviet society under Stalin's rule. "That there were hardships goes without saying," she wrote regarding the shipping of recalcitrant peasants to Siberia during agricultural collectivization. Even if the worst stories were completely true, she maintained, "I can only say . . . that that is too bad. It would have been easier for the world of 'liberals' to accept and learn from Russia if no one had been imprisoned or executed." She acknowledged that dictatorship was "repulsive" but insisted—despite her own experience with a repressive government during World War I—that specific circumstances could warrant it.[14]

Such opinions naturally inflamed Meta's critics and led to frequent local news stories about her clashes with Socialist leadership. But Meta spoke out less often as her health faltered, and her controversial political views never eclipsed her lifetime of community service. She was still an active Milwaukee school-board director and university regent into the mid-1930s, when she worked to guarantee the right of married women to teach, among other efforts. Near the end of her life she received tributes for her school-board service and for her dedication to the woman-suffrage movement. In 1939 hundreds of Meta's friends and colleagues in education attended a dinner held in her honor after her retirement from the school board. The speakers praised her idealism and her courage during her thirty years as a director. Her contributions to the suffrage movement were recognized in 1930, when her name was added to the state roll of honor, and in 1942 at a Susan B. Anthony dinner.[15]

During her final years, Meta suffered from a heart ailment. After retiring from the school board she lived quietly on the farm near Thiensville with Doris; Doris's husband, Frank Hursley; and Doris's three daughters. There Meta began writing her autobiography, working mostly alone in bed. She died on June 16, 1944. On April 26, 1945, friends held a memorial meeting in her honor at

[14] Frink Notes; Berger, I Saw Russia, 4, 18–23.

[15] Newspaper clippings, roll 33, VLB Papers (microfilm); "Mrs. Berger's Work Praised," Milwaukee Journal, April 26, 1939; "Tributes Paid to Mrs. Berger by 800 at Fete," Milwaukee Sentinel, April 26, 1939; Catherine Duncan, "State Roll of Honor," Forward: Bulletin of the Wisconsin League of Women Voters 9 (April 1930): 6; "Meta Berger, Long School Leader, Dies," Milwaukee Sentinel, June 17, 1944.

Milwaukee's Grand Avenue Congregational Church. Among those present were Marshall Field, publisher of the *Chicago Sun,* and William T. Evjue, publisher of Madison's *Capital Times,* both of whom spoke at the meeting. But the most fitting tribute was a simple one delivered by her old friend Miriam Frink, corresponding secretary for the memorial committee. "When Mrs. Meta Berger died," Frink wrote, "Wisconsin lost one of her most valuable citizens, a woman whose practical idealism, wide humane interests, and great courage won her the admiration and warm affection of hosts of men and women in all walks of life."[16]

[16] Frink, "How I Happened to Work with Mrs. Victor Berger"; Miriam Frink to Louise P. Bilty et al., December 14, 1944, roll 33, VLB Papers (microfilm).

Index

Page numbers in bold indicate biographical notes.